AQA GCSE

WORKING WITH THE ANTHOLOGY
Achieve a C
Teacher Guide

Lesson Plans: **David Grant**
Controlled Assessment: **Peter Thomas**

www.pearsonschoolsandfecolleges.co.uk

✓ Free online support
✓ Useful weblinks
✓ 24 hour online ordering

0845 630 33 33

Contents

Introduction iv

GradeStudio vii

Chapter 1: Character and voice

Getting to know the poems 2

Contemporary poems
- The Clown Punk by Simon Armitage — 4
- Checking Out Me History by John Agard — 6
- Horse Whisperer by Andrew Forster — 8
- Medusa by Carol Ann Duffy — 10
- Singh Song by Daljit Nagra — 12
- Brendon Gallacher by Jackie Kay — 14
- Give by Simon Armitage — 16
- Les Grands Seigneurs by Dorothy Molloy — 18

Poems from the literary heritage
- Ozymandias by Percy Bysshe Shelley — 20
- My Last Duchess by Robert Browning — 22
- The River God by Stevie Smith — 24
- The Hunchback in the Park by Dylan Thomas — 26
- The Ruined Maid by Thomas Hardy — 28
- Casehistory: Alison (head injury) by U. A. Fanthorpe — 30
- On a Portrait of a Deaf Man by John Betjeman — 32

Looking at the poems individually: what have you learned? 34
Comparing the 'Character and voice' poems (1) 36
Comparing the 'Character and voice' poems (2) 38
Writing in the exam 40

Chapter 2: Place

Getting to know the poems 42

Contemporary poems
- The Blackbird of Glanmore by Seamus Heaney — 44
- A Vision by Simon Armitage — 46
- The Moment by Margaret Atwood — 48
- Cold Knap Lake by Gillian Clarke — 50
- Price We Pay for the Sun by Grace Nichols — 52
- Neighbours by Gillian Clarke — 54
- Crossing the Loch by Kathleen Jamie — 56
- Hard Water by Jean Sprackland — 58

Poems from the literary heritage
- London by William Blake — 60
- The Prelude (extract) by William Wordsworth — 62
- The Wild Swans at Coole by W. B. Yeats — 64
- Spellbound by Emily Brontë — 66
- Below the Green Corrie by Norman McCaig — 68
- Storm in the Black Forest by D. H. Lawrence — 70
- Wind by Ted Hughes — 72

Looking at the poems individually: what have you learned? 74
Comparing the 'Place' poems (1) 76
Comparing the 'Place' poems (2) 78
Writing in the exam 80

Chapter 3: Conflict

Getting to know the poems 82

Contemporary poems
- Flag by John Agard — 84
- Out of the Blue (extract) by Simon Armitage — 86
- Mametz Wood by Owen Sheers — 88
- The Yellow Palm by Robert Minhinnick — 90
- The Right Word by Imtiaz Dharker — 92
- At the Border by Choman Hardi — 94
- Belfast Confetti by Ciaran Carson — 96
- Poppies by Jane Weir — 98

Poems from the literary heritage
- Futility by Wilfred Owen — 100
- The Charge of the Light Brigade by Alfred, Lord Tennyson — 102
- Bayonet Charge by Ted Hughes — 104
- The Falling Leaves by Margaret Postgate Cole — 106
- Come On, Come Back by Stevie Smith — 108
- next to of course god america by e. e. cummings — 110
- Hawk Roosting by Ted Hughes — 112

Looking at the poems individually: what have you learned? 114
Comparing the 'Conflict' poems (1) 116
Comparing the 'Conflict' poems (2) 118
Writing in the exam 120

Chapter 4: Relationships

Getting to know the poems 122

Contemporary poems
- The Manhunt by Simon Armitage — 124
- Hour by Carol Ann Duffy — 126
- In Paris with You by James Fenton — 128
- Quickdraw by Carol Ann Duffy — 130
- Ghazal by Mimi Khalvati — 132
- Brothers by Andrew Forster — 134
- Praise Song for My Mother by Grace Nichols — 136
- Harmonium by Simon Armitage — 138

Poems from the literary heritage
- Sonnet 116 by William Shakespeare — 140
- Sonnet 43 by Elizabeth Barrett Browning — 142
- To His Coy Mistress by Andrew Marvell — 144
- The Farmer's Bride by Charlotte Mew — 146
- Sister Maude by Christina Rossetti — 148
- Nettles by Vernon Scannell — 150
- Born Yesterday by Philip Larkin — 152

Looking at the poems individually: what have you learned? 154
Comparing the 'Relationships' poems (1) 156
Comparing the 'Relationships' poems (2) 158
Writing in the exam 160

Chapter 5: The unseen poem

What to look for when reading and annotating an unseen poem 162
Writing a response in the exam (1) 164
Writing a response in the exam (2) 165

Chapter 6: Controlled Assessment 166

Introduction

The new specification

September 2010 sees the first teaching of the new AQA GCSE English Literature specification, which will be notable for, among other things, the shift from a linear specification to a unitised one and the introduction of Controlled Assessment to replace coursework.

There are three examined units totalling 75% of the overall GCSE, and one Controlled Assessment unit worth 25%. As you will see from the outline below, you have a degree of choice available to you in terms of which unit you choose to do the Controlled Assessment in.

Unit 1 Exploring Modern Texts

What is the exam worth?	40% of the total marks.
How long is this exam?	1 hour 30 mins.
What is Section A of the exam?	Modern Prose or Drama.
What is Section A worth?	20% of the total marks.
How long should students spend on Section A?	45 mins.
What is Section B of the exam?	Exploring Cultures.
What is Section B worth?	20% of the total marks.
How long should students spend on Section B?	45 mins.

Unit 2 Poetry Across Time

Candidates taking Unit 2 will be tackling the Anthology as an external assessment, as opposed to the Controlled Assessment option available in Unit 5.

What is the exam worth?	35% of the total marks.
How long is this exam?	1 hour 15 mins.
What is Section A of the exam?	Poetry cluster from the Anthology.
What is Section A worth?	23% of the total marks.
How long should students spend on Section A?	45 mins.
What is Section B of the exam?	Responding to an unseen poem.
What is Section B worth?	12% of the total marks.
How long should students spend on Section B?	30 mins.

Unit 3 The Significance of Shakespeare and the English Literary Heritage

What is this unit worth?	25% of the total marks.
How is it assessed?	Controlled Assessment.
How long should I spend teaching this unit?	About 25% of the teaching time for the whole course.
What will students be assessed on?	Students will produce one piece of work that makes links between a Shakespeare play and an English Literary Heritage text from any genre.
How are tasks set?	AQA will release a set of tasks each year on 1 April. Centres are then free to choose and contextualise these tasks to suit their students.
When will students be assessed?	You can choose to assess students at any point during the course.

Unit 4 Approaching Shakespeare and the English Literary Heritage
Candidates taking Unit 4 would be tackling Shakespeare as an external assessment, rather than the Controlled Assessment route available through Unit 3.

What is the exam worth?	35% of the total marks.
How long is this exam?	1 hour 15 mins.
What is Section A of the exam?	Shakespeare.
What is Section A worth?	20% of the total marks.
How long should students spend on Section A?	45 mins.
What is Section B of the exam?	Prose from the English Literary Heritage.
What is Section B worth?	15% of the total marks.
How long should students spend on Section B?	30 mins.

Unit 5 Exploring Poetry
Candidates taking Unit 5 will be tackling the Anthology through Controlled Assessment, as opposed to the external assessment route available in Unit 2.

What is this unit worth?	25% of the total marks.
How is it assessed?	Controlled Assessment.
How long should I spend teaching this unit?	About 25% of the teaching time for the whole course.
What will students be assessed on?	Students will produce one piece of work that makes links between a range of poems.
What poems need to be studied?	The range of poetry must cover contemporary and English Literary Heritage poetry. You may use poems from the Anthology for this unit, although this is not essential.
How are tasks set?	AQA will release a set of tasks each year on 1 April. Centres are then free to choose and contextualise these tasks to suit their students.
When will students be assessed?	You can choose to assess students at any point during the course.

So, the choice available to you is essentially around where you want to tackle the Controlled Assessment: through the study of poetry, or through the study of Shakespeare and the English Literary Heritage.

Using this Teacher Guide
This Teacher Guide supports the *AQA Working with the Anthology: Achieve a C Student Book* and also references the Digital Anthology resources available to you. The Student Book and Teacher Guide have been designed to help students raise their achievement in Unit 2 or Unit 5 of the AQA GCSE English Literature specification. They are tailored to the requirements of the specification to help students achieve grades E–B*. The principal focus of these resources is on Unit 2. However, students taking Unit 5 will find most of the content relevant and helpful.

The Teacher Guide is broken down into two broad sections:
1 Visual lesson plans
2 Controlled Assessment.

Visual lesson plans (pages 2–165)
With their unique, easy-to-follow layout, the visual lesson plans support the teaching of the Student Book content. They show how the print and digital resources can be used together to deliver engaging lessons that help improve students' grades. They include close references to the resources available, free to you, on the AQA Digital Anthology at http://anthology.aqa.org.uk/ Each lesson plan includes:
- a starter activity, to introduce the learning in the lesson
- suggestions for how to carry out the Student Book activities, including group, paired and independent work
- advice on how to use the GradeStudio features to enrich learning
- guidance on how to incorporate any extra assets – such as the worksheets that appear on the CD-ROM or the Digital Anthology resources – into the lesson
- plenary activities to round-off the lesson and check/consolidate understanding
- suggested answers to the Student Book activities, to save you valuable time.

Controlled Assessment (pages 166–175)
At the end of the Teacher Guide, there is a specific section on the Controlled Assessment element of the AQA GCSE English Literature specification. This section assumes that the majority of centres will tackle the Anthology through the externally examined route, and therefore concentrates on Unit 3 (The Significance of Shakespeare and the English Literary Heritage).

Written by the people responsible for developing the Unit 3 Controlled Assessments, this section includes:
- clear explanation of the requirements of the Controlled Assessment
- detailed breakdown of the different types of tasks available to you
- advice on choosing, setting and teaching the tasks, tailored to the different ability levels of your students
- guidance on how to apply the new mark schemes, including exemplar answers from students.

What's on the CD-ROM?
This Teacher Guide is accompanied by a CD-ROM. This contains:
- the worksheets referenced in the visual lesson plans
- interactive GradeStudio activities
- versions of the lesson plans in Microsoft Word, for customisation.

GradeStudio

GradeStudio is a unique resource designed to help students achieve their best with sample questions, graded answers and examiner tips. GradeStudio has been designed to help improve students' answers to exam questions and ultimately their grades.

GradeStudio features throughout the Student Book with extensive examiner guidance and opportunities for students to reflect on, and improve, their learning. In addition to this, interactive GradeStudio activities can be found on the CD-ROM that accompanies the Teacher Guide. These interactive activities build on the GradeStudio material in the Student Book and are ideal for whole class teaching.

The main features of GradeStudio include:
- A real examiner helps you to guide your students through sample answers and mark schemes and helps them assess their own and their peers' work.
- An easy-to-use slider helps students to understand the mark scheme and grade requirements.
- The activities have been written specifically to match the grade-bands of each Student Book. Every question has sample answers for relevant grades so these activities are suitable for E–B grade candidates.
- Each activity and sample answer can be printed out to aid preparation and to be used as you work through the activities front of class.

There are three types of interactive GradeStudio activity on this CD-ROM:

1 Write a sample answer and self assess

Learning objective:
- To help students self assess their work against the mark scheme and identify how to achieve higher marks.

This activity is an opportunity for students to assess their own work with the examiner's help. Students can time themselves typing an answer to the set question or they can paste in an answer they have already written to the question. When they have finished writing, they choose the grade they think they have achieved from the mark scheme. The examiner helps them to check whether they have reached this grade with a series of questions. Finally, the student can rework their answer with the feedback or print it out for the teacher to check. The answer they have written can also be saved.

1 Students are asked if they want to time themselves answering the question. Alternatively they can skip this and paste an answer they have already written to this question.

2 Students can analyse the question and highlight relevant details.

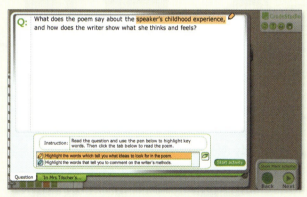

GradeStudio

3 Students type/paste their answer in the space provided and select which grade they think it has achieved.

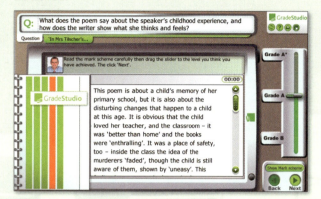

4 Students are prompted to highlight where they have met criteria of the mark scheme and/or answer multiple choice questions.

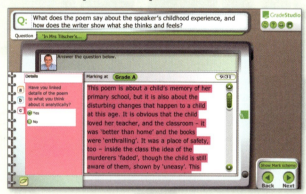

5 Students can then compare their answer with an answer written by the examiner at that grade for further self assessment opportunities.

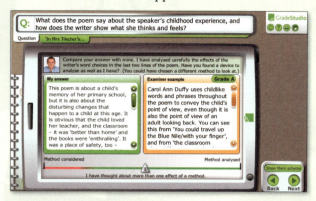

2 Improving a sample answer

Learning objective:
- To show how to move answers up a grade.

This activity is an excellent way to show students, of all abilities, how to improve answers to achieve the next grade. The teacher selects a grade. The class will suggest improvements to the sample answer which can be typed on to your whiteboard. The printout for this activity allows each student to write down their own improvements in the classroom or at home.

You can then see how the examiner would improve the answer and compare the suggestions to those made by the class.

1 Initially, students can analyse the question and highlight relevant details.

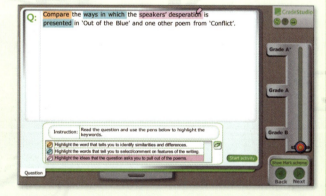

viii   © Pearson Education Limited 2010

2 The teacher annotates and discusses how to improve the sample answer with the class. The examiner will then reveal his suggestions and the class can discuss why this improved the grade.

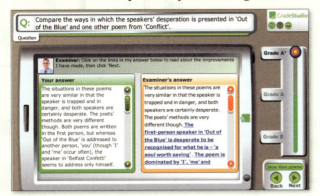

3 The mark scheme can be revealed at any time.

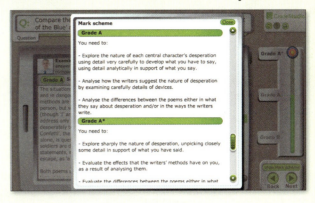

3 Mark a sample answer

Learning objective:
- To understand the mark scheme.

This activity will help you and your students pull apart a sample answer with a highlighting tool. Your students will then assess the strengths and weaknesses of each section by answering a series of questions. At the end of their analysis the students can suggest the grade of the sample answer.

This activity gives the students a chance to be the examiner and really understand how the questions are marked.

1 Initially, students can analyse the question and highlight relevant details.

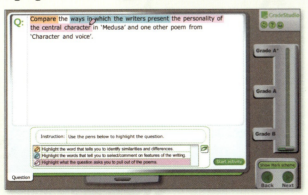

2 Students highlight parts of the sample answer when prompted by the examiner. Based on this analysis students decide the grade the answer deserves, which is checked by the examiner.

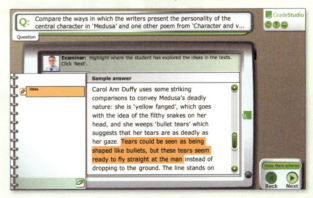

Chapter 1 Character and voice

Getting to know the poems

Assessment Objectives
- **AO1:** respond to texts critically and imaginatively; select and evaluate relevant textual detail to illustrate and support interpretations
- **AO2:** explain how language, structure and form contribute to writers' presentation of ideas, themes and settings
- **AO3:** make comparisons and explain links between texts, evaluating writers' different ways of expressing meaning and achieving effects

Learning Objectives
- To become familiar with the poems as a whole
- To start to make links between the poems

Required resources
- Student Book, pages 2–4
- Worksheets 1.1, 1.2

1 Starter

a Focus on the title of this cluster.

Ask students for definitions of:
- Character: an imaginary person in a work of fiction; someone's nature or personality – what they are 'like'.
- Voice: the way someone speaks, their accent, tone of voice, choice of language.

Record students' definitions on the whiteboard for reference during the lesson.

b Ask students to suggest **two** strong but **very different** characters from recent films or well-known TV programmes, e.g. soap operas. You may want to prompt them with images of current soap characters taken from the Internet.

c Ask students to choose **two** who would have strong characters on which they could comment, then ask them to note down words to describe:
- their chosen characters
- the way these characters speak.

What connections can the students make between character and voice?

Distribute **Worksheet 1.1** to support and to record students' responses.

2 Introduction

a Read through and clarify with the class the focus and purpose of this and subsequent lessons.

b Draw students' attention to the Assessment Objectives that this lesson will support (an explanation of these is available on page v of the Student Book).

c Ask students to locate the cluster in their Anthology.

3 Activity 1

ACTIVITY 1

Read all the 'Character and voice' poems in your AQA Anthology. Just notice what they seem to be about – don't worry about trying to make sense of every line.

a Divide the class into pairs according to ability and allocate poems accordingly, e.g:

More accessible
- Horse Whisperer
- Ozymandias
- Give
- Brendon Gallacher
- On a Portrait of a Deaf Man

Intermediate
- Clown Punk
- Checking Out Me History
- The Ruined Maid
- Les Grands Seigneurs
- Singh Song

More challenging
- My Last Duchess
- The River God
- The Hunchback in the Park
- Casehistory: Alison (head injury)

b Give pairs 5 minutes to read their allocated poem, giving clear prior warning that they will be asked to feed back information and comments to the whole class. Use the prompts below to focus discussion and feedback. (You may want to note these prompts on the board.)
- How difficult is the poem to understand?
- What is the poem about?
- What can you say about the nature of the central character(s)?

c Read each poem to the class or listen to the recordings from the Digital Anthology, then take feedback from the relevant group to ensure understanding. Encourage students to take notes in their anthology or exercise book, recording their first impressions of each poem.

4 Preparation for Activity 2

Ask the class to think of different ways in which these or any other poems can be compared. Note them on the whiteboard. These may echo the categories outlined in the Student Book, or you could add others, e.g. the nature of the central character, the voice of the poem, and whether it uses the first or third person.

5 Activity 2

a Distribute copies of **Worksheet 1.2** and look at the comparison table in Activity 2 on page 3 of the Student Book. Clarify the terms of comparison if necessary. As a class, decide which of the categories on the whiteboard (from the preparation) it will be most useful to focus on. Ask students to add them to the blank columns on the worksheet.

b Reshuffle students into groups of three or four. Clarify with them the precise requirements of this task. Depending on the ability of the class, there are a number of possible approaches. You could:
- set a clear timescale, e.g. 20 minutes for the entire activity, or 3–5 minutes for each heading, taking feedback to ensure understanding
- group the different headings, e.g.
  - titles
  - meaning
  - beginnings and endings
  - length
  - language and imagery
  - rhythm and rhyme
- rather than trying to compare all 15 poems, ask students to put them into pairs, e.g. two with similar content or language choices, or two with very different structures or viewpoints. Encourage students to note what leaps out at them rather than hunt for answers. This is very much an initial activity to familiarise and demystify.

6 Activity 3

Get students to complete this activity in pairs or groups of three. Depending on the time available, ask a range of groups to show and explain their A3 paper to the rest of the class. Try to choose groups that have taken different approaches.

7 Plenary

Take specific feedback on individual poems and points of comparison, then ask students:
- What are your first impressions of this cluster?
- What have you found easier or harder than you expected?
- What support do you feel you will need?

Chapter 1 Character and voice

The Clown Punk
by Simon Armitage

Assessment Objectives
- **AO1:** respond to texts critically and imaginatively; select and evaluate relevant textual detail to illustrate and support interpretations
- **AO2:** explain how language, structure and form contribute to writers' presentation of ideas, themes and settings

Learning Objectives
- To develop students' responses to the poem
- To relate the Assessment Objectives to the poem

Required resources
- Poem text, available on CD-ROM and video/audio online at http://anthology.aqa.org.uk
- Student Book, pages 6, 142–143
- Worksheets 1.3, 1.4, 1.5
- Images of stereotypical clown and punk, if available

1 Starter: exploring images

a Write the words 'clown' and 'punk' on the board. Illustrative images from the Internet may be helpful. Ask students to contribute their thoughts on these, then reflect on:
- their feelings/reactions
- any connections between their responses to the two individuals.

b How do students respond to the two words when they are placed together to describe one person? What expectations do they have of this character and the poem that they are about to read?

2 Activity 1

a Using the Digital Anthology, listen to/watch/read the poem to the class. Clarify any points of understanding.

b Students complete questions 1–8 independently. Take feedback to share, ensure and develop understanding. Display the poem using the Digital Anthology, annotating the text with students' responses using Wordbox.

c Ask students to write a sentence or two summing up the content or meaning of the poem. They can begin: *'The Clown Punk' is about…* .

d Students then add a sentence or two, commenting on the character of the clown punk and the poet's attitude to him.

Initial responses — ACTIVITY 1
1. The poem is about a man who Armitage calls the clown punk. Why do you think he has given him this name?
2. The **speaker** describes a time when the clown punk 'slathers his daft mush on the windscreen'. Explain what he did in your own words.
3. What details tell you that the clown punk is poor?
4. Armitage compares the clown punk to 'a basket of washing that got up and walked'. What does this suggest about his appearance?
5. Why might the children 'wince and scream' at the clown punk?
6. What will happen to the clown punk when he gets older?
7. There are a lot of references to colour in the poem. Find one, and decide what the colour makes you think about the clown.
8. What do you think the writer wants you to feel about the clown punk at the end of the poem? For example, does he want you to laugh at him? Feel sorry for him? Be scared of him? Write a sentence or two explaining your answer.

3 Activity 2

1 Give students 3 minutes to list examples from the poem. Take feedback, circling them on the displayed copy of the poem using Wordbox. List the qualities which the poet's choice of language suggests, e.g. unintelligent, dirty, badly dressed, etc.

2 Display the whole poem, but highlight the final couplet. Remind students of the previous mention of windscreen, when the Clown Punk wiped his 'daft mush' on it. Why, then, would the speaker hope for rain?

Words/phrases to explore (AO1 and AO2) — ACTIVITY 2
1. Write down all the words you can find in the poem which Armitage uses to describe the clown punk, such as 'a basket of washing' and 'deflated'. What do all the words you have found suggest about the speaker's attitude to the clown punk?
2. Think carefully about the phrase 'let it rain' at the end of the poem. What do you think the speaker means? Try to think of two different possible answers.

4 GradeStudio

a Read the GradeStudio extract to the class. Ask: How has the writer of the sample answer shown 'awareness of a writer making choices of language and/or structure and/or form'?

b How could students add to this response to show 'identification of effect(s) of writer's choices of language and/or structure and/or form intended/achieved' and so achieve a D grade? For example: *The poet is describing the man negatively.*

c How could students add a further sentence to show 'explanation of effect(s) of writer's uses of language and/or structure and/or form and effects on readers' and so achieve a C grade? For example: *The image suggests that, like a basket of washing, his clothes are all mixed up and dirty.*

d The students select a second short quotation that will allow them to explore the poet's use of language and its effect on the reader. They then write a paragraph about it using point-evidence-explanation.

> Activity 1, question 4
> In the poem, the writer uses a simile by comparing the punk to 'a basket of washing'.

5 Comparison activities, page 32

Note: In order to do these activities, students would need to have completed their work on 'The Hunchback in the Park'.

a Distribute or display **Worksheet 1.3**. Students complete it independently or as a class to support the use of connectives.

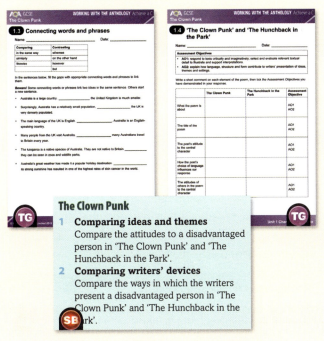

The Clown Punk
1 **Comparing ideas and themes**
Compare the attitudes to a disadvantaged person in 'The Clown Punk' and 'The Hunchback in the Park'.
2 **Comparing writers' devices**
Compare the ways in which the writers present a disadvantaged person in 'The Clown Punk' and 'The Hunchback in the Park'.

b In pairs or independently, students complete **Worksheet 1.4**, linking their response to the poems with the relevant Assessment Objective. Take feedback on any areas that students found difficult to grasp or to comment on.

c Students use their notes from **Worksheet 1.4** to write three or four key points comparing the attitudes in the poems. They should write **in complete sentences using connectives**. Take feedback, compiling notes on the board. As a class, students find evidence from each poem to support each point.

d Ask students to select three points with supporting evidence from those on the board.

e The students add a sentence or two to each point/piece of evidence, explaining and commenting on how the writers have created these powerful characters.

f Students use the grade descriptors on pages 142–143 of the Student Book to assess their own or a partner's work.

Suggested answers

Activity 1

1 'Clown' suggests the man is an object of humour or mockery, and perhaps refers to his appearance; 'punk' suggests, again, his appearance or perhaps his threatening behaviour. Both suggest a lack of respect for the man.

2 The clown punk pressed his face to the windscreen of the narrator's car in a threatening way.

3 Details that suggest the clown punk's poverty include:
- He is on the 'shonky' side of town.
- 'Like a basket of washing' suggests he is not well dressed.
- His dog is 'on a rope'.

4 A basket of washing is, clearly, not human – the comparison dehumanises the man. It also suggests that his clothes are mismatched, dirty, and that he is so thin his clothes appear to be empty.

5 He is disturbing and scary.

6 He will become 'deflated' and 'shrunken', suggesting a withered and wrinkled face.

7
- 'indelible ink' suggests that the clown punk is covered in tattoos (referred to later in the poem), making him seem even less human
- 'pixel' suggests that the clown punk is a computer image, made up of dots of colour, rather than a real person
- 'dyed brain' suggests that the ink of the tattoos has affected his intelligence as well as his skin.

8 All are arguable. Likely responses will be either positive or negative: revulsion, fear, mockery or sympathy.

Activity 2

1 town clown, basket of washing, towing a dog on a rope, deflated, shrunken, sad tattoos, daft mush, dyed brain. All are negative and suggest mockery and disrespect.

2
- The poet is vindictively hoping the clown punk will get wet.
- The poet wants it to rain so that the windscreen wipers will erase the picture of the clown punk from his memory.
- The poet wants the rain to clean his windscreen where the clown punk has slathered his 'mush' on it.

Comparison activities

Key points for this activity are provided in **Worksheet 1.5**.

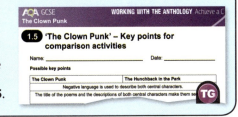

6 Plenary

Take feedback on 'The Clown Punk', annotating the poem displayed on the whiteboard using Wordbox. Focus on relevant key features, e.g:
- content
- interpretation
- language
- structure
- tone.

If students have studied and compared 'The Hunchback in the Park', take feedback on relevant key similarities and differences in content, interpretation, language, structure or tone.

Chapter 1 Character and voice

Checking Out Me History by John Agard

Assessment Objectives
- **AO1:** respond to texts critically and imaginatively; select and evaluate relevant textual detail to illustrate and support interpretations
- **AO2:** explain how language, structure and form contribute to writers' presentation of ideas, themes and settings

Learning Objectives
- To develop students' responses to the poem
- To relate the Assessment Objectives to the poem

Required resources
- Poem text, available on CD-ROM and video/audio online at http://anthology.aqa.org.uk
- Student Book, page 7
- Worksheets 1.3, 1.6, 1.7a 1.7b, 1.8

1 Starter

a Before looking at the Student Book, distribute or display the **top half only** of **Worksheet 1.6**. Ask students if they can name the historical figures described. For the first, they may name Florence Nightingale; for the second, Winston Churchill, the Duke of Wellington or Horatio Nelson; for the third, Nelson Mandela, Mahatma Gandhi or Martin Luther King.

b Now reveal the lower half of the worksheet. How many of these historical figures have students heard of? Why is this? Aim for a response that recognises that most UK students are taught white European/American history.

2 Activity 1

a Using the Digital Anthology, listen to/watch/read the poem to the class. Clarify any points of understanding.

b Students complete questions 1–5 independently. Take feedback to share, ensure and develop understanding. Display the poem using the Digital Anthology, annotating the text with students' responses using Wordbox.

c Take feedback, focusing on the point that Agard is using his poem to make.

d Ask students to write a sentence or two summing up the content or meaning of the poem. They can begin: 'Checking Out Me History' is about... .

3 Activity 2

Take a range of responses from students. Initial responses may focus on teachers. Aim towards the broadest possible answer, acknowledging that history is inextricably linked with culture and the values it perpetuates through education.

Words/phrases to explore (AO1 and AO2) — ACTIVITY 2

Agard begins the poem with 'Dem tell me', and repeats it at the beginning of the last stanza. Who are 'dem' by the end of the poem, do you th...

4 GradeStudio

a Read the GradeStudio extract to the class. Ask: How has the writer of the sample answer shown 'details linked to interpretation'?

b Ask students to select other short quotations that reflect Agard's point of view and the effect he wants to have on the reader, e.g. the references to nursery rhymes and children's stories. The students then use those quotations to write a point-evidence-explanation paragraph exploring Agard's point of view.

GradeStudio
Sample answer
To achieve a C on this AO2 descriptor, you need to show **explanation of effects of writer's use of language.** To do this, you need to explain clearly what the effect is on you as the reader, not just say what the device is. The following extract from a sample answer would hit the grade C requirement.

> Activity 1, question 3a
> The writer describes Mary Seacole as 'a healing star' and 'a yellow sunrise'. These metaphors suggest something high in the sky, and shining, so she's like a hero, somebody to look up to, as the speaker clearly does.

5 Comparison activities, page 32

Note: In order to do these activities, students would need to have completed their work on 'Brendon Gallacher' and 'Horse Whisperer.'

1 a In pairs or independently, students complete **Worksheet 1.7a**, linking their response to the poems with the relevant Assessment Objective. Take feedback on any areas that students found difficult to grasp or to comment on.

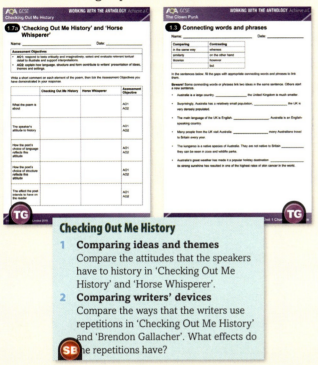

Checking Out Me History

1 Comparing ideas and themes
Compare the attitudes that the speakers have to history in 'Checking Out Me History' and 'Horse Whisperer'.

2 Comparing writers' devices
Compare the ways that the writers use repetitions in 'Checking Out Me History' and 'Brendon Gallacher'. What effects do the repetitions have?

b Students use their notes from **Worksheet 1.7a** to write three or four key points comparing the two poems' attitudes to history. They should write **in complete sentences using connectives**. Display **Worksheet 1.3** to support them.

c Take feedback, compiling notes on the board. As a class, students find evidence from each poem to support each point.

d Ask students to select three points with supporting evidence from those on the board.

e Students add a sentence or two to each point/piece of evidence, explaining and commenting on how the writers have presented their ideas.

2 Repeat the above sequence, using **Worksheet 1.7b** to explore how repetition is used in the poems.

6 Plenary

Take feedback on 'Checking Out Me History', annotating the displayed poem using Wordbox. Focus on relevant key features, e.g:
- content
- language
- tone
- interpretation
- structure

If students have studied and compared 'Horse Whisperer' and/or 'Brendon Gallacher', take feedback on relevant key similarities and differences in content, interpretation, language, structure or tone.

Suggested answers

Activity 1

1 • **Real events:** the Norman invasion of Britain in 1066; the discovery of the hot-air balloon; Lord Nelson; the Battle of Waterloo; Columbus's arrival in America in 1492; Florence Nightingale.
  • **Characters from children's stories:** Dick Whittington and his cat; Robin Hood.
  • **Nursery rhymes:** 'Hey Diddle Diddle' ('the cow jumped over the moon, the dish ran away with the spoon'); 'Old King Cole'.

2 Toussaint L'Ouverture; Nanny de Maroon; Shaka; the Spanish invasion of the Caribbean in 1492; Mary Seacole.

3 **a** vision, beacon, see-far, dream, hopeful, freedom, great, brave, healing star, yellow sunrise.
  b Short lines add impact and emphasis to these figures who Agard clearly admires and wants to draw attention to.

4 **a** 'see-far' and 'fire-woman' suggest she is mythical.
  b 'struggle' and 'freedom' suggest something real.
  c 'fire', 'stream' and 'river' suggest she is like a force of nature, at one with her land.

5 '[check] out me own history/…[carve] out me identity'. Agard suggests he will research his own history to help him understand who he is.

Activity 2

A range of possible responses, from *teachers* to *every member of our culture who ignores the contributions and achievements of people from Agard's culture*.

Comparison activities

Keys points for this activity are provided in **Worksheet 1.8**.

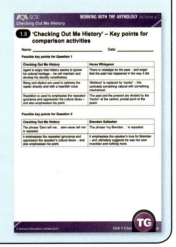

Chapter 1 Character and voice

Horse Whisperer by Andrew Forster

Assessment Objectives
- **AO1:** respond to texts critically and imaginatively; select and evaluate relevant textual detail to illustrate and support interpretations
- **AO2:** explain how language, structure and form contribute to writers' presentation of ideas, themes and settings

Learning Objectives
- To develop students' responses to the poem
- To relate the Assessment Objectives to the poem

Required resources
- Poem text, available on CD-ROM and video/audio online at http://anthology.aqa.org.uk
- Student Book, page 8
- Worksheets 1.3, 1.9, 1.10, 1.11

1 Starter
Display only the title of the poem. What associations does it have for the class? If the term is not familiar, explain it is someone who is seemingly able to communicate directly with horses. How do they think someone who claimed to be able to talk to animals would have been regarded, **a)** two hundred years ago, **b)** today?

2 Activity 1
a Using the Digital Anthology, listen to/watch/read the poem to the class. Clarify any points of understanding.

b Students complete questions 1–7 independently. Take feedback. Annotate the displayed text with students' responses using Wordbox.

c Take the class's initial response to the poem, commenting on the presentation of character and voice in the poem.

d Ask students to write a sentence or two summing up the content or meaning of the poem. They can begin with: *'The Horse Whisperer' is about…* .

Initial responses — ACTIVITY 1
1. What different things does the whisperer do to help the horses, or the people who owned them?
2. **a** Make a list of the things the speaker says and thinks about horses.
   b For each item in your list, write down what this shows about her attitude to horses.
3. How does the speaker see herself? What sort of character does she think she is? Look at what she says about herself, and the words she uses to describe what she does.
4. Why do you think the whisperer's 'secret' in the first **stanza** worked? Why would it draw the horses to her?
5. What was the 'legacy of whispers' do you think?
6. The first two stanzas describe how people used to want the whisperer, because 'They shouted for me'. What changed this? Look in the third stanza for the clue. Why do you think it led to the whisperers being driven out?
7. Which word in the fourth stanza suggests that the whisperer is almost like the horses?

3 Activity 2
a Display the last four lines of the poem in close-up.

b Students discuss the question in pairs, writing their response in full sentences to ensure clarity of thought and their ability to express it. Take feedback, annotating the displayed quotation using Wordbox. Aim to validate all interpretations supported with evidence from elsewhere in the poem and/or explanation.

Words/phrases to explore (AO1 and AO2) — ACTIVITY 2
Look at the end of the poem.
1. How does the writer create a sense of the horses being alive by the words he uses here? Look at the type of words he uses and the repetition of sound and **rhythm**.
2. Why would the whisperer know about the breath and veins? Think about where she would stand.

4 GradeStudio
a Read the GradeStudio extract to the class. Ask: How has the writer of the sample answer shown an 'explanation of the effect(s) of writer's uses of language and/or form and/or structure and effects on readers'?

b Ask students to select another quotation that reflects the poet's choice of language, form or structure and its effect on the reader, e.g. the language she uses to describe her skills: 'secret', 'legacy of whispers'; or comparing the language used to describe the situation before and after the tractors came. Students then write a point-evidence-explanation paragraph exploring the effect of their chosen quotation.

GradeStudio Sample answer
To achieve a C on this AO2 descriptor, you need to show **explanation of effect(s) of writer's uses of language and/or structure and/or form.** The following extract from a sample answer would hit the grade C requirement.

Activity 1, question 7
'Stampede' is quite a normal word to use to describe the hasty exit of a lot of people, but in this poem 'stampede' makes you think of the horses, because really it applies to animals – so it seems as though the whisperers were driven out like the animals they treated.

5 Comparison activities, page 32

Note: In order to do these activities, students would need to have completed their work on 'The Hunchback in the Park' and 'My Last Duchess'.

1 a In pairs or independently, students complete **Worksheet 1.9**, linking their response to the poems with the relevant Assessment Objective. Take feedback on any areas that students found difficult to grasp or to comment on.

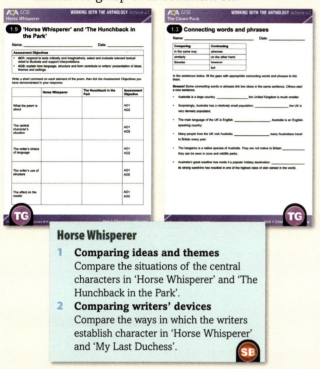

Horse Whisperer

1 **Comparing ideas and themes**
Compare the situations of the central characters in 'Horse Whisperer' and 'The Hunchback in the Park'.

2 **Comparing writers' devices**
Compare the ways in which the writers establish character in 'Horse Whisperer' and 'My Last Duchess'.

b Using their notes from **Worksheet 1.9**, students write three or four key points comparing the main characters in the poems. They should write **in complete sentences using connectives**. Display **Worksheet 1.3** to support them.

c Take feedback, compiling notes on the board. As a class, students find evidence from each poem to support each point.

d Ask students to select three points with supporting evidence from those on the board.

e Students add a sentence or two to each point/piece of evidence, explaining and commenting on how the writers have presented their points of view.

2 Repeat the above sequence, using **Worksheet 1.10** to explore how character is established.

6 Plenary

Take feedback on 'Horse Whisperer', annotating the poem displayed on the whiteboard using Wordbox. Focus on relevant key features, e.g:
- content
- language
- tone.
- interpretation
- structure

If students have studied and compared 'The Hunchback in the Park' and/or 'My Last Duchess', take feedback on relevant similarities and differences in content, interpretation, language, structure or tone.

Suggested answers

Activity 1

1 When horses were restless, or refused to pull the plough, she would encourage them with a piece of 'spongy tissue'. If they were frightened of something, e.g. they reared at burning straw, he would use a frog's wishbone to 'give them a new fear' from which he would lead them.

2 Respectful and admiring ('shimmering muscles… pride'); combative ('helpless children'); affectionate and nostalgic ('still I miss them').

3 Initially, the speaker has a clear sense of her own value ('they shouted for me… the life blood'). She talks of the tools of her trade as a 'secret' and a 'legacy of whispers' suggesting her work is mysterious, perhaps almost magical. However, she shows a bitter relish in her power once rejected ('the tools of revenge').

4 Perhaps it encourages the horse's maternal instinct?

5 Her horse whispering knowledge.

6 Tractors replaced horses as working farm animals so the whisperers are no longer needed – and their 'skills' came to be regarded as witchcraft.

7 stampede.

Activity 2

1 A range of positive language is used. The even rhythm of 'The searing breath, glistening veins, steady tread' reflects the rhythm of their movement, but the rhythm is broken, and so emphasises in conjunction with its repetition, 'the pride' she feels.

2 'breath' and 'veins' suggest the horse whisperer standing by the horse's head, suggesting closeness, both physical and emotional.

Comparison activities

Key points for this activity are provided in **Worksheet 1.11**.

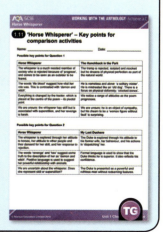

AQA GCSE Working with the Anthology: Achieve a C   9

Chapter 1 Character and voice

Medusa
by Carol Ann Duffy

Assessment Objectives
- **AO1:** respond to texts critically and imaginatively; select and evaluate relevant textual detail to illustrate and support interpretations
- **AO2:** explain how language, structure and form contribute to writers' presentation of ideas, themes and settings

Learning Objectives
- To develop students' responses to the poem
- To relate the Assessment Objectives to the poem

Required resources
- Poem text, available on CD-ROM and video/audio online at http://anthology.aqa.org.uk
- Student Book, page 9
- Worksheets 1.3, 1.12, 1.13, 1.14, 1.15
- Images of Medusa from the Internet, if possible (see starter activity)

1 Starter: exploring images

a Read the story of Medusa on **Worksheet 1.12** (more modern retellings are available).

b Display a range of images of Medusa from the Internet, e.g. Caravaggio's *Medusa*, Cellini's *Perseus with the Head of Medusa*, Böcklin's *Medusa*, Rubens' *Tête de Méduse*. Ask the students how Medusa is portrayed.

2 Activity 1

a Using the Digital Anthology, listen to/watch/read the poem to the class. Clarify any points of understanding. Does the poem meet students' expectations, having seen the images and read a retelling of the story? Ask: What is surprising in the poem?

b Students complete questions 1–7 independently. Take feedback to share, ensure and develop understanding. Display the poem using the Digital Anthology, annotating the text with students' responses using Wordbox.

c Discuss with students: Is this poem a retelling of the story of Medusa from the Gorgon's point of view? Look for responses that recognise that this is the story of an elderly, bitter, jealous woman whom Duffy describes as if she were Medusa, using the myth as a metaphor.

d Ask students to write a sentence or two summing up the content or meaning of the poem. They can begin: *'Medusa' is about…*.

3 Activity 2

a Distribute **Worksheet 1.13** for students to record their **top three** answers. Encourage the use of supporting evidence/explanation.

b Take feedback, highlighting and annotating the poem.

Words/phrases to explore (AO1) — ACTIVITY 2

Which phrase in the poem best sums up Medusa's state of mind? Make sure that you can find more than one reason for your choice

4 GradeStudio

a Read the GradeStudio extract to the class. Ask: How has the writer of the sample answer shown 'appreciation/consideration of writers' uses of language and/or structure and/or form and effects on readers'?

b Ask students to select another quotation that reflects the poet's choice of language, form or structure and its effect on the reader, e.g. the use of repetition and rhetorical questions in the penultimate stanza. Students then write a point-evidence-explanation paragraph exploring the effect of their chosen quotation.

GradeStudio
Sample answer
To achieve a B on this AO2 descriptor, you need to show **appreciation/consideration of writers' uses of language and/or structure and/or form and effects on readers**. To do this, you need to say at least two things about a writer's choice. The following extract from a sample answer would hit the grade B requirement.

Activity 1, question 7b
The last line being on its own makes the threat seem immediate, and the last word 'now' makes the reader imagine the end of the poem is the moment when he turns to stone.

5 Comparison activities, page 32

Note: In order to do these activities, students would need to have completed their work on 'Les Grands Seigneurs'.

a In pairs or independently, students complete **Worksheet 1.14**, linking their response to the poems with the relevant Assessment Objective. Take feedback on any areas that students found difficult to grasp or to comment on.

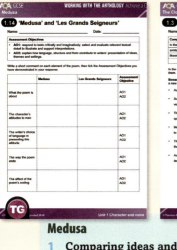

Medusa
1. **Comparing ideas and themes**
   Compare the attitudes to men in 'Medusa' and 'Les Grands Seigneurs'.
2. **Comparing writers' devices**
   Compare the effects of the ways the endings are written in 'Medusa' and 'Les Grands Seigneurs'.

b Ask students to use their notes from **Worksheet 1.14** to write three or four key points comparing the attitudes to men and the effects of the endings in the two poems. They should write **in complete sentences using connectives**. Display **Worksheet 1.3** to support them.

c Take feedback, compiling notes on the board. As a class, students find evidence from each poem to support each point.

d Ask students to select three points with supporting evidence from those on the board.

e Students add a sentence or two to each point/piece of evidence, explaining and commenting on how the writers have presented their ideas.

6 Plenary

Take feedback on 'Medusa', annotating the poem displayed on the whiteboard using Wordbox. Focus on relevant key features, e.g:
- content
- language
- tone.
- interpretation
- structure

If students have studied and compared 'Les Grands Seigneurs', take feedback on relevant key similarities and differences in content, interpretation, language, structure or tone.

Suggested answers

Activity 1

1. She suspects her husband is being unfaithful and, it is implied, she tries to kill him.
2. 'snakes', 'Greek God', turning living creatures to stone, a mirror, a Gorgon, a shield, a sword, 'Look at me now'.
3. Suspicion, doubt, jealousy. Her thoughts are described as snakes that 'hissed and spat on my scalp'.
4. Her breath is 'soured', her lungs are 'grey bags'. The overriding image is one of decay and discolouration, suggesting not only age but some kind of corrosion caused by her foul mouth.
5. She describes herself as 'yellow fanged' (continuing the theme of decay and discolouration) and her tears as 'bullets'.
6. Medusa is threatening to turn him to stone. This is better for her because he will not be able to 'stray'; he is unable to leave her.
7. **a** 'your girls, your girls'. The repetition suggests Medusa's growing anger and resentment.
   b The line's isolation at the end of the poem gives it emphasis, drama and immediacy, as though this is the moment when she confronts her Greek god with her gaze.
   c It refers to the fact that she is no longer fragrant and young; but also implies a command, an order, so that he will be turned to stone.

Activity 2

All answers are arguable with supporting evidence and explanation.

Comparison activities

Key points for this activity are provided in **Worksheet 1.15**.

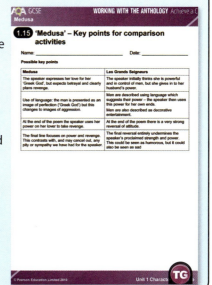

Chapter 1 Character and voice

Singh Song by Daljit Nagra

Assessment Objectives
- **AO1:** respond to texts critically and imaginatively; select and evaluate relevant textual detail to illustrate and support interpretations
- **AO2:** explain how language, structure and form contribute to writers' presentation of ideas, themes and settings

Learning Objectives
- To develop students' responses to the poem
- To relate the Assessment Objectives to the poem

Required resources
- Poem text, available on CD-ROM and video/audio online at http://anthology.aqa.org.uk
- Student Book, page 10
- Worksheets 1.3, 1.16, 1.17, 1.18, 1.19

1 Starter
Write the words 'Asian shopkeeper' on the whiteboard. Ask students to suggest the words, thoughts, ideas and associations that this phrase conjures for them, carefully challenging and moderating any extreme stereotyping before recording them on the board.

2 Activity 1

a Using the Digital Anthology, listen to/watch/read the poem to the class. Clarify any points of understanding.

b Take students' initial response to the poem, commenting on the character and life of Singh. To what extent does this poem meet expectations of a poem written in the *persona* of an Asian shopkeeper? What are the surprising features?

c Students complete questions 1–7 independently. Take feedback to share, ensure and develop understanding. Display the poem using the Digital Anthology, annotating the text with students' responses using Wordbox.

d Ask students to write a sentence or two summing up the content or meaning of the poem. They can begin: 'Singh Song' is about… .

Initial responses — ACTIVITY 1
1 Although there are other voices in the poem, the main voice is Singh's. What does the poem reveal about his life? Think about:
 • what he has to do • how he is treated by other people.
2 What is revealed about Singh's character? Think about:
 • his response to other people • his attitude to his bride.
3 What is revealed about Singh's bride? Think about:
 • what she does • her appearance • her attitude to other people.
4 Look at the **stanza** beginning 'Late in de midnight hour'. Which words and phrases suggest an atmosphere of romance here, and which words and phrases seem to show the opposite?
5 Look at the conversation between Singh and his bride. How are their words typical of each of them?
6 The last line of the poem is 'Is priceless baby'. Can you think of more than one meaning for the word 'priceless' here? Why do you think the writer decided to end with this word?
7 The voice in the poem speaks in Indian English. Which words do you think are **dialect words** (words from a specific region), rather than the writer just showing accent (how the words are spoken)?

3 Activity 2
Students can use **Worksheet 1.16** to develop their responses to this task. Take feedback to share, ensure and develop understanding.

Words/phrases to explore (AO1) — ACTIVITY 2
What do you think are the most important things in Singh's life, and what doesn't he care about? Write these in a list, using details from the poem. Then turn your list into a paragraph of writing to answer the question.

4 GradeStudio

a Read the GradeStudio extract to the class. Ask: How has the writer of the sample answer shown an 'explained response to element(s) of text'?

b How could students rewrite or add to this response to show 'sustained response to element(s) of text' and so achieve a C grade? Ask them to add a sentence or two in which they select evidence to support the point and comment on the way the writer has written about this character. For example: *The shoppers call it 'di worst Indian shop/on di whole Indian road' but Singh does not care about his shop, only about his love for his 'newly bride'.*

c Students select another quotation that will allow them to explore their response to the character in the poem. They then use that quotation to write a point-evidence-explanation paragraph exploring its effect.

GradeStudio Sample answer
To achieve a D on this AO2 descriptor, you need to show **explained response to element(s) of text**. This means you need to explain why you think what you think. The following extract from a sample answer would hit the grade D requirement.

Activity 1, question 1
I think Singh must be a hopeless shopkeeper, because he doesn't label his goods properly, his shop is dirty, and he closes when he feels like it to be with his horrible bride.

12 © Pearson Education Limited 2010

5 Comparison activities, page 32

Note: In order to do these activities, students would need to have completed their work on 'My Last Duchess' and 'The River God'.

1 a In pairs or independently, students complete **Worksheet 1.17**, linking their response to the poems with the relevant Assessment Objective. Take feedback on any areas that students found difficult to grasp or to comment on.

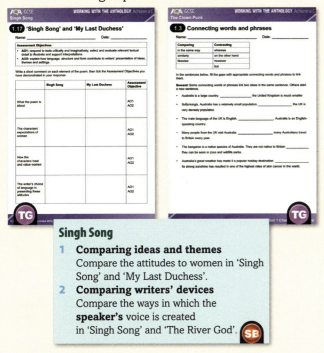

Singh Song

1 **Comparing ideas and themes**
Compare the attitudes to women in 'Singh Song' and 'My Last Duchess'.

2 **Comparing writers' devices**
Compare the ways in which the **speaker's** voice is created in 'Singh Song' and 'The River God'.

b Ask students to use their notes from **Worksheet 1.17** to write three or four key points comparing the attitudes to women in the poems. They should write **in complete sentences using connectives**. Display **Worksheet 1.3** to support them.

c Take feedback, compiling notes on the board. As a class, students find evidence from each poem to support each point.

d Ask students to select three points with supporting evidence from those on the board.

e The students then add a sentence or two to each point/evidence, explaining and commenting on how the writers have presented their points of view.

2 Repeat the above sequence, using **Worksheet 1.18** to explore the speakers' voices in the poems.

6 Plenary

Take feedback on 'Singh Song', annotating the poem displayed on the whiteboard using Wordbox. Focus on relevant key features, e.g:
- content
- language
- tone
- interpretation
- structure

If students have studied and compared 'My Last Duchess' and/or 'The River God', take feedback on relevant key similarities and differences in content, interpretation, language, structure or tone.

Suggested answers

Activity 1

1.
   - Singh runs his father's shop, working very long hours.
   - Shoppers accuse him of running the worst Indian shop in the Indian Road.

2. Singh does not seem bothered by the accusations of his shoppers and, despite her behaviour and appearance, seems besotted by his 'newly bride'.

3.
   - While he is working, she is upstairs on the computer, negotiating prices.
   - Her appearance is eccentric: 'red crew cut', 'Tartan sari', 'donkey jacket' – not traditional Indian clothing.
   - She swears at Singh's mum, laughs at his dad; so apparently has no respect for Singh's family. However, she chases girls who steal sweets from the shop, implying a respect for Singh.

4.
   - Romantic: 'whispering', 'silver', 'beaches', 'moon'.
   - Unromantic: 'precinct', 'concrete', 'stool', 'chocolate bars', 'half-price signs'.

5. She is perhaps more business-orientated, although entering into this nightly, romantic exchange; he is purely romantic, his thoughts constantly focused on her.

6. It could mean it is unpriced, i.e. has no price label on it – or that it is beyond price. It suggests a rejection of his business in favour of his love for his wife.

7. The majority of the poem reflects accent rather than dialect, although there are a small number of examples, e.g. 'newly bride', 'brightey moon'.

Activity 2

Most important: his 'newly bride', food shared with his wife ('chapatti… chutney'), his relationship with his wife ('vee hav made luv'), romance ('di brightey moon').

Does not care about: the customers' complaints ('di worst Indian shop'), his bride's attitude to his parents ('she effing at my mum… making fun at my daddy').

Comparison activities

Key points for this activity are provided in **Worksheet 1.19**.

Chapter 1 Character and voice

Brendon Gallacher
by Jackie Kay

Assessment Objectives
- **AO1:** respond to texts critically and imaginatively; select and evaluate relevant textual detail to illustrate and support interpretations
- **AO2:** explain how language, structure and form contribute to writers' presentation of ideas, themes and settings

Learning Objectives
- To develop students' responses to the poem
- To relate the Assessment Objectives to the poem

Required resources
- Poem text, available on CD-ROM and video/audio online at http://anthology.aqa.org.uk
- Student Book, page 11
- Worksheets 1.3, 1.20, 1.21, 1.22

1 Starter
Ask if any students had imaginary friends when they were young. Aim for some kind of conclusion as to why children invent them: to make life more interesting, to make up for something lacking, perhaps because of loneliness.

2 Activity 1
a Using the Digital Anthology, listen to/watch/read the poem to the class. Clarify any points of understanding.

b Students complete questions 1–6 independently. Display the poem using the Digital Anthology, annotating the text with students' responses using Wordbox. They can record their responses to questions 2 and 3 together on **Worksheet 1.20**. Take feedback to share, ensure and develop understanding.

c Take students' initial responses to the poem, commenting on the character and voice of the speaker.

d Ask students to write a sentence or two summing up the content or meaning of the poem. They can begin: 'Brendon Gallacher' is about… .

Initial responses — ACTIVITY 1

1 'My Brendon Gallacher' is repeated throughout the poem. Why do you think the writer includes it three times in the opening **stanza**?

2 In the first stanza the writer creates a contrast between the **speaker's** family and Brendon's by balancing the two as she writes. The first is 'He was seven and I was six.' Write down as many other balances like this from the first stanza as you can.

3 What clue does the first line of the second stanza give for another possible reason for the child inventing Brendon? What does that tell you about the child's life?

4 'how his mum drank and his daddy was a cat burglar.' Why do you think the child creates this?

5 a What additional things about Brendon that might appeal to the speaker are mentioned in the last stanza?
   b Do they suggest anything about the child?

6 Why do you think the writer repeats the words 'oh' and 'Brendon' in the last line? What does this repetition tell you about how the child is feeling?

3 Activity 2
a Students identify examples of simple language and sentences. Take feedback.

b Students then work in pairs, suggesting typical features of children's language. Take feedback, listing them on the board. How many of these features are used in the poem?

Words/phrases to explore (AO2) — ACTIVITY 2

The line 'how his mum drank and his daddy was a cat burglar' sounds like a child speaking. How does the writer create the language and thoughts of a child? Look for simple words and sentences.

4 GradeStudio
a Read the GradeStudio extract to the class. Ask: How has the writer of the sample answer shown 'appropriate comment on ideas/themes'?

b Ask students to identify another possible opportunity to comment on the ideas or themes in the poem. For example, the kind of exciting, dangerous friend that the speaker invents.

c Students select a quotation that reflects their response to the task above. They then use that quotation to write a point-evidence-explanation paragraph exploring its effect.

GradeStudio

Sample answer — C

To achieve a C on this AO2 descriptor, you need to show **appropriate comment on ideas/themes**. The following extract from a sample answer would hit the grade C requirement.

'And he died then' is a moment of shock for the reader – not only the realisation that Brendon was an 'imaginary friend', but that he was a friend so real as to be living for the child. The loss is very real for her, therefore.

5 Comparison activities, page 32

Note: In order to do these activities, students would need to have completed their work on 'On a Portrait of a Deaf Man'.

a In pairs or alone, students complete **Worksheet 1.21**, linking their response to the poem with the relevant Assessment Objective. Take feedback on any areas that students found difficult to grasp or to comment on.

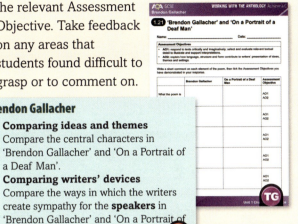

Brendon Gallacher
1 **Comparing ideas and themes**
Compare the central characters in 'Brendon Gallacher' and 'On a Portrait of a Deaf Man'.
2 **Comparing writers' devices**
Compare the ways in which the writers create sympathy for the **speakers** in 'Brendon Gallacher' and 'On a Portrait of a Deaf Man'.

b Ask students to use their notes from **Worksheet 1.21** to write three or four key points comparing the central characters and the ways in which sympathy is created in the two poems. They should write **in complete sentences using connectives**. Display **Worksheet 1.3** as support.

c Take feedback, compiling notes on the board. As a class, students find evidence from each poem to support each point.

d Ask students to select three points with supporting evidence from those on the board.

e The students add a sentence or two to each point/piece of evidence, explaining and commenting on how the writers have presented their points of view.

6 Plenary

Take feedback on 'Brendon Gallacher', annotating the poem displayed on the whiteboard using Wordbox. Focus on relevant key features, e.g:
- content
- language
- tone.
- interpretation
- structure

If students have studied and compared 'On a Portrait of a Deaf Man', take feedback on relevant key similarities and differences in content, interpretation, language, structure or tone.

Suggested answers

Activity 1

1 The repetition emphasises his importance to the speaker; and constant use of 'my' emphasises her possession of him.

2 **The speaker** is Scottish, six years old, has one brother, his father is a Communist Party worker.
Brendon Gallacher is Irish, seven years old, has six brothers, his father (a cat burglar) is in prison. Suggests perhaps that the speaker wishes she had a larger family and a father with a more dangerous, glamorous job. She also perhaps likes the idea of an older friend.

3 Suggests she took comfort from his presence – perhaps because she feared the river.

4 Perhaps adds an element of danger and excitement to her staid life.

5 a/b 'his spiky hair', 'impish grin', and his 'flapping ear' suggest someone untidy, excitingly dangerous, mischievous and fun, and someone who would listen.

6 a/b It suggests her sadness and regret at his 'death' – and emphasises her love for him.

Activity 2

Simple language/sentence structure is used throughout. Also:
- use of repetition
- short sentences suggest a gasping child in a hurry
- longer sentences are joined using simple connectives (and, when, where)
- strange linking of short, half-explanations: 'he's got big holes in his trousers' immediately followed by 'I like meeting him by the burn'.

Comparison activities

Key points for this activity are provided in **Worksheet 1.22**.

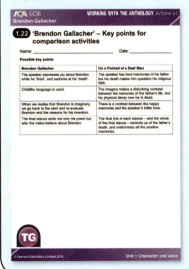

Chapter 1 Character and voice

Give by Simon Armitage

Assessment Objectives
- **AO1:** respond to texts critically and imaginatively; select and evaluate relevant textual detail to illustrate and support interpretations
- **AO2:** explain how language, structure and form contribute to writers' presentation of ideas, themes and settings

Learning Objectives
- To develop students' responses to the poem
- To relate the Assessment Objectives to the poem

Required resources
- Poem text, available on CD-ROM and video/audio online at http://anthology.aqa.org.uk
- Student Book, page 12
- Worksheets 1.3, 1.23, 1.24, 1.25

1 Starter
Write the word 'homeless' on the board and ask students for their responses. Depending on their response, ask them to broaden their thinking by considering others' attitudes. Aim for a range of views, from deeply sympathetic to the opposite.

2 Activity 1

a Using the Digital Anthology, listen to/watch/read the poem to the class. Clarify any points of understanding.

b Students complete questions 1–7 independently. Take feedback to share, ensure and develop understanding. Display the poem using the Digital Anthology, annotating the text with students' responses using Wordbox.

c Take students' initial responses to the poem, commenting on the character, voice and attitude of the speaker.

d Ask students to write a sentence or two summing up the content or meaning of the poem. They can begin: *'Give' is about...*.

ACTIVITY 1
Initial responses
1 What is the **speaker's** situation, exactly? Why do you think he is desperate?
2 Who do you think the beggar is speaking to? Try to think of more than one possibility, and then check through the poem to see if the beggar's words make sense for each possibility.
3 What does the other person think of the beggar? Find a detail from the poem to back up your point.
4 How does the beggar feel about having to beg? How do you know?
5 How does the reader know that the beggar is desperate? Look at the middle of the poem, not just the end, and trace the way the voice moves from one thing to the next.
6 a There are lots of patterns in this poem. Look at the first two lines, which form a sentence, and the next two lines, which also form a sentence. How are they very alike in the words the writer has chosen?
   b The sentences end with the two words 'here' and 'yours'. Why do you think the writer has decided to end with these?
   c How does **rhyme** emphasise these two words?
7 Now look at the last two lines.
   a What do you notice about the length of sentences?
   b Is there any rhyme or **half-rhyme** in these lines?
   c What is the effect of these last two lines?

3 Activity 2
Give students 2 minutes to discuss this activity in pairs and write down as many possible interpretations as they can: not only of the word 'change' but more specifically the kind of change that the beggar is hoping for. If necessary, allow a further 2 minutes for students to consider what the beggar thinks should 'change'. Take feedback to share, ensure and develop understanding.

ACTIVITY 2
Words/phrases to explore (AO1)
Look again at line 10. What 'change' does the speaker mean? Think about two possible meanings of the word.

4 GradeStudio

a Read the GradeStudio extract to the class. Ask: How has the writer of the sample answer shown 'thoughtful consideration of ideas/themes'? How has s/he offered more than one idea about the ideas in the poem?

b Ask students to identify another possible opportunity to comment on the ideas and themes in the poem. For example, to whom the poem is addressed, or what the beggar is actually begging for.

c Students select a quotation that reflects their response to the task above. They then use that quotation to write a point-evidence-explanation paragraph exploring its effect.

GradeStudio
Sample answer C
To achieve a C on this AO2 descriptor, you need to show **appropriate comment on ideas/themes**. To do this, you need to make a clear statement about an idea in the poem. The following extract from a sample answer would hit the grade C requirement:

Activity 1, question 5
The beggar doesn't like his situation, and seems resentful – he's made a deliberate choice of of the person to approach, and 'That's big of you' seems almost aggressive.

5 Comparison activities, page 32

Note: In order to do these activities, students would need to have completed their work on 'Medusa' and 'The Clown Punk'.

1 **a** In pairs or independently, students complete **Worksheet 1.23**, linking their response to the poem with the relevant Assessment Objective. Take feedback on any areas that students found difficult to grasp or to comment on.

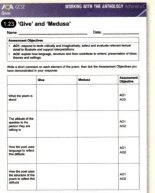

Give

1 **Comparing ideas and themes**
Compare the attitudes of the voices in 'Give' and 'Medusa' to the person they are speaking to.

2 **Comparing writers' devices**
Compare the writing of the last two lines of 'Give' with the last two lines of 'The Clown Punk'. Look at the length of the sentences, the effects of the full stops and the rhymes, and the effects of the last four words of each poem.

b Ask students to use their notes from **Worksheet 1.23** to write three or four key points comparing the attitudes of the voices in the two poems. They should write **in complete sentences using connectives**. Display **Worksheet 1.3** to support them.

c Take feedback, compiling notes on the board. As a class, students find evidence from each poem to support each point.

d Ask students to select three points with supporting evidence from those on the board.

e They then add a sentence or two to each point/piece of evidence, explaining and commenting on how the writers have presented their points of view.

2 Repeat the above sequence, using **Worksheet 1.24** to explore the final couplet of each poem.

6 Plenary

Take feedback on 'Give', annotating the poem displayed on the whiteboard using Wordbox. Focus on relevant key features, e.g:
- content
- language
- tone.
- interpretation
- structure

If students have studied and compared 'Medusa' and/or 'The Clown Punk', take feedback on relevant key similarities and differences in content, interpretation, language, structure or tone.

Suggested answers

Activity 1

1 A homeless person, begging for money.

2 A range of possibilities:
- the person – perhaps a shopkeeper – whose doorway s/he has been sleeping in
- the reader being confronted by this representation of homelessness: the poem is the 'public place' in which the beggar has chosen to 'make a scene'.

3 The other person shows some sympathy for the beggar by offering tea.

4 Resentment is suggested by emphasising the beggar's situation: 'on the street, under the stars' and with the hyperbolic sarcasm of the lengths to which he will go for money: 'swallow swords, eat fire'.

5 The beggar says he will do almost anything for money, his offers growing with his desperation: from coppers to silver to gold. He is literally and figuratively begging on his knees.

6 **a** Short sentences.
b 'give'/'big'; 'tea'/'knees'; 'big'/'beg'; 'you'/'you'.
c Further weight is added to these two words: they are the concluding rhyme to the two couplets which open the poem.

Activity 2

The word 'change' suggests not only coins but also a change in the beggar's circumstances, in society's attitude to the homeless, and perhaps to the society itself that allows people to fall into homelessness and begging.

Comparison activities

Key points for this activity are provided in **Worksheet 1.25**.

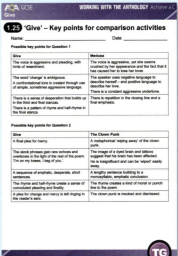

Chapter 1 Character and voice

Les Grands Seigneurs by Dorothy Molloy

Assessment Objectives
- **AO1:** respond to texts critically and imaginatively; select and evaluate relevant textual detail to illustrate and support interpretations
- **AO2:** explain how language, structure and form contribute to writers' presentation of ideas, themes and settings

Learning Objectives
- To develop students' responses to the poem
- To relate the Assessment Objectives to the poem

Required resources
- Poem text, available on CD-ROM and video/audio online at http://anthology.aqa.org.uk
- Student Book, page 13
- Worksheets 1.3, 1.26, 1.27, 1.28

1 Starter
Ask students to think about the future:
- Do they expect to get married at some point in their lives?
- How do they think their attitudes to the opposite sex will change when they are married/commit to a partner?
- How do they expect their own behaviour to change when they are married/commit to a partner?

Record on the board the effect that students feel marriage and/or commitment to a partner has on people.

2 Activity 1
a Using the Digital Anthology, listen to/watch/read the poem to the class. Clarify any points of understanding, in particular the meaning of the title: a French phrase meaning 'The Great Lords', often used ironically.

b Students complete questions 1–4 independently. Take feedback to share, ensure and develop understanding. Display the poem using the Digital Anthology, annotating the text with students' responses using Wordbox.

c Take the class's initial response to the poem, commenting on the character and voice of the speaker.

d Ask students to write a sentence or two summing up the content or meaning of the poem. They can begin: 'Les Grands Seigneurs' is about....

3 Activity 2
Ask students to discuss and record their responses in pairs. Take feedback to share and ensure understanding. Is the poem an accurate representation of marriage and the relationship between men and women? How does this equate with our expectations of sexual equality?

4 GradeStudio
a Read the GradeStudio extract to the class. Ask: How has the writer of the sample answer shown an 'awareness of ideas/themes'?

b How could students rewrite or add to this response to show 'appropriate comment on ideas/themes' and so achieve a C grade? Discuss as a whole class. Give students 3 minutes to write an additional sentence or two. For example: *Before marriage, she treated men as 'rocking horses' which suggests they were <u>her</u> playthings. The poem is suggesting that marriage can precisely reverse the roles of women and men.*

c Ask students to identify another possible opportunity to make appropriate comment on the poem's ideas/themes. For example, exploring the things to which the speaker compares men before her marriage to identify her attitude and approach to men.

d Students select a quotation that reflects their response to the task above. They then use that quotation to write a point-evidence-explanation paragraph exploring its effect.

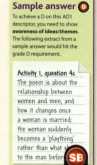

5 Comparison activities, page 33

Note: In order to do these activities, students would need to have completed their work on 'Medusa' and 'My Last Duchess'.

1 a In pairs or independently, students complete **Worksheet 1.26**, linking their response to the poem with the relevant Assessment Objective. Take feedback on any areas that students found difficult to grasp or to comment on.

Les Grands Seigneurs

1 **Comparing ideas and themes**
Compare the attitudes to men in 'Les Grands Seigneurs' and 'Medusa'.

2 **Comparing writers' devices**
Compare the ways in which voice is created in 'Les Grands Seigneurs' and 'My Last Duchess'.

b Ask students to use their notes from **Worksheet 1.26** to write three or four key points comparing the attitudes to men. They should write **in complete sentences using connectives**. Display **Worksheet 1.3** to support them.

c Take feedback, compiling notes on the board. As a class, students find evidence from each poem to support each point.

d Ask students to select three points with supporting evidence from those on the board.

e They then add a sentence or two to each point/piece of evidence, explaining and commenting on how the writers have presented their points of view.

2 Repeat the above sequence, using **Worksheet 1.27** to explore the ways in which voice is created in the poems.

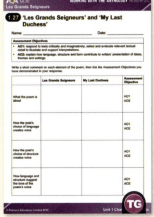

6 Plenary

Take feedback on 'Les Grands Seigneurs', annotating the poem displayed on the whiteboard using Wordbox. Focus on relevant key features, e.g:
- content
- language
- tone.
- interpretation
- structure

If students have studied and compared 'Medusa' and/or 'My Last Duchess', take feedback on relevant key similarities and differences in content, interpretation, language, structure or tone.

Suggested answers

Activity 1

1 Men serve the role of protection and entertainment for the speaker; she is their 'queen'.

2 Animals (birds, in particular), ships, toys/entertainers ('rocking-horses'/'hurdy-gurdy monkey-men').

3 **a** She was their untouchable ruler.
   b 'buttresses', 'castellated towers', 'bowers', 'sailing ships', 'hurdy-gurdy monkey-men'.

4 **a** The use of 'But'.
   b Use of slang ('bedded', 'fluff'), the conversational tone of the brackets and direct address to the reader.
   c They imply that she is no longer in charge but entirely subservient to her husband: their roles have swapped.
   d The connection between 'bedded' and 'overnight' imply a sexual element in this change.

Activity 2

It suggests her power over men was based on bluff and that her role in her marriage is more in keeping with her true self.

Comparison activities

Key points for this activity are provided in **Worksheet 1.28**.

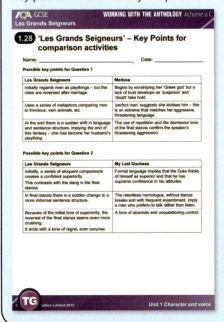

AQA GCSE Working with the Anthology: Achieve a C 19

Chapter 1 Character and voice

Ozymandias by Percy Bysshe Shelley

Assessment Objectives
- **AO1:** respond to texts critically and imaginatively; select and evaluate relevant textual detail to illustrate and support interpretations
- **AO2:** explain how language, structure and form contribute to writers' presentation of ideas, themes and settings

Learning Objectives
- To develop students' responses to the poem
- To relate the Assessment Objectives to the poem

Required resources
- Poem text, available on CD-ROM and video/audio online at http://anthology.aqa.org.uk
- Student Book, page 14
- Worksheets 1.3, 1.29, 1.30
- Images from the Internet, if available (see starter activity)

1 Starter: exploring images

a Display a suitable image of a commemorative statue from the Internet, if possible. For example, Nelson (at the top of his column), Winston Churchill (outside the Houses of Parliament), Saddam Hussain (in Baghdad).

b Discuss: Why are statues erected in honour of people?

c Ask: How does it change your view if you know that the person represented by the statue ordered its creation and erection?

2 Activity 1

a Using the Digital Anthology, listen to/watch/read the poem to the class. Clarify any points of understanding.

b Students complete questions 1–7 independently. Take feedback to share, ensure and develop understanding. Display the poem using the Digital Anthology, annotating the text with students' responses using Wordbox.

c Take students' initial response to the poem, commenting on the poet's intention.

d Ask students to write a sentence or two summing up the content or meaning of the poem. They can begin: *'Ozymandias' is about....*

Initial responses — ACTIVITY 1
1 Ozymandias was a great king. What tells you this in the poem?
2 Find and write down the **adjectives** in lines 2 and 4. What picture do they create of the statue?
3 What do the ends of line 4 and line 5 suggest about the nature of the king?
4 How do you think the king treated his subjects? Try to find a detail to support your view.
5 a 'Look on my works, Ye Mighty, and despair!' What did Ozymandias mean when he had this written on his statue?
  b What does it mean now that the statue has been destroyed?
6 Line 12 begins 'Nothing beside remains.' This is the shortest sentence in the poem.
  a Why do you think Shelley has used such a short sentence?
  b Why do you think he has placed it after the previous thought, 'Look on my works, Ye Mighty, and despair!'?
7 Find the adjectives in the last two lines. What do they emphasise?

3 Activity 2

a Ask students to discuss and record their responses in pairs. Take feedback to share and ensure understanding.

b Take the discussion further. Ask: Why is the poem set at one remove from the reader – the majority of the poem spoken in the voice of a traveller who told the story to the narrator?

Words/phrases to explore (AO1 and AO2) — ACTIVITY 2
1 At the beginning of the poem the traveller is 'from an antique land'. Why do you think the writer isn't more exact about the place?
2 What difference would it make to the poem if he was more exact, and made it about a specific place?

4 GradeStudio

a Read the GradeStudio extract to the class. Ask: How has the writer of the sample answer shown an 'explanation of effect(s) of writer's uses of language and/or structure and/or form and effects on readers'? What two things has s/he said about the writer's choice?

b Ask students to identify another possible opportunity to analyse a detail of Shelley's language. For example, the implications about the character of Ozymandias, or the short sentence in line 12.

c Students select a quotation that reflects their response to the task above. They then use that quotation to write a point-evidence-explanation paragraph exploring its effect.

GradeStudio Sample answer
To achieve a C on this AO2 descriptor, you need to show **explanation of effect(s) of writers' uses of language and/or structure and/or form and effects on readers**. The following extract from a sample answer would hit the grade C requirement because it explains the effect of the use of certain words.

Activity 1, question 7
In the last line the words 'level' and 'stretch far away' emphasise how complete the destruction is, because it suggests that absolutely nothing is breaking the surface of the sand, where there used to be a great civilisation.

5 Comparison activities, page 33

Note: In order to do these activities, students would need to have completed their work on 'My Last Duchess'.

a In pairs or independently, students complete **Worksheet 1.29**, linking their response to the poems with the relevant Assessment Objective. Take feedback on any areas that students found difficult to grasp or to comment on.

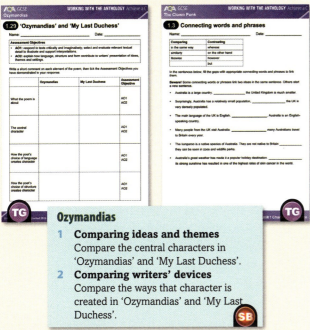

Ozymandias

1 **Comparing ideas and themes**
Compare the central characters in 'Ozymandias' and 'My Last Duchess'.
2 **Comparing writers' devices**
Compare the ways that character is created in 'Ozymandias' and 'My Last Duchess'.

b Students use their notes from **Worksheet 1.29** to write three or four key points comparing the central characters and the ways that they are created in the two poems. They should write **in complete sentences using connectives**. Display **Worksheet 1.3** to support them.

c Take feedback, compiling notes on the board. As a class, students find evidence from each poem to support each point.

d Ask students to select three points with supporting evidence from those on the board.

e Students add a sentence or two to each point/piece of evidence, explaining and commenting on how the writers have presented their points of view.

6 Plenary

Take feedback on 'Ozymandias', annotating the poem displayed on the whiteboard using Wordbox. Focus on relevant key features, e.g:
- content
- language
- tone.
- interpretation
- structure

If students have studied and compared 'My Last Duchess', take feedback on relevant key similarities and differences in content, interpretation, language, structure or tone.

Suggested answers

Activity 1

1 The inscription on the base of the statue suggests that this was how Ozymandias saw himself. 'vast' also implies the once great scale – and arrogance – of Ozymandias and his kingdom.

2 'trunkless', 'half sunk', 'shattered' emphasise the collapse of the statue and of his kingdom – and the transience of all human activity.

3 They suggest that Ozymandias was a powerful, cruel and overbearing king.

4 'sneer of cold command' – 'sneer' suggests his contempt for his people, 'cold' his unemotional ruthlessness, 'command' his expectations of absolute obedience.

5 a/b At the time it was written on the statue, it stood as a warning to Ozymandias' mighty enemies. Now the statue has fallen, it acts as a warning to those who think they are mighty: that their might will not last and that all things must pass.

6 a Such a short sentence has been used for emphasis: there is literally nothing else to describe.
 b The proud boast inscribed on the statue's pedestal is immediately negated. Placing it at the start of the line gives further emphasis.

7 'colossal', 'boundless', 'bare', 'lone', 'level', all emphasise the vast emptiness which now occupies the space where Ozymandias' kingdom once stood.

Activity 2

'antique' implies an ancient civilisation such as Greece, Rome or Egypt. The lack of exactness gives the poem a greater universality: this is not just about the fall of an empire; it is about the fall of all empires, and of all human achievement.

Comparison activities

Keys points for this activity are provided in **Worksheet 1.30**.

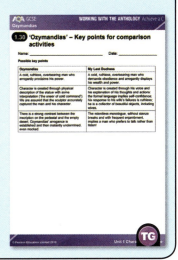

AQA GCSE Working with the Anthology: Achieve a C 21

Chapter 1 Character and voice

My Last Duchess
by Robert Browning

Assessment Objectives:
- **AO1:** respond to texts critically and imaginatively; select and evaluate relevant textual detail to illustrate and support interpretations
- **AO2:** explain how language, structure and form contribute to writers' presentation of ideas, themes and settings

Learning Objectives:
- To develop students' responses to the poem
- To relate the Assessment Objectives to the poem

Resources required:
- Poem text, available on CD-ROM and video/audio online at http://anthology.aqa.org.uk
- Student Book, page 15
- Worksheets 1.3, 1.31, 1.32, 1.33, 1.34

1 Starter

a Display or distribute **Worksheet 1.31**. Give students 5 minutes to consider and note down their responses to the questions in pairs.

b Take feedback, gathering responses on the board.
- Who will the narrator of the poem be?
- What does the word 'last' imply? Look for possible interpretations implying either 'final' or 'the most recent', with the implied suggestion that he has dispensed with his previous 'model' and is about to 'update'.
- What can be inferred about the character of the narrator from the title alone?

2 Activity 1

a Using the Digital Anthology, listen to/watch/read the poem to the class. Clarify any points of understanding.

b Students complete questions 1–5 independently. Take feedback to share, ensure and develop understanding. Display the poem using the Digital Anthology, annotating the text with students' responses using Wordbox.

c Return to the notes taken on the board during the Starter. Consider with the students whether the evidence from the poem supports the interpretations of the title discussed.

d Ask students to write a sentence or two summing up the content or meaning of the poem. They can begin: *'My Last Duchess' is about...* .

3 Activity 2

a Give students 5 minutes to discuss their response to the task in pairs, noting their thoughts. Take feedback to share and ensure understanding.

b Use this discussion to gather and note on the board a range of vocabulary to describe the Duke, e.g. arrogant, cold, calculating, ruthless, merciless.

c Give students a further 5 minutes to write a paragraph on the character of the Duke, using the quotation 'for me'.

Words/phrases to explore (AO1) — ACTIVITY 2
1. The last two words of the poem are 'for me'. Why do you think the writer chose these as the last words?
2. How do they form a suitable end for the whole poem? You could write a paragraph about the Duke starting from those words.

4 GradeStudio

a Read the GradeStudio extract to the class. Ask: How has the writer of the sample answer shown a 'sustained response to elements of text'?

b Ask students to identify another possible opportunity to explore the Duke's character. For example, the Duke's description of the Duchess's behaviour, or those things which the Duchess 'ranked' as equal to 'my gift of a nine-hundred-years-old name'.

c Students select a quotation that reflects their response to the task above. They then use that quotation to write a point-evidence-explanation paragraph exploring its effect.

GradeStudio Sample answer
To achieve a C on this AO1 descriptor, you need to show **sustained response to elements of text**. The following extract from a sample answer would hit the grade C requirement.

The Duke appears to admire other people, like Frà Pandolf, but really he only admires himself. He is the only person allowed to draw back the curtain over the picture, and he chooses 'never to stoop' as that would lessen his importance in his own eyes. He demands that others admire him too, and when the Duchess dares to 'approve' of anybody else, the Duke thinks they are 'fools' and disapproves of her so much it seems that he had her ki

5 Comparison activities, page 33

Note: In order to do these activities, students would need to have completed their work on 'Les Grands Seigneurs' and 'The River God'.

1. **a** In pairs or independently, students complete **Worksheet 1.32**, linking their response to the poem with the relevant Assessment Objective. Take feedback on any areas that students found difficult to grasp or to comment on.

    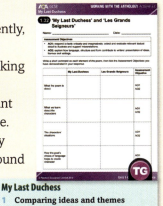

    b Ask students to use their notes from **Worksheet 1.32** to write three or four key points comparing the characters' situations in the two poems. They should write **in complete sentences using connectives**. Display **Worksheet 1.3** to support them.

    c Take feedback, compiling notes on the board. As a class, students find evidence from each poem to support each point.

    d Ask students to select three points with supporting evidence from those on the board.

    e The students then add a sentence or two to each point/piece of evidence, explaining and commenting on how the writers have presented their points of view.

2. Repeat the above sequence, using **Worksheet 1.33** to explore the voices created in the two poems.

6 Plenary

Take feedback on 'My Last Duchess', annotating the poem displayed on the whiteboard using Wordbox. Focus on relevant key features, e.g:
- content
- language
- tone.
- interpretation
- structure

If students have studied and compared 'Les Grands Seigneurs' and/or 'The River God', take feedback on relevant key similarities and differences in content, interpretation, language, structure or tone.

Suggested answers

Activity 1

1. He seems powerful and ruthless, e.g. 'if they durst…'.

2. **a** No facts are given about the Duchess, only the Duke's point of view regarding her behaviour.

   b The Duke describes other people flattering her, smiling at her, presenting her with gifts. It seems she was popular and, perhaps, beautiful.

   c She was easily flattered ('She had/A heart… too soon made glad'); she did not value the Duke's gift of marriage more highly than other gifts; she smiled freely at the Duke and at everyone else.

   d The Duke feels he deserves respect and deference – particularly from his wife. The Duchess enjoyed the attention and flattery she received and was, perhaps, unwilling to be as subservient as her husband demanded.

3. His family name is 900 years old and should be highly respected, especially by his wife to whom he has given it. He does not consider that he has 'skill/In speech' which, judging by the language and fluency of this monologue, seems to be false modesty – or an excuse for not verbally correcting his wife's behaviour. He considers such correction beneath him ('I choose/Never to stoop').

4. 'There she stands' implies she is still alive; before the next line reminds us that we are only looking at a portrait. We presume she has been killed.

5. He is to re-marry, suggesting that he will continue to marry until he finds a wife who is suitably subservient and respectful – and ruthlessly despatch any who do not meet his standards.

   He then points out the bronze statue of Neptune taming a sea-horse. The metaphorical implication is that the Duke regards himself as a god and the Duchess as a creature to be tamed. The pointing out of the statue immediately after the Duchess's portrait places them on a par: both are beautiful objects to be collected, displayed and boasted about.

Activity 2

The final two words leave no doubt about the Duke's sense of self-importance. Everything in his life is done to suit him, or for his pleasure. Anything which does not do this is disposed of.

Comparison activities

Key points for this activity are provided in **Worksheet 1.34**.

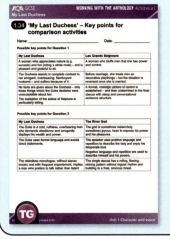

Chapter 1 Character and voice

The River God
by Stevie Smith

Assessment Objectives
- **AO1:** respond to texts critically and imaginatively; select and evaluate relevant textual detail to illustrate and support interpretations
- **AO2:** explain how language, structure and form contribute to writers' presentation of ideas, themes and settings

Learning Objectives
- To develop students' responses to the poem
- To relate the Assessment Objectives to the poem

Required resources
- Poem text, available on CD-ROM and video/audio online at http://anthology.aqa.org.uk
- Student Book, page 16
- Worksheets 1.3, 1.35, 1.36
- Images of gods, if available (see starter activity)

1 Starter: exploring images

a If possible, show students some artists' representations of gods, such as Michelangelo's *Creation of Adam*, Blake's *God Judging Adam*, Crane's *The Horses of Neptune*.

b Ask: What do the pictures suggest about gods? What are the artists' – and the students' – perceptions of gods?

c Gather descriptive vocabulary on the whiteboard, e.g. powerful, omnipotent, vengeful, angry, mysterious, supernatural.

2 Activity 1

a Using the Digital Anthology, listen to/watch/read the poem to the class. Clarify any points of understanding.

b Students complete questions 1–6 independently. Take feedback to share, ensure and develop understanding. Display the poem using the Digital Anthology, annotating the text with students' responses using Wordbox.

c Take the class's initial response to the poem, commenting on the character and voice of the river god.

d Ask students to write a sentence or two summing up the content or meaning of the poem. They can begin: 'The River God' is about….

Initial responses — ACTIVITY 1

1. What sort of character does the god seem to be to you? Think about:
   - what he enjoys
   - his attitude to the woman
   - what he thinks of himself
   - the words he uses to show what he thinks.
2. How does the writer make the voice seem like a god? Look at the attitudes the voice has, and the words it uses. 'Where my fish float by' suggests he owns them, for example. What else can you find?
3. The river god is a spirit of water. Find as many references to water and rivers as you can, starting with the second line.
4. Look at lines 17–18. What is the god's attitude to the things in his river here? Look carefully at both lines.
5. Look at the **rhyme** in the poem.
   a. How does the **rhyme scheme** change in the last four lines?
   b. Why do you think the writer chooses to rhyme 'bed' and 'head'?
   c. 'Head' and 'her' do not rhyme. Why do you think the writer chose not to rhyme the last two lines?
   d. What effect does the last line have? Notice that it's a sentence all in one line.
6. Look at the repetitions and **exclamations** in the poem, like 'yippity-yap'. What effects do they have on your impression of him?

3 Activity 2

a Students can work on this independently followed by feedback, or as a class discussion. Emphasise the importance of evidence to support points of view.

b Use feedback/discussion to validate, eliminate or add to the vocabulary collected on the whiteboard during the starter activity, describing the character of the river god.

Words/phrases to explore (AO1 and AO2) — ACTIVITY 2
What overall effect does the voice of the god have on you, the reader? Do you like him, or not?

4 GradeStudio

a Read the GradeStudio extract to the class. Ask: How has the writer of the sample answer shown 'a considered/qualified response to text'?

b What other examples of this kind of contrast or contradiction can students find in the poem? For example, the contrast of the river's age and smell with the lady's golden hair and beauty.

c What effect does this contrast have? Ask students to write a paragraph following the same point-evidence-explanation structure.

GradeStudio
Sample answer B
To achieve a B on this AO1 descriptor, you need to make a **considered response**. To do this, you need to think about more than one thing. The following extract from a sample answer would hit the grade B requirement:

> Activity 1, question 1
> In some ways the god seems to be kind, as he blesses the fish and seems to like people swimming, and having fun. It is very sinister fun, though, as it includes a deliberate drowning and imprisonment of the body.

5 Comparison activities, page 33

Note: In order to do these activities, students would need to have completed their work on 'Medusa'.

a In pairs or independently, students complete **Worksheet 1.35**, linking their response to the poems with the relevant Assessment Objective. Take feedback on any areas that students found difficult to grasp or to comment on.

The River God

1. **Comparing ideas and themes**
   Compare the central characters in 'The River God' and 'Medusa'.
2. **Comparing writers' devices**
   Compare the ways the characters in 'The River God' and 'Medusa' are shown to have power.

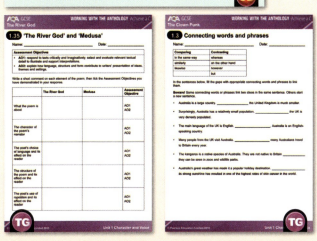

b Students use their notes from **Worksheet 1.35** to write three or four key points comparing the central characters and the ways their power is created in the two poems. They should write **in complete sentences using connectives**. Display **Worksheet 1.3** to support them.

c Ask students to select three points for each question in the activity with supporting evidence from the board.

d Students add a sentence or two to each point/piece of evidence, explaining and commenting on how the writers have presented their ideas.

6 Plenary

Take feedback on 'The River God', annotating the poem displayed on the whiteboard using Wordbox. Focus on relevant key features, e.g:
- content
- language
- tone.
- interpretation
- structure

If students have studied and compared 'Medusa', take feedback on relevant key similarities and differences in content, interpretation, language, structure or tone.

Suggested answers

Activity 1

1.
   - He enjoys the fish who swim in him and the people who bathe, especially women.
   - He seems to love the woman he drowned – he thinks she is beautiful and does not want her to leave him.
   - He thinks he is smelly and old, but he has 'plenty of go'.
   - The language he uses is simple suggesting the simple – perhaps naive, almost childlike – pleasure he takes in himself and in his victim.

2. The river god is kind to his own creatures: 'I bless their swimming'. But he is brutal and vindictive to those who anger him:
   'I can drown the fools
   Who bathe too close to the weir, contrary to rules.
   …As I throw them up now and then in the spirit of clowning.'

3. 'pebbles', 'reedy', 'pools', 'fish', 'float', 'swimming', 'bathe', 'drown', 'weir', 'flow', 'water runs cold', 'deep river bed', 'weed', 'reed', 'wash'.

4. It suggests a great pride and love for his 'beautiful river bed' while 'hold her' suggests, perhaps, tenderness for the 'beautiful lady' – or perhaps imprisonment.

5. **a** The rhyme scheme has changed from abab to abba.
   b It connects the lady, the river, her 'sleep' and her death.
   c/d A final rhyming couplet often gives a sense of conclusion. However, by choosing not to rhyme the last two lines, the writer has created a disturbing sense of lingering threat.

6.
   - Repetition of 'old' and 'smelly' adds to the disturbing tone of the poem, in direct contrast to the image of a 'golden sleepy head' which is not sleeping but dead.
   - The initial exclamations suggest joy, energy and playfulness, echoing 'merrily I flow' with 'plenty of go'. The third and final exclamation of 'Hi yih' followed by 'do not let her go' seems more anxious or even desperate.

Activity 2

Likely responses are either positive or negative: of sympathy or revulsion. Both should be supported with evidence.

Comparison activities

Key points for this activity are provided in **Worksheet 1.36**.

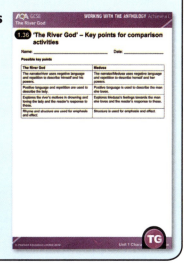

Chapter 1 Character and voice

The Hunchback in the Park
by Dylan Thomas

Assessment Objectives
- **AO1:** respond to texts critically and imaginatively; select and evaluate relevant textual detail to illustrate and support interpretations
- **AO2:** explain how language, structure and form contribute to writers' presentation of ideas, themes and settings

Learning Objectives
- To develop students' responses to the poem
- To relate the Assessment Objectives to the poem

Required resources
- Poem text, available on CD-ROM and video/audio online at http://anthology.aqa.org.uk
- Student Book, page 17
- Worksheet 1.3, 1.37, 1.38

1 Starter

Before looking at the poem, write its title on the board. What does it suggest to the students? Focus initially on the word 'hunchback', drawing out attitudes and responses to this kind of disfigurement:
- What do the students expect the poem to be about?
- Does the word 'hunchback' remind students of anyone from their own experience?
- How do the students think these people are treated by the local community?
- How might they expect a poet to treat this figure?

2 Activity 1

a Using the Digital Anthology, listen to/watch/read the poem to the class. Clarify any points of understanding.

b Students complete questions 1–7 independently. Take feedback to share, ensure and develop understanding. Display the poem using the Digital Anthology, annotating the text with students' responses using Wordbox.

c Take students' initial response to the poem, commenting on the character of the hunchback and the various attitudes to him expressed in the poem.

d Ask students to write a sentence or two summing up the content or meaning of the poem. They can begin: 'The Hunchback in the Park' is about… .

Initial responses — ACTIVITY 1
1 What are your first impressions of the hunchback? Find details from the poem to support what you think.
2 In the first **stanza**, the hunchback enters when the lock is opened, like the trees and water. This makes him seem more like part of nature than human. Now look carefully through the rest of the poem and write down examples of words and phrases that make him seem part of nature.
3 The writer also shows him as being like an animal. Starting with line 11, find examples of where the writer does this.
4 In the fourth stanza, the trees are described as a 'loud zoo'. Why? Think of as many reasons as you can. Try seeing the phrase from all the points of view in the poem – the boys, the hunchback, and the **speaker** in the poem.
5 In the fifth stanza, how does the writer get inside the minds of the boys? Think about what they are imagining.
6 In the sixth stanza, how does the writer get inside the mind of the hunchback? What does this stanza show about what he thinks?
7 a In the last stanza, what things have followed the hunchback out of the park? How?
b Now think about the word 'unmade'. How has the park been 'unmade'?

3 Activity 2

a Focus students on the first part of the question. Allow 2 minutes for pairs to discuss a range of possibilities. What evidence supports their decision? Take class feedback, aiming to come to a consensus.

b Ask students to identify and note down evidence from the poem to support their response. Take feedback to ensure understanding. How does the narrator's response to the hunchback and the boys' influence affect our response to them – and to him?

Words/phrases to explore (AO1) — ACTIVITY 2
Think again about the 'I' in the second stanza. Using details from the poem:
1 Who do you think he is, and how old is he?
2 What do you think his response is to the hunchback, and to the boys?

4 GradeStudio

a Read the GradeStudio extract to the class. Ask: How has the writer of the sample answer shown 'appropriate comment on ideas/themes'?

b Ask students to identify other features of the poem that might affect the reader's response to the hunchback. What effect do they have?

c Students write a paragraph commenting on the reader's possible response to the hunchback, following the point-evidence-explanation structure.

GradeStudio — Sample answer
To achieve a C on this AO1 descriptor, you need to show **appropriate comment on ideas/themes**. The following extract from a sample answer would hit the grade C requirement.

Activity 1, question 6
It would be easy to see the hunchback as some sort of old pervert because he imagines a woman, but the key thing is that he imagines her 'straight', 'straight and tall', unlike his 'crooked bones'. He imagines what he would like to be, just like the boys who imagine 'tigers' and 'sailors' in the woods.

5 Comparison activities, page 33

Note: In order to do these activities, students would need to have completed their work on 'The Clown Punk'.

a In pairs or independently, students complete **Worksheet 1.37**, linking their response to the poems with the relevant Assessment Objective. Take feedback on any areas that students found difficult to grasp or to comment on.

> **The Hunchback in the Park**
> 1 **Comparing ideas and themes**
>   Compare the central characters of 'The Hunchback in the Park' and 'The Clown Punk'.
> 2 **Comparing writers' devices**
>   Compare the ways the central characters are created in 'The Hunchback in the Park' and 'The Clown Punk'.

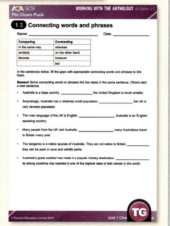

b Students use their notes from **Worksheet 1.37** to write three or four key points comparing the attitudes and endings of the two poems. They should write **in complete sentences using connectives**. Display **Worksheet 1.3** to support them.

c Take feedback, compiling notes on the board. As a class, students find evidence from each poem to support each point.

d Ask students to select three points with supporting evidence from those on the board.

e Students add a sentence or two to each point/piece of evidence, explaining and commenting on how the writers have presented their central characters.

6 Plenary

Take feedback on 'The Hunchback in the Park', annotating the poem displayed on the whiteboard using Wordbox. Focus on relevant key features, e.g:

- content
- language
- tone.
- interpretation
- structure

If students have studied and compared 'The Clown Punk', take feedback on relevant key similarities and differences in content, interpretation, language, structure or tone.

Suggested answers

Activity 1

1 The hunchback seems to live a sad, solitary life, mocked by children – but he dreams of transformation.

2 Stanza 3: The hunchback is compared to the park birds; he sits down 'Like the water'. Stanza 6: he transforms into a 'woman figure' described as 'Straight as a young elm'.

3 In stanza 5 he is described as an 'old dog sleeper' and in stanzas 2 and 7 reference is made to him sleeping in a kennel. He is compared to park birds in stanza 3.

4 It reflects the noise the boys are making, acting like 'tigers', and behaving like animals – in both senses!

5 By describing the tigers jumping 'out of their eyes', suggesting their imaginations becoming reality.

6 Similarly, the hunchback's imagination creates a 'woman figure' who grows 'Straight and tall from his crooked bones', suggesting a desire to escape from his disfigurement and his transience: a transformation to the permanence and beauty of nature.

7 a The railings, shrubberies, birds, grass, trees, lake, wild boys.

  b The poem seems to suggest that, once people are locked out of the park, the features of the park are no more: they only exist when they can be seen and experienced.

Activity 2

- The poem is based on Thomas's own experience as a child in Cwmdonkin Park, Swansea. The key evidence is 'the fountain basin where I sailed my ship', suggesting a young boy is speaking.
- The description of the 'loud' boys, suggests a wariness, or even fear of their behaviour; the description of the hunchback being taunted by the boys and sleeping in a kennel suggests sympathy for him.

Comparison activities

Key points for this activity are provided in **Worksheet 1.38**.

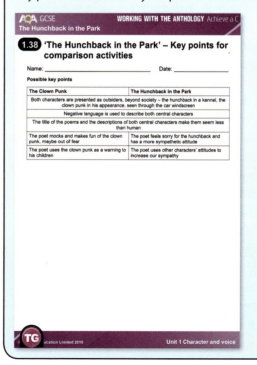

Chapter 1 Character and voice

The Ruined Maid by Thomas Hardy

Assessment Objectives
- **AO1:** respond to texts critically and imaginatively; select and evaluate relevant textual detail to illustrate and support interpretations
- **AO2:** explain how language, structure and form contribute to writers' presentation of ideas, themes and settings

Learning Objectives
- To develop students' responses to the poem
- To relate the Assessment Objectives to the poem

Required resources
- Poem text, available on CD-ROM and video/audio online at http://anthology.aqa.org.uk
- Student Book, page 18
- Worksheets 1.3, 1.39, 1.40, 1.41

1 Starter
Write the word 'reputation' on the board.
Discuss:
- Is it good to have a 'reputation'?
- What constitutes a 'good reputation' or a 'bad reputation' for boys or girls, focusing in particular on sexual activity?
- Does it differ, depending on gender?
- How is it affected if the loss of reputation is counterbalanced with financial gain (perhaps picking a relevant example from the media, e.g. a model who poses naked, undergoes surgery, but gains fame and wealth as a result)?

2 Activity 1
a Using the Digital Anthology, listen to/watch/read the poem to the class. Clarify any points of understanding.
b Students complete questions 1–7 independently. Take feedback to share, ensure and develop understanding. Display the poem using the Digital Anthology, annotating the text with students' responses using Wordbox.
c Take the class's initial response, commenting on the two characters and the issues raised by the poem. The poem was written in 1866: are these issues still relevant today?
d Ask students to write a sentence or two summing up the content or meaning of the poem. They can begin: *'The Ruined Maid' is about…*. Take feedback, clarifying that it is prostitution which has allowed Melia to transform herself.

3 Activity 2
Discuss the questions as a class. All answers are valid – however, they should be considered in the light of society's values at the time of writing. In the Victorian era, prostitution was described as 'the great social evil', while the lives and rights of working people were only just beginning to be considered a possible concern – and the rights of women were hardly considered at all. Perhaps it is this issue which Hardy is challenging in the poem.

4 GradeStudio
a Read the GradeStudio extract to the class. Ask: How has the writer of the sample answer shown a 'thoughtful consideration of ideas and themes'?
b Ask students to add another sentence to the sample answer, commenting on Hardy's intention in creating this irony. For example: *Perhaps Hardy is suggesting that prostitution is the only means of escape from the harsh labour of country life and, in doing this, is drawing our attention to the limited possibilities that women faced at this time.*
c Ask students to identify other ways in which Hardy draws attention to the contrast between the speakers, and the similarities in their situations. What effect does it have?
d Students write a paragraph using this evidence to comment on the reader's possible response to the themes and ideas of the poem, following the point-evidence-explanation structure.

5 Comparison activities, page 33

Note: In order to do these activities, students would need to have completed their work on 'Les Grands Seigneurs' and 'Singh Song'.

The Ruined Maid

1. **Comparing ideas and themes**
   Compare the ways in which women are presented in 'The Ruined Maid' and 'Les Grands Seigneurs'.
2. **Comparing writers' devices**
   Compare the ways in which conversation and **dialect** are shown in 'The Ruined Maid' and 'Singh Song'.

1 a In pairs or independently, students complete **Worksheet 1.39**, linking their response to the poem with the relevant Assessment Objective. Take feedback on any areas that students found difficult to grasp or to comment on.

b Ask students to use their notes from **Worksheet 1.39** to write three or four key points comparing the ways in which women are presented in the two poems. They should write **in complete sentences using connectives**. Display **Worksheet 1.3** to support them.

c Take feedback, compiling notes on the board. As a class, students find evidence from each poem to support each point.

d Ask students to select three points with supporting evidence from those on the board.

e The students then add a sentence or two to each point/piece of evidence, explaining and commenting on the ways in which the writers have presented their points of view.

2 Repeat the above sequence, using **Worksheet 1.40** to explore how dialect is used.

6 Plenary

Take feedback on 'The Ruined Maid', annotating the poem displayed on the whiteboard using Wordbox. Focus on relevant key features, e.g:
- content
- language
- tone.
- interpretation
- structure

If students have studied and compared 'Les Grands Seigneurs' and/or 'Singh Song', take feedback on relevant key similarities and differences in content, interpretation, language, structure or tone.

Suggested answers

Activity 1

1. **a/b** Melia: a well-dressed, apparently socially elevated, woman who was once a farm worker but is now a prostitute; and a country girl, with whom she used to work 'digging potatoes'.

2. Her 'fair garments' and prosperity, her bracelets and feathers, her language fit for 'high company', her complexion, her gloves, her apparent happiness. All she admires is Melia's appearance: she **looks** like a 'lady'.

3. **a/b** The country girl describes Melia's hands as having been 'like paws' when she knew her. The implication is that she is no longer a farm labourer. The term 'lady' implies someone of a higher class. Ironically, as a prostitute, Melia does not fulfil the moral requirements needed to be a 'lady'.

4. The country girl's speech contains much more informal language and slang ('spudding up docks'). Melia's language is much more formal ('Some polish is gained') and has a slightly superior tone, suggested in her use of 'one' and 'we' when referring to ladies; this is at its clearest in the final lines, in her patronising use of 'my dear' and the ironic (or perhaps revealing) use of 'ain't'.

5. The use of rhyming couplets reflects the simplicity of the country girl's admiration for Melia and creates pace, suggesting her gabbled surprise at seeing Melia so transformed.

6. The repetition of 'ruin' and 'said she' in every fourth line, rhyming with the country girl's third line, 'ties' Melia's inevitable response to her friend's highly vocal admiration as a kind of punchline.

7. Melia's response is fuller once the other girl's speech moves from admiration to envy ('I wish I had…'). It seems to emphasise that the only escape from the hard labour of farm work is prostitution.

Activity 2

It could be argued that the country girl's position is as lowly and awkward as Melia's, albeit with more financial and physical, rather than moral, degradation.

Comparison activities

Key points for this activity are provided in **Worksheet 1.41**.

AQA GCSE Working with the Anthology: Achieve a C   29

Chapter 1 Character and voice

Casehistory: Alison (head injury)
by U. A. Fanthorpe

Assessment Objectives
- **AO1:** respond to texts critically and imaginatively; select and evaluate relevant textual detail to illustrate and support interpretations
- **AO2:** explain how language, structure and form contribute to writers' presentation of ideas, themes and settings

Learning Objectives
- To develop students' responses to the poem
- To relate the Assessment Objectives to the poem

Required resources
- Poem text, available on CD-ROM and video/audio online at http://anthology.aqa.org.uk
- Student Book, page 19
- Worksheets 1.3, 1.42, 1.43, 1.44

1 Starter

a Ask students to imagine themselves in later life, looking back at a photograph of themselves taken today. **Worksheet 1.42** may help clarify this task. Ask:
- What do you see when you look at the photograph today?
- How might that perception change when you look back later? Will you still think the same way about:
  - your appearance
  - your future (which when they look back will have become their past!)?

b Ask students to write two or three sentences as themselves in 50 years' time, commenting on a photograph taken today.

2 Activity 1

a Using the Digital Anthology, listen to/watch/read the poem to the class.

b Students complete questions 1–7 independently. Take feedback to share, ensure and develop understanding. Display the poem using the Digital Anthology, annotating the text with students' responses using Wordbox.

c Take the class's initial response to the poem, commenting on the character, voice and situation of the speaker.

d Ask students to write a sentence or two summing up the content or meaning of the poem. They can begin: *'Casehistory: Alison (head injury)' is about….*

3 Activity 2

Give students 5 minutes to discuss, identifying evidence to support each of their assertions. Take feedback to share and ensure understanding.

4 GradeStudio

a Read the GradeStudio extract to the class. Ask: How has the writer of the sample answer shown 'identification of effect(s) of writer's choices of language and/or structure and/or form intended/achieved'?

b How could students rewrite or add to this response to show 'explanation of effect(s) of writer's uses of language and/or structure and/or form and effects on readers' and so achieve a C grade? For example: *It is on its own suggesting her isolation from the past, sounding like a sad echo of her thoughts in the first stanza.*

c Ask students to identify other quotations which will allow them to explore the writer's choices, e.g. the poem's introductory line *(She looks at her photograph)*, or the repetition in stanza 8.

d Students write a paragraph using this evidence to comment on the reader's possible response to the poem, following the point-evidence-explanation structure.

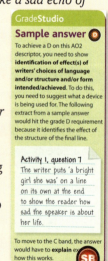

© Pearson Education Limited 2010

5 Comparison activities, page 33

Note: In order to do these activities, students would need to have completed their work on 'Medusa'.

a Working in pairs or independently, students complete **Worksheet 1.43**, linking their response to the poems with the relevant Assessment Objective. Take feedback on any areas that students found difficult to grasp or to comment on.

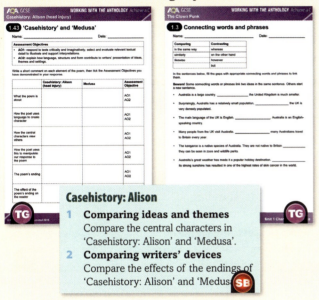

Casehistory: Alison
1 **Comparing ideas and themes**
Compare the central characters in 'Casehistory: Alison' and 'Medusa'.
2 **Comparing writers' devices**
Compare the effects of the endings of 'Casehistory: Alison' and 'Medusa'.

b Students use their notes from **Worksheet 1.43** to write three or four key points comparing the attitudes to men and the effects of the endings of the two poems. They should write **in complete sentences using connectives**. Display **Worksheet 1.3** to support them. Students repeat this for comparing the effects of the endings of the two poems.

c Take feedback, compiling notes on the board. As a class, students find evidence from each poem to support each point.

d Ask students to select three points with supporting evidence from those on the board.

e Students add a sentence or two to each point/piece of evidence, explaining and commenting on how the poets have presented their points of view.

6 Plenary

Take feedback on 'Casehistory: Alison (head injury)', annotating the poem displayed on the whiteboard using Wordbox. Focus on relevant key features, e.g:
- content
- language
- tone.
- interpretation
- structure

If students have studied and compared 'Medusa', take feedback on relevant key similarities and differences in content, interpretation, language, structure or tone.

Suggested answers

Activity 1

1 Alison has suffered a head injury which has affected her memory. She can no longer remember her past and cannot retain information for any length of time.

2 It sets the scene, helps the situation come into focus and, ultimately, builds our sympathy in this direct comparison between the hope of her youth and the reality of her future.

3 a She cannot remember her past because of her head injury.
  b It emphasises that she was a bright girl *in the past* – and is not any more.

4 It reflects a verbal pause in the narrator's address to the reader: a break to give added emphasis – in conjunction with the word 'lugs' – to the narrator's physical state: she can hardly walk up the stairs.

5 She knows – and can remember and has therefore come to terms with the fact – that her father is dead. The older Alison learns of his death anew every morning and will 'never get over what/I do not remember.'

6 This 'list of three' emphasises the range of her achievements as a younger woman. Using 'her' not 'me' emphasises that the narrator sees herself as a different person.

7 The final line is emphasised by its solitariness; also perhaps suggesting a kind of regretful, wistful afterthought as it repeats the assertion from the first stanza. Although she was a bright girl, she did not know that her life would reach this point – and this makes the shock of her present situation all the greater.

Activity 2

She feels sorry for her younger self who does not know that 'I am her future' – that she will come to be in this position.

Students are likely to sympathise with Alison's situation: her father's death, her immobility, and having forgotten everything that her younger self was smiling at. They may also respond with admiration: despite her situation, she seems happy with herself ('comforting fat') and entirely accepting and open about her 'damaged brain'.

Comparison activities

Key points for this activity are provided in **Worksheet 1.44**.

Chapter 1 Character and voice

On a Portrait of a Deaf Man
by John Betjeman

Assessment Objectives
- **AO1:** respond to texts critically and imaginatively; select and evaluate relevant textual detail to illustrate and support interpretations
- **AO2:** explain how language, structure and form contribute to writers' presentation of ideas, themes and settings

Learning Objectives
- To develop students' responses to the poem
- To relate the Assessment Objectives to the poem

Required resources
- Poem text, available on CD-ROM and video/audio online at http://anthology.aqa.org.uk
- Student Book, page 20
- Worksheets 1.3, 1.45, 1.46, 1.47

1 Starter

a Discuss with students: What happens to us after we die? Give students 2 minutes to note their own views and those of others of which they are aware, including any evidence to support them.

b Take feedback, recording students' responses and supporting evidence on the whiteboard. Emphasise that the aim of this activity is not to come to a definite conclusion, to dismiss some views and support others, but to explore the breadth of human belief.

2 Activity 1

a Using the Digital Anthology, listen to/watch/read the poem to the class. Clarify any points of understanding.

b Students complete questions 1–7 independently. Take feedback to share, ensure and develop understanding. Display the poem using the Digital Anthology, annotating the text with students' responses using Wordbox.

c Take students' initial response to the poem, commenting on the character, voice, thoughts and feelings of the narrator.

d Ask students to write a sentence or two summing up the content or meaning of the poem. They can begin: 'On a Portrait of a Deaf Man' is about....

Initial responses — ACTIVITY 1

1 What does the **speaker** of the poem feel about his father overall? Find evidence to support what you think. You could start with the first adjective in the poem.
2 List all of the activities which the 'deaf man' used to like. How do these work to create the character of the 'deaf man'?
3 How does the writer play with the idea of eating in a gruesome way in the second **stanza**?
4 The fourth stanza is also deliberately gruesome. How does the writer use **rhyme** to add to the effect? Look at what he connects together with rhyme.
5 Now look at the seventh stanza. Like stanzas 2 and 4, there is a gruesome idea here about the corpse.
   a How are these stanzas structured in a similar way?
   b How does the writer use rhyme to add to the effect?
6 There is another rhyme in the last stanza which works in a similar way. What two things does the rhyme connect? How do they contrast with each other as well?
7 The poem finishes with the line 'I only see decay.' How does the whole poem and the **imagery** in it lead up to this last word?

3 Activity 2

Give students 3 minutes to work in pairs on a written response to the question, supported with evidence from the poem. Take feedback to share and ensure understanding.

Words/phrases to explore (AO1) — ACTIVITY 2

John Betjeman was in many ways a religious man. What do you think the last sentence of the poem says about his belief?

4 GradeStudio

a Read the GradeStudio extract to the class. Ask: How has the writer of the sample answer shown 'effective use of details to support interpretation'?

b Ask students to identify other quotes which will allow them to explore their interpretation of the poem, e.g. the contrast of the living body and the dead body in stanzas 2, 4, and 7.

c Students write a paragraph using this evidence to explore their interpretation of the poem, following the point-evidence-explanation structure.

GradeStudio

Sample answer — C

To achieve a C on this AO1 descriptor, you need to show **effective use of details to support interpretation**. The following extract from a sample answer would hit the grade C requirement.

Activity 1, question 7

The speaker is determined to show the realities of what happens to the body after death, to show that there is no life after death. His eyes are full of 'maggots', his 'finger-bones/Stick through his finger-ends', and his mouth is full of earth. All this leads to the word at the end of the poem, 'decay'.

5 Comparison activities, page 33

Note: In order to do these activties, students would need to have completed their work on 'Brendon Gallacher' and 'Ozymandias'.

1 a Working in pairs or independently, students complete **Worksheet 1.45**, linking their response to the poem with the relevant Assessment Objective. Take feedback on any areas that students found difficult to grasp or to comment on.

> **On a Portrait of a Deaf Man**
> 1 **Comparing ideas and themes**
>   Compare the feelings of the speakers in 'On a Portrait of a Deaf Man' and 'Brendon Gallacher'.
> 2 **Comparing writers' devices**
>   Compare the effects of the endings of 'On a Portrait of a Deaf Man' and 'Ozymandias'.

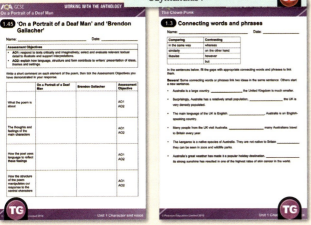

b Ask students to use their notes from **Worksheet 1.45** to write three or four key points comparing the feelings of the speakers in the two poems. They should write **in complete sentences using connectives**. Display **Worksheet 1.3** to support them.

c Take feedback, compiling notes on the board. As a class, students find evidence from each poem to support each point.

d Ask students to select three points with supporting evidence from those on the board.

e The students then add a sentence or two to each point/pieces of evidence, explaining and commenting on the ways in which the writers have presented their points of view.

2 Repeat the above sequence, using **Worksheet 1.46** to explore the endings of the poems.

6 Plenary

Take feedback on 'On a Portrait of a Deaf Man', annotating the poem displayed on the whiteboard using Wordbox. Focus on relevant key features, e.g:
- content
- language
- tone.
- interpretation
- structure

If students have studied and compared 'Brendon Gallacher' and/or 'Ozymandias', take feedback on relevant key similarities and differences in content, interpretation, language, structure or tone.

Suggested answers

Activity 1

1 The poem suggests the speaker feels affectionately about his father: e.g. 'kind… egg-shaped head… discreetly loud… smiled… wise'.

2 Activities are: shooting, eating in 'old City dining rooms', long country walks, being outdoors in Cornwall, painting landscapes. The image is of a well-to-do city gentleman who enjoyed the countryside.

3 The stanza moves from an image of eating food, to a wide open mouth full of soil in the grave.

4 The rhyme of 'wise' and 'eyes' emphasises the replacement of wisdom in his eyes with maggots.

5 a The first two lines focus on a positive activity or facet of his father's character; the final two lines focus on his decaying corpse.

  b The dead body is linked to the living body through specific reference to a body part: his mouth in stanza 2; his eyes in stanza 4; his fingers in stanza 7. In each case the rhyme emphasises the contrasting state of his body.

6 The physical decay of his body is contrasted with the spiritual salvation God promises – and in which the speaker seems unable to believe.

7 The theme of physical decay after death runs throughout the poem.

Activity 2

The poet finds it hard to reconcile the loss of his father with his religious belief. It implies a great love and respect for his father that it can bring about this questioning of his faith.

Comparison activities

Key points for this activity are provided in **Worksheet 1.47**.

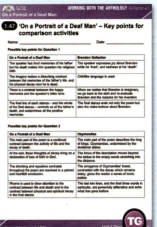

Chapter 1 Character and voice

Looking at the poems individually: what have you learned?

Assessment Objectives
- **AO1:** respond to texts critically and imaginatively; select and evaluate relevant textual detail to illustrate and support interpretations
- **AO2:** explain how language, structure and form contribute to writers' presentation of ideas, themes and settings

Learning Objectives
- To recap and explore students' responses to the poem

Required resources
- Student Book, page 21
- Worksheet 1.48, ideally enlarged to A3

1 Starter

Looking at the poems individually: what have you learned?

a Explain to students that this lesson will consolidate, recap and explore their knowledge and understanding of, and response to, the 15 poems they have explored.

b Give students 3 minutes to complete the following task in silence:
Without looking at their anthology or any notes, how many of the poems can they remember from those they have explored over the last 15 lessons? They can either note down the titles (and poets, if possible) or give a brief description of the poems' content: *The one about… .*

c List the 15 poems aloud so students can check their answers. Ask students to add titles to the poems where the content but not the title had been remembered.

d Take feedback. How many poems could students remember? Based on the class's response as a whole, were some more memorable than others? Why?

The poems

The Clown Punk *Simon Armitage*	**Brendon Gallacher** *Jackie Kay*	**The River God** *Stevie Smith*
Checking Out Me History *John Agard*	**Give** *Simon Armitage*	**The Hunchback in the Park** *Dylan Thomas*
Horse Whisperer *Andrew Forster*	**Les Grands Seigneurs** *Dorothy Molloy*	**The Ruined Maid** *Thomas Hardy*
Medusa *Carol Ann Duffy*	**Ozymandias** *Percy Bysshe Shelley*	**Casehistory: Alison (head injury)** *U. A. Fanthorpe*
Singh Song *Daljit Nagra*	**My Last Duchess** *Robert Browning*	**On a Portrait of a Deaf Man** *John Betjeman*

2 Activity 1

a Explain that Question 1 of the activity will consolidate students' thinking from the Starter activity.

b Read Question 1 aloud, then ask students to choose the **five** poems they responded to most strongly – it is likely that these will be the first five they listed in the Starter. Ask them to add a sentence explaining why they found each poem memorable: it may be an activity, a word, a line, an idea, a character, or a title which has sparked their engagement. Ask volunteers to share with the class.

c Read Question 2. Ask: Are your answers to this question likely to feature the same poems as Question 1? Why?

d Give students 5 minutes to list the **five** poems they found it easiest to offer an interpretation about, using their notes from the last 15 lessons. Take feedback to ensure understanding. Ask: Is it easier to talk and write about poems that are simpler to understand? Or is there more to be said (and more marks to be gained!) by exploring a variety of different interpretations of more complex poems?

Assessment Objective 1 (AO1) — ACTIVITY 1

1 Which of these poems did you **respond** to most strongly? You may have liked it, or disliked it, or found it the most interesting, or horrible. You may have a number of things to say about it.

2 Which poems did you find it easiest to offer an **interpretation** about? In other words, you had an opinion about a poem's meaning and could argue from the text and **select detail** to support your opinion. For instance, you might have found it easy to argue that the shopkeeper in 'Singh Song' neglects his shop because he is ordered about by his bride.

Suggesting more than one interpretation of a poem, or parts of a poem, gives you opportunities to score more marks. For instance, there are several ways in which you could respond to the shopke

3 Activity 2

Give students 20 minutes to complete questions 1 and 2 of the activity. They can record their responses on **Worksheet 1.48**. Point out that if they cannot think of anything significant in a particular area within, say, 30 seconds, then it does not suggest a ready understanding: they should move on to a new feature or poem. Take feedback to ensure and develop understanding.

Assessment Objective 2 (AO2) — ACTIVITY 2

1. Which features of **language**, **structure** or **form** did you understand best? The most promising ones to write about in the exam will be the ones where you have most to say. For instance, you might have found several things to say about:
   - the effect of the repetitions in 'Checking Out Me History' (language)
   - the repetition of 'a bright girl she was' at the end of 'Case history: Alison' (structure)
   - the effects of the rhyme at the end of 'The Clown Punk' (form).

   When answering this question, it would be best if you chose your own examples rather than using the ones above!

2. What **ideas** did you pick out in the poems? Again, the best answers will probably identify more than one idea in a poem, or several aspects of one idea. For instance, you might have identified attitudes to women in 'Les Grands Seigneurs' or 'My Last Duchess'. Which poems contain ideas about history?

1.48 What have you learned?

Name: _____   Date: _____

Title	Language	Structure	Form	Ideas
The Clown Punk – Simon Armitage				
Checking Out Me History – John Agard				
Horse Whisperer – Andrew Forster				
Medusa – Carol Ann Duffy				
Singh Song – Daljit Nagra				
Brendon Gallacher – Jackie Kay				
Give – Simon Armitage				
Les Grands Seigneurs – Dorothy Molloy				
Ozymandias – Percy Bysshe Shelley				
My Last Duchess – Robert Browning				
The River God – Stevie Smith				
The Hunchback in the Park – Dylan Thomas				
The Ruined Maid – Thomas Hardy				
Casehistory: Alison – U.A. Fanthorpe				
On a Portrait of a Deaf Man – John Betjeman				

4 Plenary

Ask students:
- Based on your exploration of content, interpretation, language, structure, form and ideas, which are the most memorable, exam-friendly poems in the 'Character and voice' cluster? Do they have any significant links or points of comparison?
- Which poems are particularly difficult to write about?
- Which poems do you feel you need to give more (of your own) time to?

5 Further Work

a. Students identify the **five** poems that have the fewest entries on **Worksheet 1.48**.

b. Students complete each column for each poem, using **Worksheet 1.48** and their notes.

1.48 What have you learned?

Name: _____   Date: _____

Title	Language	Structure	Form	Ideas
The Clown Punk – Simon Armitage				
Checking Out Me History – John Agard				
Horse Whisperer – Andrew Forster				
Medusa – Carol Ann Duffy				
Singh Song – Daljit Nagra				
Brendon Gallacher – Jackie Kay				
Give – Simon Armitage				
Les Grands Seigneurs – Dorothy Molloy				
Ozymandias – Percy Bysshe Shelley				
My Last Duchess – Robert Browning				
The River God – Stevie Smith				
The Hunchback in the Park – Dylan Thomas				
The Ruined Maid – Thomas Hardy				
Casehistory: Alison – U.A. Fanthorpe				
On a Portrait of a Deaf Man – John Betjeman				

Chapter 1 Character and voice

Comparing the 'Character and voice' poems (1)

Assessment Objectives
- **AO3:** make comparisons and explain links between texts, evaluating writers' different ways of expressing meaning and achieving effects

Learning Objectives
- To develop students' abilities to compare the poems
- To relate the Assessment Objectives to the poems
- To develop students' writing skills for the exam

Required resources
- Poem texts, available on CD-ROM and video/audio online at http://anthology.aqa.org.uk
- Student Book, pages 22–23
- Worksheet 1.49

1 Starter

a Read the explanation of the Assessment Objective on page 22 of the Student Book, clarifying understanding of the Assessment Objective's demands.

b Explain to students that, in this lesson, they are going to compare 'The Clown Punk' and 'The Hunchback in the Park'.

c Display both poems on the whiteboard, side by side, using Wordbox in the Digital Anthology. Re-read the poems.

d Ask students to describe the content of each poem, providing evidence where appropriate. Draw the characters and events on the board as they are described, annotating with quotations. Depending on your artistic skills, you may want to ask a volunteer student to take this role!

Assessment Objective:

The Assessment Objective you will be focusing on in this part of the chapter is:

 make comparisons and explain links between texts, evaluating writers' different ways of expressing meaning and achieving effects.

2 Activity 1

a Using **Worksheet 1.49**, students record all the similarities and differences they can think of in the two poems in the first column on the worksheet. The second column is for their responses to Activity 2.

b Take feedback, ideally compiling students' responses on a copy of the worksheet projected onto the whiteboard, using Wordbox.

ACTIVITY 1

Think about the ideas and themes in the two poems. List as many similarities and differences as you can. Think about:
- what both the main characters in the poems have in common
- how other people respond to the two characters
- how the two main characters differ.

36 © Pearson Education Limited 2010

3 Activity 2

Explain that this is an opportunity for students to develop their points of comparison, using **Worksheet 1.49**. Use the example in the Student Book and perhaps one other from the class's responses compiled on the whiteboard. Remind students of the need for evidence to support each point. Take feedback, again compiling notes on the whiteboard.

ACTIVITY 2

Using your list of similarities and differences from Activity 1, decide how different each of the poems are for each point you made. For example, the young people in both poems react badly to the main character – but exactly how do they react, and how do you think these reactions are different?

Your answer needs to be based on the q[uotations] or refer to specific parts of the po[ems]

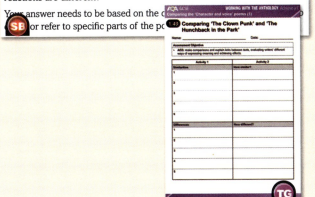

4 Activity 3

a Recap the key features of similarity/difference compiled on the whiteboard.

b Explain to students that this is an opportunity to explore the **effect** of the differences they noted in Activity 2.

c Clarify the three key areas outlined in the activity:
   • the way the characters are described
   • the use of rhyme
   • the endings of the poems.

d Using their notes from **Worksheet 1.49** and the notes compiled on the whiteboard, ask students, working in pairs, to select **one** of these three areas on which they feel they can comment and write a sentence or two explaining and commenting on the different effects achieved in the poems. If time allows, students can select a second area.

ACTIVITY 3

Now you need to compare the differences in the ways the poems are written.
• What comparisons did you find in the poems? What sort of things do they describe? Are the comparisons similar in what they describe, or in the effects they have when you read them?
• Which of the poems use **rhyme**? Why do you think the writers of the poems use rhyme, or not?
• Compare the endings of the two poems. How does each ending finish the poem off, both in what it says and the ways it is said? Are there any similarities between the two endings, do you think?

5 Plenary

a Take feedback on Activity 3, focusing on one area at a time. Discuss each pair's contribution as a whole class: Have they identified a significant difference and commented on its effect? Add to the compiled notes on the whiteboard.

b Based on the popularity of each of the three areas, which do students feel are easier or harder to comment on?

c Do students feel they have enough material to write three or four paragraphs comparing how the two characters are created in the poems? If so, give 1 minute for students to select the three or four key points they would use. Take feedback to share and develop thinking.

Suggested answers

Activities 1/2

Similarities:
• Both central characters are 'outcasts'.
• Both are dehumanised by the poem's title and others' attitudes to them.
• Both are described negatively.

Differences:
• The speaker in 'The Hunchback in the Park' gives a much more sympathetic portrayal.
• The speaker in 'The Clown Punk' dismisses the punk; the speaker in 'The Hunchback in the Park' shows sympathy, describing the hunchback's dreams of transformation.
• The clown punk is an object of fear to children, the hunchback is an object of fun.
• The punk is aggressive, the hunchback is passive.

Comparison activities
• Negative description: Hunchback described as an 'old dog', Clown Punk as 'a basket of washing'.
• Both poems use rhyme and half-rhyme loosely and irregularly.
• The clearest example of rhyme is the final, rhyming couplet of 'The Clown Punk' – an emphatic rhyme, almost a punchline to the poem, suggesting the finality of the speaker's dismissal of this strange, disturbing aggressive character. The final rhyme of 'The Hunchback in the Park' is less conclusive (park… dark), suggesting the inevitability of his return to his kennel, despite his dreams of transformation.

Chapter 1 Character and voice

Comparing the 'Character and voice' poems (2)

Assessment Objectives
- **AO3:** make comparisons and explain links between texts, evaluating writers' different ways of expressing meaning and achieving effects

Learning Objectives
- To develop students' abilities to compare the poems
- To relate the Assessment Objectives to the poems
- To develop students' writing skills for the exam

Required resources
- Poem texts, available on CD-ROM and video/audio online at http://anthology.aqa.org.uk
- Student Book, pages 22–25, 142–143

1 Starter

Assessment Objective:
The Assessment Objective you will be focusing on in this part of the chapter is:
AO3 make comparisons and explain links between texts, evaluating writers' different ways of expressing meaning and achieving effects.

a Recap the comparison process from the previous lesson.
b Read the explanation of the Assessment Objective on page 22 of the Student Book, clarifying understanding of the Assessment Objective's demands.
c Explain to students that in this lesson, they are going to continue to compare 'The Clown Punk' and 'The Hunchback in the Park', then use this process to develop their comparison skills further.
d Display both poems on the whiteboard, side by side, using Wordbox in the Digital Anthology. Re-read the poems.

2 GradeStudio

a Read the GradeStudio E grade extract to the class. Ask: How has the writer of the sample answer made 'some comment(s) on similarities/differences, with detail'?
b Read the GradeStudio D extract to the class. How do the additional sentences give 'structured comments on similarities/differences, with detail'?
c Looking at the grade descriptors on pages 142–143 of the Student Book, what would students have to do to raise this D to a C?
d Give students 5 minutes to add a sentence or two – or rewrite those in the exemplar – in order to show 'sustained focus on similarities/differences' and so achieve a C.

3 Activity 4

a Read the activity instructions, discussing each bullet point as a class.
b Give students 5 minutes to note their own thoughts on the three bullet points.
c Take feedback to ensure and develop understanding.
d Give students 10 minutes to write a paragraph comparing these two details.
e Remind students of their recent work on the GradeStudio extracts. Students swap paragraphs with a partner. Using the grade descriptors on pages 142–143, what grade would they award their partner's paragraph? How would they suggest it could be improved to achieve a higher grade?

ACTIVITY 4

One of the best ways to score well when comparing poems is to compare two details, one from each poem, that you can say a lot about when you put them together. It doesn't matter whether you're comparing what the details are about, or the ways they're written, though if you're dealing with both it will provide more to say.

For instance, let's suppose that you chose these two details from these poems:

like a basket of washing that got up and walked	Like the park birds he came early Like the water he sat down
(The Clown Punk)	(The Hunchback in the Park)

You could say that these are both **similes**, but that would only be a simple link between the details, which is in the F band of marks. What more can you find to say? Think about:
- the places where the two characters are, and how the comparisons fit the places
- what the comparisons say about the characters – what they look like or what they are like as people
- how the lines, and the way they are arranged, suit walking (Clown Punk) or sitting (Hunchback)

You should have enough material now to write a good paragraph comparing the two details.

GradeStudio
Sample answer E
To hit one of the AO3 descriptors at grade E, you need to make **some comment(s) on similarities/differences, with detail**. The following extract from a sample answer would hit the grade E requirement.

> The two characters are compared to things that belong to the places where they are. The clown punk is compared to a basket of washing, which seems more like a town thing, but the hunchback is compared to the birds and the water in the park that he goes to every day.

GradeStudio
Sample answer D
To hit one of the AO3 descriptors at grade D, you need to make some **structured comments on similarities/differences, with detail**. The following extract from a sample answer would hit the grade D requirement.

> The two characters are both compared to things that belong to the places where they are. The clown punk is compared to a basket of washing, which seems more like a town thing, but the hunchback is compared to the birds and the water in the park that he goes to every day. The ways the lines are written make the hunchback seem more organised, though: 'Like the park birds' then 'like the water' on the next line sounds like two organised movements, not happening very quickly. The lines about the clown punk don't seem as organised, and the 'basket of washing' isn't an organised idea at all.

38 © Pearson Education Limited 2010

4 Activity 5

a The students now move on to compare 'On a Portrait of a Deaf Man' and 'Casehistory: Alison'. Display both poems on the whiteboard, side by side, using Wordbox. Re-read the poems.

b What initial points of comparison, similarities and differences, can students suggest?

c Students work independently, recording their response to questions 1–4, one at a time. Encourage students to record as wide a range of responses as possible.

d Take feedback after each question, discussing and developing a whole class response, then giving students a minute or two to add to their written response.

5 Activity 6

a Explain that, although there are other points of comparison, you are going to look at the endings of the poems in this activity.

b Discuss the bullet pointed questions as a whole class, compiling responses on the whiteboard.

c Read the GradeStudio exemplars on page 25 of the Student Book. Ask students to identify how the C has identified and explored similarities and differences – and the B has further developed the comparison.

d Give students 10 minutes to write a point-evidence-explanation paragraph exploring the poem's endings.

6 Plenary

a Students swap their written response to Activity 6 with a partner and, using the grade descriptors on pages 142–143 of the Student Book, decide what grade their partner's response should be awarded.

b Working together, students identify one way in which they could improve or add to their writing to aim for the next grade up.

c Take feedback, summarising those key areas which students have identified as targets to achieve in order to raise their grade.

Suggested answers

Activity 4

The Clown Punk	The Hunchback in the Park
Appropriate to the 'shonky side of town' setting	Appropriate to the park setting
Suggests dirt and dishevelled appearance	Suggests he is a part of, and in tune with, nature
Enjambment suggests movement	Although unpunctuated, the sense of the lines suggests end stopping

Activity 5

1 Both poems focus on damage and loss – of a loved one, or of self. The Deaf Man is dead; Alison is physically and mentally damaged by a head injury. Both speakers have lost their father, though this incidental in 'Casehistory'.

2 In 'Portrait of a Deaf Man', the father's death has caused the speaker to lose his religious faith. The death of his father focuses the son on what has been lost – there is comparison throughout of his father's habits with his now decaying body. In 'Casehistory', however, Alison has lost her memory, making her past 'dead' to her.

3 Both express their thoughts with some resentment and bitterness.

4 • Betjeman uses rhyme to link what his father was with the decay he has now succumbed to, e.g. loud/shroud, looked so wise/maggots in his eyes.
  • Fanthorpe's choice of form – long and short lines alternated – reflects the disjointed thoughts and thought processes of the speaker. It is much more conversational and reflective in tone, contrasting with the inevitability of the rhyme and the ironically light hearted tone of Betjeman's poem.

Activity 6

- His religious faith is dispelled by the death and decay of his father. The rhyme suggests the connection between these two events.
- It suggests a solitary, final reflection on the past – and on her loss.
- 'decay' emphasises what has swept away the speaker's faith – the physical loss of his father. 'was' emphasises the 'past' that Alison has lost.

AQA GCSE Working with the Anthology: Achieve a C 39

Chapter 1 Character and voice

Writing in the exam

Assessment Objectives
- **AO1:** respond to texts critically and imaginatively; select and evaluate relevant textual detail to illustrate and support interpretations
- **AO2:** explain how language, structure and form contribute to writers' presentation of ideas, themes and settings
- **AO3:** make comparisons and explain links between texts, evaluating writers' different ways of expressing meaning and achieving effects

Learning Objectives
- To develop students' ability to structure a successful exam response

Required resources
- Poem text, available on CD-ROM and video/audio online at http://anthology.aqa.org.uk
- Student Book, pages 26–31, 142–143
- Worksheets 1.50, 1.51

1 Starter

a Write the word 'planning' on the board. Ask: What are the advantages and disadvantages of using the first 5 minutes of exam time to plan a written response? Give students 2 minutes to record their thoughts.

b Take feedback. Aim to refute the argument that planning takes up valuable writing time, and that your plan is not marked. Point out that your response **is** marked – and a well-planned response gets the best mark.

2 Writing your response – planning and structuring

Read the sequence of read-think-write-edit to the class, pausing to discuss whether the students agree or disagree that each of these stages is vital. Discuss with students if there is anything that can be cut out of this process to speed it up and still achieve the best possible grade. Conclude with students that all stages in the process are vital to getting the best possible grade.

3 Putting it into practice

a Read the material from the Student Book to the class, pausing to clarify understanding where needed.

b Do students think that this is a successful plan? How might they improve it? Point out that the task has to be completed in a limited time, so anything that is added may well mean that something else must be cut. Remind the class that this guide was written by the Chief Examiner – so it's good advice!

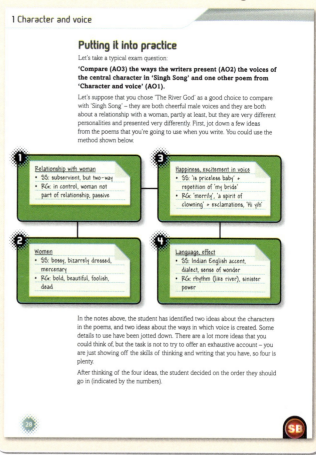

40 © Pearson Education Limited 2010

4 GradeStudio

a Close the Student Book and distribute or display **Worksheet 1.50**. Note that two of the paragraphs focus on specific Assessment Objectives, while the answer as a whole focuses on AO3: the comparison of the two poems.

b Using the grade descriptors on pages 142–143 of the Student Book (also available on **Worksheet 1.51**), ask students to work in pairs to decide which grade they would award Student A and Student B, matching specific features from the mark scheme to specific evidence from each response to justify their decision.

c Take feedback, continually aiming to re-affirm the Assessment Objectives: the importance of responding to, and comparing, the details, ideas, themes, language, structure and form of the poems.

d Return to the Student Book and read through the Examiner comments. Do the class's marks and justifications tally with the Chief Examiner's?

5 Sample exam question

Depending on the confidence of your class, this can be tackled as homework, as entirely independent work, or planned as a class prior to independent writing.

a Ask students to spend 2 minutes noting down the sequence of thinking they would follow before writing. For example:
  1 Read the question **carefully**.
  2 Identify which parts of the question relate to which Assessment Objective.
  3 Consider which poem to compare 'Give' with. Think of two or three possibilities. Which will allow you to demonstrate your skill and understanding most fully? Choose one.
  4 Note down points comparing the themes and ideas in the poems.
  5 Note down points comparing details in the poems.
  6 Note down points comparing the writer's choice of language, form and/or structure in the poems and its effect on the reader.

b Give students 10 minutes to follow this sequence, completing their essay plan. Point out that, although this should take 5 minutes in the exam, this is practice to help get students up to exam pace!

> You are now ready to tackle an exam question. Here's one to try:
> Compare how characters in difficulties are presented in 'Give' and one other poem from 'Character and voice'.
> When you've written your answer you could mark it, or get a partner to mark it, using the mark scheme on page 142.

6 Plenary

Students swap plans. Does their partner's plan cover all the necessary Assessment Objectives and explore the poem in enough developed detail? What grade do they think the essay based on this plan will achieve? Why? Take feedback, focusing on the grade awarded and the peer marker's justification for that grade. Does the class agree that the grade is justified?

7 Further work

Students can write up their essay in their own time. The following lesson can then be spent peer-marking the essays using the grade descriptors on pages 142–143 of the Student Book – also available on **Worksheet 1.51** – then listening as a class to the peer-marker's choices of:
- the most successful point targeting AO1
- the most successful point targeting AO2
- the most successful point targeting AO3.

AQA GCSE Working with the Anthology: Achieve a C

Chapter 2 Place

Getting to know the poems

Assessment Objectives
- **AO1:** respond to texts critically and imaginatively; select and evaluate relevant textual detail to illustrate and support interpretations
- **AO2:** explain how language, structure and form contribute to writers' presentation of ideas, themes and settings
- **AO3:** make comparisons and explain links between texts, evaluating writers' different ways of expressing meaning and achieving effects

Learning Objectives
- To become familiar with the cluster as a whole
- To start to make links between the poems

Required resources
- Student Book, pages 34–36
- Worksheet 2.1, ideally enlarged to A3 size
- A3 paper

1 Starter

a Focus on the title of this cluster.

b Ask students: If you were to write a poem focusing on a place, where would you choose? Some prompts may help: Your local area? Somewhere you have visited or been on holiday? Somewhere you used to live?

c Take feedback, including an explanation of why they made this choice.

d If time allows, ask students to write the first line(s) of their poem. Ask volunteers to share with the class.

2 Introduction

a Read through and clarify with the class the focus and purpose of this and subsequent lessons.

b Draw students' attention to the Assessment Objectives which this lesson will support (an explanation of them is available on page 34 of the Student Book).

c Ask students to locate the cluster in their Anthology.

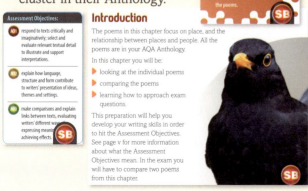

3 Activity 1

Read all the 'Place' poems in your AQA Anthology. Just notice what they seem to be about – don't worry about trying to make sense of every line.

a Divide the class into pairs according to ability, with poems allocated accordingly. For example:

More accessible
- The Blackbird of Glanmore
- Crossing the Loch
- The Prelude (extract)
- A Vision
- Spellbound

Intermediate
- Price We Pay for the Sun
- Cold Knap Lake
- The Wild Swans at Coole
- Hard Water
- Wind

More challenging
- The Moment
- Neighbours
- London
- Below The Green Corrie
- Storm in the Black Forest

b Give pairs 5 minutes to read their allocated poem, giving clear prior warning that they will be asked to feed back information and comments to the whole class. Use the prompts below to focus discussion and feedback. (You may want to note these prompts on the board.)
- How difficult is the poem to understand?
- What is the poem about?
- What can you say about the presentation of place?

c Read each poem to the class, then take feedback from the relevant group to ensure understanding. Encourage students to take notes in their Anthology or exercise book, recording their first impressions of each poem.

4 Preparation for Activity 2

Ask the class to think of different ways in which these or any other poems can be compared. Note them on the whiteboard, e.g. a description of place, an event or experience at a particular place, an impartial voice, a point to make, the use of descriptive language.

5 Activity 2

a Distribute copies of **Worksheet 2.1** and look at the comparison table in Activity 2 on page 35 of the Student Book. Clarify the terms of comparison if necessary. As a class, decide which of the categories on the whiteboard (from the preparation) it will be most useful to focus on. Ask students to add them to the blank columns on the worksheet.

b Reshuffle students into groups of three or four. Clarify with them the precise requirements of this task. Depending on the ability of the class, there are a number of possible approaches. You could:
- set a clear timescale, e.g. 20 minutes, for the entire activity, or allow 3–5 minutes for each heading, taking feedback after each to ensure understanding
- group some of the headings, e.g.
  - titles
  - what the poems are about
  - beginnings and endings
  - length
  - language and imagery
  - rhythm and rhyme
- rather than trying to compare all 15 poems, ask students to put them into pairs, e.g. two with similar content or language choices, or two poems with very different structures or viewpoints.

Encourage students to note what leaps out at them rather than hunt for answers. This is very much an initial response to familiarise and demystify.

6 Activity 3

Get students to complete this activity in pairs or groups of three. Depending on the time available, ask a range of groups to show and explain their A3 copies of **Worksheet 2.1** to the rest of the class. Try to choose groups that have taken different approaches.

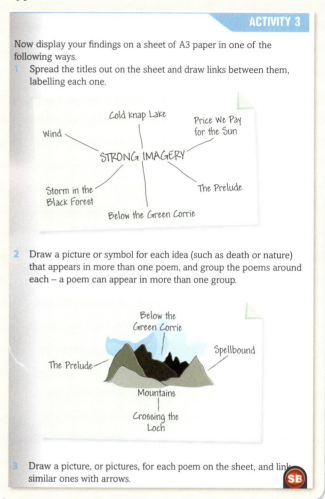

7 Plenary

Take specific feedback on individual poems and points of comparison, then ask students:
- What are your first impressions of this cluster?
- What have you found easier or harder than they expected?
- What support do you feel you will need?

Chapter 2 Place

The Blackbird of Glanmore
by Seamus Heaney

Assessment Objectives
- **AO1:** respond to texts critically and imaginatively; select and evaluate relevant textual detail to illustrate and support interpretations
- **AO2:** explain how language, structure and form contribute to writers' presentation of ideas, themes and settings

Learning Objectives
- To develop students' responses to the poem
- To relate the Assessment Objectives to the poem

Required resources
- Poem text, available on CD-ROM and video/audio online at http://anthology.aqa.org.uk
- Student Book, page 38
- Worksheets 1.3, 2.2, 2.3, 2.4

1 Starter

a Explain that you are going to look at a Heaney poem very quickly in order to give some background context to the poem you are going to explore in more detail.

b Display and read **Worksheet 2.2**, which contains the poem 'Mid-Term Break'.

c Discuss the context of 'Mid-Term Break': Heaney was called back from boarding school to attend the funeral of his four-year-old brother, killed in a road accident. Ask: How does the poem convey Heaney's sadness, anger and disorientation?

2 Activity 1

a Using the Digital Anthology, listen to/watch/read 'The Blackbird of Glanmore' to the class.

b Students complete questions 1–7 independently. Take feedback to share, ensure and develop understanding.

c Take students' initial response to the poem, commenting on the presentation of place in the poem.

d Ask students to write a sentence or two, summing up the content or meaning of the poem. They can begin: *'The Blackbird of Glanmore' is about... .*

3 Activity 2

a Display the poem using the Digital Anthology.

b Students discuss the activity question in pairs, writing their response in full sentences to ensure clarity of thought and their ability to express it.

c Take feedback, annotating the poem using Wordbox. Aim to gather and annotate all references to the blackbird and its connection with the speaker's brother, validating all views supported with evidence and/or explanation.

Words/phrases to explore (AO1 and AO2) — ACTIVITY 2
'In the ivy when I leave'. How is the blackbird made to seem as though it's always there in the whole poem?

4 GradeStudio

a Read the GradeStudio extract to the class. Ask: How has the writer of the extract shown an 'explained response to element(s) of text'?

b How could students add to this answer, in order to show a 'sustained response to element(s) of text' and so achieve a C? For example: *The blackbird seems to represent the speaker's memories of his father and in particular his brother, who are always with him.*

c Where else in the poem is there an opportunity for students to explore their response to the poem? For example, the description of the brother in the fifth stanza or the feelings of the speaker in the poem.

d Ask students to select a short quotation that will allow them to explore their response to the poem. The students then write a paragraph about it, using point-evidence-explanation.

44   © Pearson Education Limited 2010

5 Comparison activities, page 64

Note: In order to do these activities, students would need to have completed their work on 'The Wild Swans at Coole'.

a In pairs or independently, students complete **Worksheet 2.3**, linking their response to the poems with the relevant Assessment Objective. Take feedback on any areas which students found difficult to grasp or to comment on.

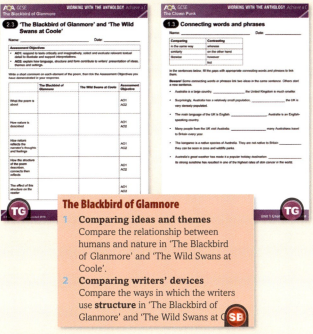

b Students use their notes from **Worksheet 2.3** to write three or four key points comparing the relationship between humans and nature and the use of structure in the two poems. They should write **in complete sentences using connectives**. Display **Worksheet 1.3** to support them.

c Take feedback, compiling notes on the board. As a class, students find evidence from each poem to support each point.

d Students select three points with supporting evidence from those on the board.

e Students add a sentence or two to each point/piece of evidence, explaining and commenting on how the writers have presented their points of view.

6 Plenary

Take feedback on 'The Blackbird of Glanmore', annotating the poem displayed on the whiteboard using Wordbox. Focus on relevant key features, e.g:

- content
- language
- tone
- interpretation
- structure

If students have studied and compared 'The Wild Swans at Coole', take feedback on relevant key similarities and differences in content, interpretation, language, structure or tone.

Suggested answers

Activity 1

1. The speaker is visiting his family home. While there he sees a blackbird. He remembers his father who lived there, and his brother who died in an accident, aged four.

2. • Use of short phrases and commas slows the pace to the pause of the full stop.
   • Alliteration ('park', 'pause') gives a sense of deliberate pause.
   • Repetition of 'breathe' suggests a further slowing of pace and the passing of time.

3. **a** To join his father in death.
   b He was 'A little stillness dancer… Cavorting through the yard' on Heaney's arrival.
   c It suggests that Heaney sees the ghost of his brother in the blackbird – or perhaps alludes to his brother following his father or himself everywhere – even in death.

4. The neighbour 'never liked yon bird'. He says the bird was 'up on the ridge for weeks' after the accident – again suggesting some kind of spiritual connection between the lost brother and the blackbird.

5. **a/b** 'The automatic lock/Clunks shut'. The use of plosives (the hard 'c' and 't') contribute onomatopoeically.

6. **a/b** It implies that, to the blackbird, Heaney in the land of the living is not quite real – and that the blackbird, as the ghostly presence of his brother, sees him as a shadow from 'the other side'.

7. It suggests a pause for thought and reflection – perhaps suggesting a glance back as he leaves – and emphasises the permanent presence of the blackbird.

Activity 2

The opening and closing stanzas focus on the bird and frame the poem with its presence. The connection between the bird and his brother, and the remembered neighbour's words, maintain its presence throughout the poem.

Comparison activities

Key points for this activity are provided in **Worksheet 2.4**.

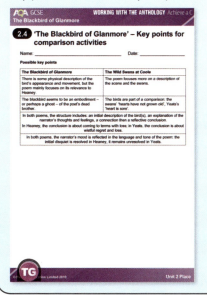

Chapter 2 Place

A Vision
by Simon Armitage

Assessment Objectives
- **AO1:** respond to texts critically and imaginatively; select and evaluate relevant textual detail to illustrate and support interpretations
- **AO2:** explain how language, structure and form contribute to writers' presentation of ideas, themes and settings

Learning Objectives
- To develop students' responses to the poem
- To relate the Assessment Objectives to the poem

Required resources
- Poem text, available on CD-ROM and video/audio online at http://anthology.aqa.org.uk
- Student Book, page 39
- Worksheets 1.3, 2.5, 2.6, 2.7, 2.8

1 Starter

a Ask students to work in pairs and note, or draw, the key features of their ideal town or city of the future. Display the prompt questions on **Worksheet 2.5** as a stimulus.

b Take feedback. Do students feel this ideal could become a reality? If so, how? If not, why not?

2 Activity 1

a Using the Digital Anthology, listen to/watch/read the poem to the class. Clarify any points of understanding.

b Students complete questions 1–6 independently. Take feedback to share, ensure and develop understanding.

c Take students' initial response to the poem, commenting on the presentation of place in the poem.

d Ask students to write a sentence or two, summing up the content or meaning of the poem. They can begin: 'A Vision' is about… .

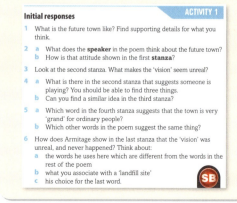

3 Activity 2

a Display the first line of the poem in close-up using the Digital Anthology.

b Students discuss the activity question in pairs, writing their response in full sentences to ensure clarity of thought and their ability to express it. Take feedback, annotating the displayed quotation using Wordbox.

Words/phrases to explore (AO1 and AO2) — ACTIVITY 2

Look at the first line again. How exactly does this line set up the whole poem? Think about what it says and the choices Armitage has made of words and punctuation.

4 GradeStudio

a Read the GradeStudio extract to the class. Ask: How has the writer of the sample answer shown an 'appreciation/consideration of writers' uses of language and/or structure and/or form and effects on readers'?

b Ask: Where else in the poem are we encouraged towards a particular response? For example, the playful language of the second stanza or the more damning language of the final stanza.

c Ask students to select a short quotation that will allow them to explore the writer's use of language and its effect on the reader. The students then write a paragraph about it, using point-evidence-explanation.

5 Comparison activities, page 64

Note: In order to do these activities, students would need to have completed their work on 'London' and 'Wind'.

A Vision
1. **Comparing ideas and themes**
   Compare the views of society shown in 'A Vision' and 'London'.
2. **Comparing writers' devices**
   Compare how the writers of 'A Vision' and 'Wind' capture the mood of the poems in the opening lines.

1. a In pairs or independently, students complete **Worksheet 2.6**, linking their response to the poems with the relevant Assessment Objective. Take feedback on any areas which students found difficult to grasp or to comment on.
   b Students use their notes from **Worksheet 2.6** to write three or four key points comparing the two writers' views of society in the poems. They should write **in complete sentences using connectives**. Display **Worksheet 1.3** to support them.
   c Take feedback, compiling notes on the board. As a class, students find evidence from each poem to support each point.
   d Students select three points with supporting evidence from those on the board.
   e Students add a sentence or two to each point/piece of evidence, explaining and commenting on how the writers have presented their points of view.
2. Repeat the above sequence, using **Worksheet 2.7** exploring the mood of the poems in the opening lines.

6 Plenary

Take feedback on 'A Vision', annotating the poem displayed on the whiteboard using Wordbox. Focus on relevant key features, e.g:
- content
- language
- tone.
- interpretation
- structure

If students have studied and compared 'London' and/or 'Wind', take feedback on relevant key similarities and differences in content, interpretation, language, structure or tone.

Suggested answers

Activity 1
1. The future town is a seemingly perfect place. It is 'beautiful'. It sounds very modern 'smoked glass and tubular steel… electric cars' and full of fun 'board game… fairground rides… toys…'. It is a place of 'dreams'.
2. a It was a dream that was never going to become reality.
   b The first line clearly indicates that the display described in the following three lines of the poem never came to fruition.
3. The adjective 'board-game', the 'fairground rides' and 'dreams' similes, the noun 'toys'.
4. a 'board-game', 'fairground' and 'toys'.
   b 'fuzzy-felt grass' and 'model drivers'.
5. a 'boulevard'.
   b • 'smoked glass and tubular steel' and 'cantilevered by light' imply modern architectural splendour
      • the overly formal language of 'modes of transportation' implies modern marvels.
6. a The language of the final stanza is less playful and much more negative: 'north wind' and 'riding the air' imply something ephemeral that has been blown away.
   b 'landfill' implies that the project has been thrown away.
   c 'extinct' implies this future will not only never be realised, but is no longer even a living possibility.

Activity 2

The first line indicates that this possible balsa-wood model of the future, which would have been beautiful, was not an accurate vision of the future.

The use of the past tense 'was', in contrast with the word 'future', immediately intrigues. The word 'once', between the pause of the comma and the finality of the full stop, ironically and emphatically places this thought further in the past.

Comparison activities

Key points for this activity are provided in **Worksheet 2.8**.

Chapter 2 Place

The Moment
by Margaret Atwood

Assessment Objectives
- **AO1:** respond to texts critically and imaginatively; select and evaluate relevant textual detail to illustrate and support interpretations
- **AO2:** explain how language, structure and form contribute to writers' presentation of ideas, themes and settings

Learning Objectives
- To develop students' responses to the poem
- To relate the Assessment Objectives to the poem

Required resources
- Poem text, available on CD-ROM and video/audio online at http://anthology.aqa.org.uk
- Student Book, page 40
- Worksheets 1.3, 2.9, 2.10

1 Starter

a Write the words 'human beings', 'nature' and 'progress' on the board.

b Give students 3 minutes to decide – and write – which is the odd one out and why.

c Take feedback. Aim for a discussion of people's attitude to nature – particularly in the light of current environmental concerns – and a response which indicates that the natural world is often a casualty of human 'progress'.

2 Activity 1

a Using the Digital Anthology, listen to/watch/read the poem to the class. Clarify any points of understanding.

b Students complete questions 1–7 independently. Take feedback to share, ensure and develop understanding.

c Take students' initial response to the poem, commenting on the presentation of place in the poem.

d Ask students to write a sentence or two, summing up the content or meaning of the poem. They can begin: *'The Moment' is about…*.

4 GradeStudio

a Read the GradeStudio extract to the class. Ask: How has the writer of the sample answer shown 'awareness of a writer making choice(s) of language and/or form and/or structure'?

b How could students add to the sentence to achieve 'identification of effect(s) of writer's choices of language and/or structure and/or form intended/achieved' needed and so achieve a D? For example: *…to emphasise man's arrogance in claiming ownership of the land.*

c How could students add to or rewrite this to achieve the 'explanation of effect(s) of writer's uses of language and/or structure and/or form and effects on readers' needed for a C? For example: *It's like a satisfied pause before the rest of the poem shows how wrong mankind is.*

d Where else in the poem is there an opportunity for students to explore the writer's choice of language or structure? For example, the contrasting movement of the first and second stanza, or the final emphatic line.

d Ask students to select a short quotation that will allow them to explore the poet's use of language or structure and its effect on the reader. The students then write a paragraph about it using point-evidence-explanation.

3 Activity 2

a Display the poem on the board using the Digital Anthology.

b Students discuss the activity questions in pairs, writing their response in full sentences to ensure clarity of thought and their ability to express it.

c Take feedback, annotating the displayed poem using Wordbox. Encourage and validate a wide variety of interpretation and response.

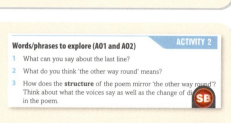

48 © Pearson Education Limited 2010

5 Comparison activities, page 64

Note: In order to do these activities, students would need to have completed their work on 'Wind'.

The Moment
1. **Comparing ideas and themes**
   Compare the relationship between man and nature in 'The Moment' and 'Wind'.
2. **Comparing writers' devices**
   Compare the ways in which the writers of 'The Moment' and 'Wind' suggest the power of nature.

a In pairs or independently, students complete **Worksheet 2.9**, linking their response to the poems with the relevant Assessment Objective. Take feedback on any areas which students found difficult to grasp or to comment on.

b Students use their notes from **Worksheet 2.9** to write three or four key points comparing the relationship between humans and nature and the use of personification in the two poems. They should write **in complete sentences using connectives**. Display **Worksheet 1.3** to support them.

c Take feedback, compiling notes on the board. As a class, students find evidence from each poem to support each point.

d Students select three points with supporting evidence from those on the board.

e Students add a sentence or two to each point/piece of evidence, explaining and commenting on how the writers have presented their ideas.

6 Plenary

Take feedback on 'The Moment', annotating the poem displayed on the whiteboard using Wordbox. Focus on relevant key features, e.g:
- content
- language
- tone.
- interpretation
- structure

If students have studied and compared 'Wind', take feedback on relevant key similarities and differences in content, interpretation, language, structure or tone.

Suggested answers

Activity 1

1 Man thinks he owns nature simply because he arrives somewhere, plants a flag and says 'I own this'. Man does not own nature: he is 'just a visitor'.

2 The journey through life.

3 The area becomes increasingly large, like a camera zooming out; reflecting the way in which humans regard, and crave, ownership of the land.

4 The pause creates a moment of misplaced satisfaction in humans' sense of ownership, of achievement, of belonging – before crushing that perception.

5 The movement seems to be upward, from the trees to the birds to the cliffs to the air – and then suddenly back to the level of the reader: 'you can't breathe'.

6 • The list uses longer, descriptive phrases giving a sense of grandeur.
   • The personification of the trees suggests an active response to human activities; the use of verbs creates a stronger sense of movement; the use of emotive language ('fissure… collapse') gives a sense of drama.

7 a *Announcing*.
  b This suggests man's loud, possessive arrogance.

Activity 2

1 While humans have always considered themselves the conquerors and manipulators of the natural world, this places the power firmly on nature's side. A single sentence on its own line gives an emphatic contradiction.

2 The entire poem is a negation of human arrogance. This conclusion reflects and confirms that.

3 The first stanza draws in and sets up the reader's complicity with the view presented, with an expanding focus from the individual to the national. The second stanza not only negates this but presents a change of direction – shooting upwards through destruction and back before the third stanza expresses the natural world's point of view. The two points of view – the mistaken human view and the natural view – pivot on the disorientating, dramatic second stanza.

Comparison activities

Key points for this activity are provided in **Worksheet 2.10**.

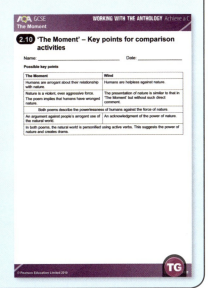

Chapter 2 Place

Cold Knap Lake
by Gillian Clarke

Assessment Objectives
- **AO1:** respond to texts critically and imaginatively; select and evaluate relevant textual detail to illustrate and support interpretations
- **AO2:** explain how language, structure and form contribute to writers' presentation of ideas, themes and settings

Learning Objectives
- To develop students' responses to the poem
- To relate the Assessment Objectives to the poem

Required resources
- Poem text, available on CD-ROM and video/audio online at http://anthology.aqa.org.uk
- Student Book, page 41
- Worksheets 1.3, 2.11, 2.12, 2.13

1 Starter
Ask students to think of their earliest or strongest childhood memory before they were five. Can they identify why this memory has 'stuck' when so many other moments have been forgotten? Was it very dramatic? Or frightening? Or beautiful? Or significant in some other way?

2 Activity 1
a Using the Digital Anthology, listen to/watch/read the poem to the class. Clarify any points of understanding.
b Students complete questions 1–6 independently. Take feedback to share, ensure and develop understanding.
c Take students' initial response to the poem, commenting on the presentation of place in the poem.
d Ask students to write a sentence or two, summing up the content or meaning of the poem. They can begin: *'Cold Knap Lake' is about… .*

Initial responses — ACTIVITY 1
1. a What happens in the first three **stanzas** of the poem?
   b Who are the different people involved in the story?
2. The first three stanzas are written from the point of view of a child. How does the poet show that it is a child's viewpoint? Think about the words she uses, and how she describes her mother.
3. 'My mother gave a stranger's child her breath.' What is the mother doing here, and how is this clearly her child's point of view?
4. 'Was I there?' comes after a gap, and is the shortest line in the poem.
   a Why is this question a surprise when you read it? Think about what it looks like when you look at the whole poem on the page.
   b How does the time of the poem alter at this point? Think about the age of 'I'.
5. The sentences in the fourth stanza are questions.
   a What is the **speaker** uncertain about?
   b Which words in the stanza suggest uncertainty, or things being lost?
6. There are some **echoes** and **half-rhymes** in the poem, but the only full **rhyme** in the poem is formed by the last two lines.
   Why do you think the poet decided to do this?
   What things is she joining together by using rhyme?

3 Activity 2
a Display the poem using the Digital Anthology.
b Give students 3 minutes in pairs to identify child-like and adult features.
c Take feedback, highlighting the poem on the whiteboard using Wordbox.

Words/phrases to explore (AO1 and AO2) — ACTIVITY 2
The last two lines seem almost like part of a nursery rhyme. What else in the poem seems to be like a children's story, and what seems very adult?

4 GradeStudio
a Read the GradeStudio extract to the class. Ask students: How has the writer of the sample answer shown an 'explanation of effect(s) of writer's use of language and/or structure and/or form and effects on readers'?
b Where else in the poem can the students find language, structure or form used to create a specific effect? For example, the description of the narrator's mother, or the movement from the third to the fourth stanza.
c Ask students to select a short quotation that will allow them to explore the writer's use of language or structure and its effect on the reader. The students then write a paragraph about it using point-evidence-explanation.

GradeStudio
Sample answer
To achieve a C on this AO2 descriptor, you need to show **explanation of effect(s) of writers' uses of language and/or structure and/or form and effects on reader**. The following extract from a sample answer would hit the grade C requirement because it explains the effect of the pause in the poem.

> The pause created by the comma after 'the child breathed' lets the reader take in that it has actually been saved. Up to that point you think that it died.

5 Comparison activities, page 64

Note: In order to do these activities, students would need to have completed their work on 'The Wild Swans at Coole' and 'Neighbours'.

Cold Knap Lake

1. **Comparing ideas and themes**
   Compare the effects of memory in 'Cold Knap Lake' and 'The Wild Swans at Coole'.
2. **Comparing writers' devices**
   Compare how Gillian Clarke shapes the endings of 'Cold Knap Lake' and 'Neighbours' to affect the reader.

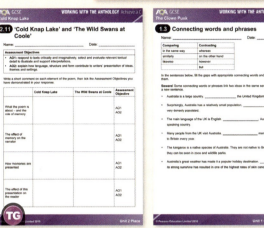

1. **a** In pairs or independently, students complete **Worksheet 2.11**, linking their response to the poems with the relevant Assessment Objective. Take feedback on any areas which students found difficult to grasp or to comment on.
   b Students use their notes from **Worksheet 2.11** to write three or four key points comparing the effects of memory in the poems. They should write **in complete sentences using connectives**. Display **Worksheet 1.3** to support them.
   c Take feedback, compiling notes on the board. As a class, students find evidence from each poem to support each point.
   d Students select three points with supporting evidence from those on the board.
   e Students add a sentence or two to each point/piece of evidence, explaining and commenting on how the writers have presented their ideas.
2. Repeat the above sequence, using **Worksheet 2.12** to explore the endings of the poems.

6 Plenary

Take feedback on 'Cold Knap Lake', annotating the poem displayed on the whiteboard using Wordbox. Focus on relevant key features, e.g:
- content
- language
- tone.
- interpretation
- structure

If students have studied and compared 'The Wild Swans at Coole' and/or 'Neighbours', take feedback on relevant key similarities and differences in content, interpretation, language, structure or tone.

Suggested answers

Activity 1

1. An apparently drowned child was pulled from a lake. The narrator's mother gave the child the kiss of life and the child recovered. The narrator's father took the child home where her own parents thrashed her for almost drowning.

2. The narrator refers to her parents taking an active part, while she watches passively. She describes her mother as 'a heroine' suggesting the narrator admires her actions.

3. The mother is giving the child the 'kiss of life'. As well as the reference to **my** mother', the phrase 'a stranger's child' rather than just 'a child' suggests a daughter's perspective.

4. **a** The first half of the poem is described from the narrator's point of view, clearly suggesting that she was there. The surprise is emphasised by the structure and position of the line: the gap before it, and its brevity, suggests a sudden and sharp questioning, a possible contradiction in the narrative.
   b The poem moves from the past into the present, from narrative to reflection.

5. **a** Whether her memory is reliable.
   b 'troubled', 'shadowy', 'cloudiness'.

6. **a** It gives the conclusion of the poem an emphatic weight and finality.
   b The rhyme returns us to the image of the girl lost underwater, now with additional meaning: the loss and unreliability of memory.

Activity 2

- 'dressed in… long green silk' and 'a heroine' 'kneeling on the earth' seem romantically fairy-tale descriptions. The return to life of this 'drowned child' has a sense of magic.
- The description of the 'wartime frock' and the 'thrashing' give a much more adult tone to the poem.
- The suggestion is that, as this story has been told and re-told, the narrator may have 'placed' herself in the memory and taken it on as one of her own. Above all, the implication is that memory is unreliable.

Comparison activities

Key points for this activity are provided in **Worksheet 2.13**.

Chapter 2 Place

Price We Pay for the Sun
by Grace Nichols

Assessment Objectives
- **AO1:** respond to texts critically and imaginatively; select and evaluate relevant textual detail to illustrate and support interpretations
- **AO2:** explain how language, structure and form contribute to writers' presentation of ideas, themes and settings

Learning Objectives
- To develop students' responses to the poem
- To relate the Assessment Objectives to the poem

Required resources
- Poem text, available on CD-ROM and video/audio online at http://anthology.aqa.org.uk
- Student Book, page 42
- Worksheets 1.3, 2.14, 2.15, 2.16

1 Starter
a Write the word 'Caribbean' on the board.
b Give students 3 minutes to note the associations and connotations of the word.
c Take feedback. Discuss: Where have you acquired these associations and ideas?

2 Activity 1
a Using the Digital Anthology, listen to/watch/read the poem to the class. Clarify any points of understanding.
b Students complete questions 1–7 independently. Take feedback to share, ensure and develop understanding.
c Take students' initial response to the poem, commenting on the presentation of place in the poem.
d Ask students to write a sentence or two, summing up the content or meaning of the poem. They can begin: *'Price We Pay for the Sun' is about… .*

Initial responses — ACTIVITY 1
1. In the poem as a whole, what is good about the islands and what isn't? Find evidence to support what you think.
2. Who do you think the 'we' and 'you' in the poem might be? Support your answer with evidence.
3. Why does Nichols repeat the word 'real'? Think about what isn't 'real'.
4. The writer compares the islands to the people who live there. Which phrase in the first **stanza** is the first to make a comparison?
5. What features of the islands that are not like 'picture postcards' are mentioned in the second stanza?
6. How are these features compared to bad things happening to the **speaker's** family?
7. a Nichols invents a word, 'sulph-furious', to describe her mother's cancer. What other words does this word come from?
   b What is she saying about the illness? Remember that she is comparing the islands' features to the inhabitants.

3 Activity 2
a Display the poem using the Digital Anthology.
b Give students 3 minutes in pairs to write their responses in complete sentences to ensure understanding and the ability to express it. Ask volunteers to share with the class.

Words/phrases to explore (AO1 and AO2) — ACTIVITY 2
Look at the last three lines of the poem and the first three. What is Nichols saying about the islands overall?

4 GradeStudio
a Read the GradeStudio extract to the class. Ask students: How has the writer of the sample answer shown that s/he has selected 'details linked to interpretation'?
b Ask students: Where else in the poem are we encouraged towards a particular interpretation? For example, her father's tears or the contrast of 'picture postcards' and 'flesh and blood'.
c Ask students to select a short quotation that will allow them to explore their interpretation of the poem with close reference to the writer's use of language and its effect on the reader. The students then write a paragraph about it, using point-evidence-explanation.

GradeStudio — Sample answer B
To achieve a B on this AO1 descriptor, you need to show **details linked to interpretation**. The following extract from a sample answer would hit the grade B requirement.

Activity 1, question 5
Nichols shows clearly that the islands, although they are beautiful, contain the possibilities of pain: the volcanoes may be 'sleeping', but they are there, and the winds become 'salty hurricanes' – people suffer, like anywhere else.

5 Comparison activities, page 64

Note: In order to do these activities, students would need to have completed their work on 'Hard Water' and 'London'.

Price We Pay for the Sun
1. **Comparing ideas and themes**
   Compare how the reality of a place is shown in 'Price We Pay for the Sun' and 'Hard Water'.
2. **Comparing writers' devices**
   Compare how a place is made to seem unpleasant in 'Price We Pay for the Sun' and 'London'.

1 a In pairs or independently, students complete **Worksheet 2.14**, linking their response to the poems with the relevant Assessment Objective. Take feedback on any areas which students found difficult to grasp or to comment on.
   b Students use their notes from **Worksheet 2.14** to write three or four key points comparing reality of a place in the poems. They should write **in complete sentences using connectives**. Display **Worksheet 1.3** to support them.
   c Take feedback, compiling notes on the board. As a class, students find evidence from each poem to support each point.
   d Students select three points with supporting evidence from those on the board.
   e Students add a sentence or two to each point/piece of evidence, explaining and commenting on how the writers have presented their points of view.
2 Repeat the above sequence, using **Worksheet 2.15** to explore negative presentation of place in the poems.

6 Plenary

Take feedback on 'Price We Pay for the Sun', annotating the poem displayed on the whiteboard using Wordbox. Focus on relevant key features, e.g:
- content
- language
- tone
- interpretation
- structure

If students have studied and compared 'Hard Water' and/or 'London', take feedback on relevant key similarities and differences in content, interpretation, language, structure or tone.

Suggested answers

Activity 1

1. Positive: they are beautiful ('picture postcards') and the weather is good ('the sun').
   Negative: image of violence ('these islands split bone'), volcanoes, hurricanes, and poverty.
2. 'We' suggests the people who live on 'These islands'. 'You' suggests the girl addressed in the final verse – 'we pay for the sun girl' – although the fact that she is not addressed directly until the end of the poem may suggest that the poem is addressed to anyone who does not see beyond the picture-postcard to the reality of the Caribbean.
3. To emphasise her point: the Caribbean is much more than the fantasy holiday destination that tourists see.
4. 'more real/than flesh and blood'.
5. Volcanoes and hurricanes.
6. Volcanoes are used as a simile for the writer's mother's breast cancer; hurricanes are a metaphor for her father's emotional upset.
7. a/b Volcanoes emit sulphurious gases; the pun using the word 'furious' adds a further connotation of aggressive cancer.

Activity 2

The Caribbean is more than a holiday destination. It is a place of poverty – but perhaps that hardship is tempered by natural advantages, which should be enjoyed.

Comparison activities

Key points for this activity are provided in **Worksheet 2.16**.

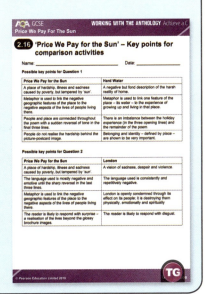

Chapter 2 Place

Neighbours
by Gillian Clarke

Assessment Objectives
- **AO1:** respond to texts critically and imaginatively; select and evaluate relevant textual detail to illustrate and support interpretations
- **AO2:** explain how language, structure and form contribute to writers' presentation of ideas, themes and settings

Learning Objectives
- To develop students' responses to the poem
- To relate the Assessment Objectives to the poem

Required resources
- Poem text, available on CD-ROM and video/audio online at http://anthology.aqa.org.uk
- Student Book, page 43
- Worksheets 1.3, 2.12, 2.17, 2.18

1 Starter
Find some footage of the Chernobyl disaster on the Internet. Before showing students the footage ask them to read the 'Poem context' on page 43 of the Student Book. Watch the footage together and answer students' questions.

2 Activity 1
a Using the Digital Anthology, listen to/watch/read the poem to the class. Clarify any points of understanding.

b Students complete questions 1–7 independently. Take feedback to share, ensure and develop understanding.

c Take students' initial response to the poem, commenting on the presentation of place in the poem.

d Ask students to write a sentence or two, summing up the content or meaning of the poem. They can begin: *'Neighbours' is about…* .

Initial responses — ACTIVITY 1
1 'That spring was late'. What other signs are there in the first **stanza** that there iws something wrong in nature?
2 Go through the poem and jot down all the other examples you can find of things being 'wrong'.
3 'A mouthful of bitter air' (fourth stanza). Why is the air described as 'bitter'? Try to think of more than one reason.
4 What does the 'box of sorrows' refer to? Read the 'Context' above again if you're not sure.
5 Why is the rain described as a 'poisoned arrow'? Think about both words.
6 What exactly do you think the writer means by 'neighbourly' in the sixth stanza? Think about where the places in the poem are, and personal relationships – what 'neighbours' means. Where can you find both ideas in this stanza?
7 Why are they looking for a bird 'with green in its voice'? Think of various associations with the word 'green'.

3 Activity 2
a Display the last three lines of the poem in close-up using the Digital Anthology.

b Give students 5 minutes in pairs to respond to the questions, recording their responses **in complete sentences** to ensure understanding and the ability to express it.

c Take feedback, annotating the displayed lines using Wordbox to ensure understanding.

Words/phrases to explore (AO1 and AO2) — ACTIVITY 2
Analyse the last three lines.
1 Why do you think the writer uses two other languages here?
2 What does the 'break of blue' imply? Think of as many reasons as you can.
3 Why do you think the lines are shorter here than in the rest of the poem? Look at the shape of the clines on the page.

4 GradeStudio
a Read the GradeStudio extract to the class. Ask: How has the writer of the sample answer shown that s/he has selected 'details linked to interpretation'?

b Ask: Where else in the poem are we encouraged towards a particular response? For example, the disturbing description of the lambs and children in the fifth stanza; the empathy of the sixth stanza.

c Ask students to select a short quotation that will allow them to explore the writer's use of language and its effect on the reader. They then write a paragraph about it, using point-evidence-explanation.

GradeStudio — Sample answer
To achieve a C on this AO1 descriptor, you need to show **effective use of details**. The following extract from a sample answer would hit the grade C requirement:

The poem is full of poison – 'gall', 'bitter air', 'the poisoned arrow', and a lamb that 'sips caesium' rather than clean milk.

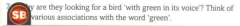

5 Comparison activities, page 64

Note: In order to do these activities, students would need to have completed their work on 'Price We Pay for the Sun' and 'Cold Knap Lake'.

1 a In pairs or independently, students complete **Worksheet 2.17**, linking their response to the poems with the relevant Assessment Objective. Take feedback on any areas which students found difficult to grasp or to comment on.

Neighbours

1 Comparing ideas and themes
Compare the unpleasant aspects of nature shown in 'Neighbours' and 'Price We Pay for the Sun'.

2 Comparing writers' devices
Compare the effects of the endings of 'Neighbours' and 'Cold Knap Lake'.

b Students use their notes from **Worksheet 2.17** to write three or four key points comparing the presentation of place in the poems. They should write **in complete sentences using connectives**. Display **Worksheet 1.3** to support them.

c Take feedback, compiling notes on the board. As a class, students find evidence from each poem to support each point.

d Students select three points with supporting evidence from those on the board.

e Students add a sentence or two to each point/piece of evidence, explaining and commenting on how the writers have presented their ideas.

2 Repeat the above sequence, using **Worksheet 2.12** to explore negative presentation of place.

6 Plenary

Take feedback on 'Neighbours', annotating the poem displayed on the whiteboard using Wordbox. Focus on relevant key features, e.g:

- content
- language
- tone
- interpretation
- structure

If students have studied and compared 'Price We Pay for the Sun' and/or 'Cold Knap Lake', take feedback on relevant key similarities and differences in content, interpretation, language, structure or tone.

Suggested answers

Activity 1

1 'spring was late', 'Birds were late to pair', and crows pecked lambs' eyes.

2 Birds dying over Finland; milk spilt in Poland; a lamb sips caesium in Wales; a child takes in poison; burnt fireman; virus and toxin.

3 The air is contaminated; relations between these countries had not been good for years during the Cold War ('some old story').

4 This is perhaps a reference to Chernobyl, the nuclear plant itself. It suggests an allusion to the Pandora story, perhaps implying that the scientific 'progress' is like Pandora's curiosity, 'lifting the lid' on the power of the atom – and bringing sorrow into the world as a result.

5 The rain carried the contamination; as such it is poisoned. 'Arrow' depicts the rain as an aggressive assault, falling from the sky.

6 It implies that the fallout from Chernobyl is showing qualities of neighbourliness by visiting, sharing itself with the surrounding countries; so connecting them, and bringing them closer together. This idea is developed in the notion that the fallout is responsible for 'twinning' or connecting these towns.

7 'Green' suggests new life, a re-growth. It refers back to the description of birds falling earlier in the poem, now making the bird a symbol of recovery as well as the disaster.

Activity 2

1 Referring back to the title and reference in the fifth stanza to 'neighbours' and twinning, the three languages reflect the democratic nature of the disaster, bringing countries and languages together.

2 A clearing of clouds from the sky suggests a return to happiness – and an end to the clouds of radioactivity blowing across Europe.

3 An emphatic, summative end to the poem. Possibly also the first hesitant attempts at communication in a foreign language.

Comparison activities

Key points for this activity are provided in **Worksheet 2.18**.

Chapter 2 Place

Crossing the Loch
by Kathleen Jamie

Assessment Objectives
- **AO1:** respond to texts critically and imaginatively; select and evaluate relevant textual detail to illustrate and support interpretations
- **AO2:** explain how language, structure and form contribute to writers' presentation of ideas, themes and settings

Learning Objectives
- To develop students' responses to the poem
- To relate the Assessment Objectives to the poem

Required resources
- Poem text, available on CD-ROM and video/audio online at http://anthology.aqa.org.uk
- Student Book, page 44
- Worksheets 1.3, 2.19, 2.20, 2.21

1 Starter

a Look at the vocabulary on **Worksheet 2.19** – or export the poem text to 'Magnets' using the Wordbox facility on the Digital Anthology. Explain to students that it is all taken from the poem they will be exploring in the lesson.

b Students sort the words into groups, either electronically, by cutting and shuffling the worksheet, or noting with pen and paper. The students then give each language group a title, summing up the kind of vocabulary it contains, e.g. movement, nature.

c Take feedback, noting relevant vocabulary groups on the whiteboard.

d Display the poem using the Digital Anthology.

e Listen to/watch/read the poem to the class. Clarify any points of understanding.

f Allocate a colour to each vocabulary group. What do students notice, e.g. the sense of movement at the start and end of the poem; the stillness at the centre; the incongruity of 'nuclear' in the language of nature?

2 Activity 1

a Students complete questions 1–7 independently. Take feedback to share, ensure and develop understanding.

b Ask students to write a sentence or two, summing up the content or meaning of the poem. They can begin: *'Crossing the Loch' is about…*

3 Activity 2

a Display the last stanza in close-up using the Digital Anthology.

b Students record their responses to the questions in complete sentences, ensuring their understanding and ability to express it.

c Take feedback, annotating the displayed poem using Wordbox where relevant, to share and develop thinking.

4 GradeStudio

a Read the GradeStudio extract to the class. How has the writer of the sample answer shown 'some response to text'?

b How could students add to this answer, in order to show an 'explained response' and so achieve a D? For example: *…because the loch glowed in the dark* and *'we watched water shine/on our fingers and oars'*.

c How could students further develop this answer, in order to show a 'sustained response' and so achieve a C? For example: *Nature is described as if it were magical, which explains why this moment was so memorable for the narrator.*

d Ask students: Where else in the poem are we encouraged towards a particular response? For example, the shock of 'nuclear hulls', the references to the travellers' later life.

e Ask students to select a short quotation that will allow them to explore their response to the text. The students then write a paragraph about it, using point-evidence-explanation.

5 Comparison activities, page 64

Note: In order to do these activities, students would need to have completed their work on 'The Prelude'.

a In pairs or independently, students complete **Worksheet 2.20**, linking their response to the poems with the relevant Assessment Objective. Take feedback on any areas which students found difficult to grasp or to comment on.

> **Crossing the Loch**
> 1 **Comparing ideas and themes**
>   Compare the experiences of rowing at night in 'Crossing the Loch' and 'The Prelude'.
> 2 **Comparing writers' devices**
>   Compare the ways in which the writers describe rowing in 'Crossing the Loch' and 'The Prelude'.

b Students use their notes from **Worksheet 2.20** to write three or four key points comparing the experience of rowing at night in the poems. They should write **in complete sentences using connectives**. Display **Worksheet 1.3** to support them.

c Take feedback, compiling notes on the board. As a class, students find evidence from each poem to support each point.

d Students select three points with supporting evidence from those on the board.

e Students add a sentence or two to each point/piece of evidence, explaining and commenting on how the writers have presented their ideas.

6 Plenary

Take feedback on 'Crossing the Loch', annotating the poem displayed on the whiteboard using Wordbox. Focus on relevant key features, e.g:
- content
- language
- tone.
- interpretation
- structure

If students have studied and compared 'The Prelude' take feedback on relevant key similarities and differences in content, interpretation, language, structure or tone.

Suggested answers

Activity 1

1 A group of friends went to the pub then decided to row to 'the cottage' across the loch. The water glows strangely with 'phosphorescence'. Although the loch was broad and tidal, they made it safely to the other side. Since then, they have grown older and had families.

2 'one night'; 'I forget'; series of questions in third stanza: 'Who rowed and who kept their peace?', 'Who hauled…', 'who first noticed…'; 'we live' and reference to children in final stanza.

3 As the boat 'lands' in the water, the water around it forms the shape of a mouth and, in taking on the shape of the boat, it seems to take on the shape of the word.

4 **a** 'hushed', 'night', 'scared', 'cold', 'hunched', 'deadheads', 'nuclear'.

  b The writer emphasises the sound of the boat and contrasts it with the silence of those in it; particularly telling is that the high spirits ('jokes') which made this seem a good idea have vanished ('hushed') and all that can now be heard is the boat and the water, the source of danger: 'splash, creak and the spill'. The feeling of 'cold' reflects fear and a drop in mood.

5 The boat is the shape of a nest; its occupants 'twitter' about the phosphorescence. The image suggests nature, excitement, innocence.

6 'Saints' has religious connotations, implying that the phosphorescence is miraculous.

7 Like a dart in shape, and glowing magically, further reinforcing the supernatural quality of the phosphorescence.

Activity 2

In later life, the people in the boat met women and men with whom they had children. The event is perhaps most memorable for the phosphorescence of the loch, but perhaps also for the communal nature of the experience, drawing this group together as an 'astonished small boat of saints' before later life dispersed them.

Comparison activities

Key points for this activity are provided in **Worksheet 2.21**.

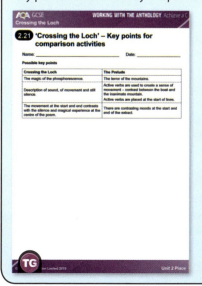

Chapter 2 Place

Hard Water by Jean Sprackland

Assessment Objectives
- **AO1:** respond to texts critically and imaginatively; select and evaluate relevant textual detail to illustrate and support interpretations
- **AO2:** explain how language, structure and form contribute to writers' presentation of ideas, themes and settings

Learning Objectives
- To develop students' responses to the poem
- To relate the Assessment Objectives to the poem

Required resources
- Poem text, available on CD-ROM and video/audio online at http://anthology.aqa.org.uk
- Student Book, page 45
- Worksheets 1.3, 2.22, 2.23, 2.24

1 Starter

a Write the phrases 'going away' and 'coming home' on the whiteboard.

b Ask students to think of the longest/furthest they have been away from home. Then ask:
- What was it like coming home – good or bad? In what ways?
- What reminds you of home/makes you glad to return?

2 Activity 1

a Using the Digital Anthology, listen to/watch/read the poem to the class. Clarify any points of understanding.

b Students complete questions 1–7 independently. Take feedback to share, ensure and develop understanding.

c Take students' initial response to the poem, commenting on the presentation of place in the poem.

d Ask students to write a sentence or two, summing up the content or meaning of the poem. They can begin: *'Hard Water' is about….* .

Initial responses — ACTIVITY 1
1. What is it about the water and her home town that the **speaker** likes? Go through the poem looking for the words and phrases that tell you this, and make a note of them.
2. a The first three lines are about a holiday experience. Why do you think there is a break after these lines?
   b What do you think has happened during the pause here.
3. What do you think the 'little fizz of anxiety' is? Think about the water and how the speaker is feeling.
4. 'It couldn't lie.' What does the water tell the truth about? Look at the next two sentences.
5. Look at the four lines beginning 'I let a different cleverness'.
   a The writer has 'book-learning', but what is the 'cleverness' of her home city? What are people like there?
   b How do these four lines use the idea of water? Look carefully at all the words.
6. Who do you think might have said 'too bloody deep for me', and why?
7. The writer is marked as 'belonging, regardless'. What does she belong to, do you think, and 'regardless' of what?

3 Activity 2

a Display the poem using the Digital Anthology to highlight the quotation, 'Flat. Straight.'

b Students discuss the questions in pairs, noting their response in complete sentences to ensure understanding and the ability to express it. Ask volunteers to share with the class.

Words/phrases to explore (AO1 and AO2) — ACTIVITY 2
Remind yourself of the words 'Flat. Straight.'
1. What do these two words apply to? Think of more than one thing.
2. How does the way the words are written add to the effect?

4 GradeStudio

a Read the GradeStudio extract to the class. Ask: How has the writer of the sample answer shown 'appropriate comment on ideas/themes'?

b Where else in the poem provides students with an opportunity to explore ideas and themes? For example, the links between the water and her home town.

c Ask students to select a short quotation which will allow them to explore the writer's ideas and themes. The students then write a paragraph about it using point-evidence-explanation.

GradeStudio
Sample answer
To achieve a C on this AO2 descriptor, you need to show **appropriate comment on ideas/themes**. The following extract from a sample answer would hit the grade C requirement.

> Activity 1, question 1
> The speaker has several attitudes to the water. She doesn't always seem to like it, because it's 'not quite clean' and the rain falls with a 'payload of acid', but in the end she seems to love it, as she sees it as 'fierce lovely water'.

5 Comparison activities, page 64

Note: In order to do these activities, students would need to have completed their work on 'A Vision' and 'Wind'.

1 a In pairs or independently, students complete **Worksheet 2.22**, linking their response to the poems with the relevant Assessment Objective. Take feedback on any areas which students found difficult to grasp or to comment on.

> **Hard Water**
> 1 **Comparing ideas and themes**
>   Compare the feelings of the speakers in 'Hard Water' and 'A Vision'.
> 2 **Comparing writers' devices**
>   Compare the ways in which the writers use the senses in 'Hard Water' and 'W

b Students use their notes from **Worksheet 2.22** to write three or four key points comparing the feelings of the speakers in the poems. They should write **in complete sentences using connectives**. Display **Worksheet 1.3** to support them.

c Take feedback, compiling notes on the board. As a class, students find evidence from each poem to support each point.

d Students select three points with supporting evidence from those on the board.

e Students add a sentence or two to each point/piece of evidence, explaining and commenting on how the writers have presented their ideas.

2 Repeat the above sequence, using **Worksheet 2.23** to explore the writers' use of the senses.

6 Plenary

Take feedback on 'Hard Water', annotating the poem displayed on the whiteboard using Wordbox. Focus on relevant key features, e.g:
- content
- language
- tone.
- interpretation
- structure

If students have studied and compared 'A Vision' and/or 'Wind', take feedback on relevant key similarities and differences in content, interpretation, language, structure or tone.

Suggested answers

Activity 1

1 The speaker likes: the water because it is 'flat' and 'straight' and 'honest'; the 'straight talk'; the taste of rain, even though it has a 'payload of acid', it 'tasted of work' and is 'blunt' like the 'straight talk'; the feeling of 'belonging'.

2 **a** To demarcate the experience of holiday from the experience of home.
   b The gap suggests the journey and therefore the distance between holiday and home.

3 Water straight from the tap sometimes fizzes as it settles; also the anxiety of returning home after a holiday – and perhaps returning to work.

4 The rain has been polluted by industry; changed to such an extent that the water has forgotten its origins, its identity – which strongly reflects the poet, reaffirming her identity in the poem.

5 **a** 'work', 'early mornings', blunt speaking.
   b The water seems to have taken on the taste of – i.e. reflect – local attitudes and habits.

6 Perhaps someone responding to the ideas in the poem; implying that the writer has over-complicated the experience of returning from holiday and drinking a glass of water.

7 A feeling of belonging to her home town, perhaps regardless of the 'book-learning' that marks her difference and, linked with it, the fierce rejection of her thinking in previous lines.

Activity 2

1 The water, the place, the people.

2 Like the straight-talking people of her town, these monosyllabic sentences are short, simple and emphatic. Their structure reflects their meaning.

Comparison activities

Key points for this activity are provided in **Worksheet 2.24**.

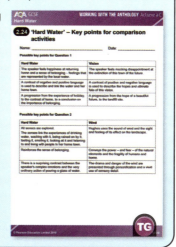

AQA GCSE Working with the Anthology: Achieve a C 59

Chapter 2 Place

London by William Blake

Assessment Objectives
- **AO1:** respond to texts critically and imaginatively; select and evaluate relevant textual detail to illustrate and support interpretations
- **AO2:** explain how language, structure and form contribute to writers' presentation of ideas, themes and settings

Learning Objectives
- To develop students' responses to the poem
- To relate the Assessment Objectives to the poem

Required resources
- Poem text, available on CD-ROM and video/audio online at http://anthology.aqa.org.uk
- Student Book, page 46
- Worksheets 1.3, 2.25, 2.26, 2.27, 228

1 Starter
Display/distribute **Worksheet 2.25**. Give students 5–10 minutes to complete the cloze activity, choosing from the vocabulary box beside the poem. Point out that there are five gaps and ten words to choose from – some words are not taken from the poem.

2 Activity 1
a Using the Digital Anthology, listen to/watch/read the poem to the class. Clarify any points of understanding.
b Students complete questions 1–7 independently. Take feedback to share, ensure and develop understanding.
c Take students' initial response to the poem, commenting on the presentation of place in the poem.
d Ask students to write a sentence or two, summing up the content or meaning of the poem. They can begin: *'London' is about… .*

Initial responses — ACTIVITY 1
1 Make a list of all the people the **speaker** sees in the streets of London. What do they all have in common?
2 Look through the whole poem, and pick out all the words that suggest grief, danger, destruction or cruelty.
3 There are a lot of repetitions of words in the poem.
  a Go through the poem carefully and make a note of them.
  b What is the overall effect of having so many repetitions, do you think?
4 'Marks of weakness, marks of woe'. What 'marks' do you think the speaker sees?
5 Look at the phrase 'mind-forged manacles'.
  a In what ways are the people in the city tied?
  b Work out what the term 'mind-forged' means. How are their bonds 'mind-forged'?
6 a What were working conditions like for early nineteenth-century chimney sweeps? (You might need to do some research to help you here.)
  b How might their cries 'appal' the church? Think what the church stands for.
7 In Blake's picture of London, everything that should be innocent and happy is not. Find three examples of this in the last few lines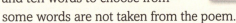

3 Activity 2
a Display the poem using Digital Anthology.
b Students discuss the question in pairs, recording their response in complete sentences to ensure understanding and the ability to express it.
c Take feedback using students' thoughts to annotate the displayed poem, focusing in particular on the reasons for their choices.

Words/phrases to explore (AO1 and AO2) — ACTIVITY 2
Of all the things that the speaker sees in London, which does he think is the worst? Which do you think is the worst? Write this down, giving reasons for your answers.

4 GradeStudio
a Read the GradeStudio extract to the class. Ask: How has the writer of the sample answer shown 'details used to support a range of comments'?
b How could students add to this answer, in order to show an 'effective use of details to support interpretation' and so achieve a C? For example: *Blake seems to be suggesting that London is responsible for all this misery.*
c Where else in the poem can students identify details which will help them explore their response to the poem? For example, the use of repetition, or the phrase 'mind-forg'd manacles'.
d Ask students to select a short quotation that will allow them to explore their response. The students then write a paragraph about it, using point-evidence-explanation.

GradeStudio — Sample answer D
To achieve a D on this AO1 descriptor, you need to use **details to support a range of comments**. The following extract from a sample answer would hit the grade D requirement.

Activity 2
Everybody in the poem seems to be unhappy, full of 'woe'. The children live in 'fear', the chimney sweepers 'cry', and the reader is also invited to feel sorry for the soldier's 'sigh'. The worst thing is not simply that the prostitutes are young, but that they even 'curse' their own bab[y]

5 Comparison activities, page 65

Note: In order to do these activities, students would need to have completed their work on 'Wind' and 'Price We Pay for the Sun'.

1 a In pairs or independently, students complete **Worksheet 2.26**, linking their response to the poems with the relevant Assessment Objective. Take feedback on any areas which students found difficult to grasp or to comment on.

London

1. **Comparing ideas and themes**
   Compare the ways things are destroyed in 'London' and 'Wind'.
2. **Comparing writers' devices**
   Compare how the writers of 'London' and 'Price We Pay for the Sun' make a place seem unpleasant.

b Students use their notes from **Worksheet 2.26** to write three or four key points comparing the way things are destroyed in the two poems. They should write **in complete sentences using connectives**. Display **Worksheet 1.3** to support them.

c Take feedback, compiling notes on the board. As a class, students find evidence from each poem to support each point.

d Students select three points with supporting evidence from those on the board.

e Students add a sentence or two to each point/piece of evidence, explaining and commenting on how the writers have presented their ideas.

2 Repeat the above sequence, using **Worksheet 2.27** to explore how the writers make a place seem unpleasant.

6 Plenary

Take feedback on 'London', annotating the poem displayed on the whiteboard using Wordbox. Focus on relevant key features, e.g:
- content
- language
- tone.
- interpretation
- structure

If students have studied and compared 'Wind' and/or 'Price We Pay for the Sun', take feedback on relevant key similarities and differences in content, interpretation, language, structure or tone.

Suggested answers

Activity 1

1. The faces of lots of people; men, infants, chimney sweepers, soldiers, harlots. All are marked with 'weakness' and 'woe'.

2. 'weakness', 'woe', 'cry', 'fear', 'manacles', 'appalls', 'sigh', 'blood', 'curse', 'blasts', 'tear', 'blights', 'plagues', 'hearse'.

3. 'mark(s)'; 'every', 'cry'; emphasises the universality of this sadness and cruelty and reflects the grinding monotony of this miserable life in the city.

4. Physical as well as mental damage to these people.

5. **a** They are imprisoned by their miserable situation.
   b Implies that this is an imprisoning of the mind – perhaps with an implication that these are 'only' in the mind and could be broken by a different way of thinking.

6. **a** Children used to be sent up to sweep smaller chimneys because they were small enough. Health and safety were not considered.
   b On the one hand it suggests that the church is horrified to see such suffering and sadness; on the other, it implies that the church, by remaining impassive to the suffering, is being blotted out by it

7. 'new-born Infants', 'Marriage' and youth ('youthful Harlots') have all been corrupted.

Activity 2

All responses are arguable. Perhaps the final image of the Harlot's curse on the new-born Infants is felt most strongly.

Comparison activities

Key points for this activity are provided in **Worksheet 2.28**.

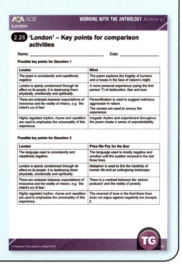

Chapter 2 Place

The Prelude (extract)
by William Wordsworth

Assessment Objectives
- **AO1:** respond to texts critically and imaginatively; select and evaluate relevant textual detail to illustrate and support interpretations
- **AO2:** explain how language, structure and form contribute to writers' presentation of ideas, themes and settings

Learning Objectives
- To develop students' responses to the poem
- To relate the Assessment Objectives to the poem

Required resources
- Poem text, available on CD-ROM and video/audio online at http://anthology.aqa.org.uk
- Student Book, page 47
- Worksheets 1.3, 2.29, 2.30
- A copy of the image *Gordale Scar* by James Ward, if available

1 Starter

a Display James Ward's painting *Gordale Scar*. (You can source this image on the Internet.)
b Point out the following to students:
- Gordale Scar is at the end of a 22-mile fault line which travels from Cumbria to the Yorkshire Dales.
- It is around 15–16 million years old.
- The Romantics (such as Wordsworth) felt it was so overpowering that it was impossible to capture its mood in paint.
- Thomas Gray, the poet, said he could only stay there for 15 minutes, but 'not without shuddering'!

c Discuss with students: How is nature presented in this painting?

2 Activity 1

a Using the Digital Anthology, listen to/watch/read the poem to the class. Clarify any points of understanding.
b Students complete questions 1–6 independently. Take feedback to share, ensure and develop understanding.
c Take students' initial response to the poem, commenting on the presentation of place in the poem.
d Ask students to write a sentence or two, summing up the content or meaning of the poem. They can begin: *'The Prelude' is about... .*

Initial responses — ACTIVITY 1

1 Write down exactly what the boy does in this extract from 'The Prelude', and why he does it.
2 a What evidence is there to suggest that the boy feels guilty for what he does? Look at the first eight lines of the extract.
   b How does his guilt come back again later in the poem?
3 The **speaker** describes the circles behind the boat melting 'into one track'. How does this suggest the distance the boat travels? Think about it from the boy's point of view in the boat.
4 Read the lines from 'But now' to 'like a swan' (lines 11–20). How does Wordsworth suggest that the boy enjoys the place and the activity in these lines? Think about what the boy does and what he sees.
5 Look at the lines from 'When, from behind' to 'Strode after me.' (lines 21–29). The mountains suddenly seem threatening. How does Wordsworth achieve this? Think about:
   a the ways the mountains are **personified** (made to seem living)
   b the adjectives used to describe the mountains.
6 The boy's mood has changed from the opening. He has two responses to what happens. What is his immediate response (look at the lines from 'With trembling oars' to 'serious mood'), and what does he think about it later (look the last 10 lines)?

3 Activity 2

a Display the poem using the Digital Anthology.
b Students work in pairs, responding to the question, writing their response **in complete sentences** to ensure understanding and their ability to express it. Ask volunteers to share their responses with the class.

Words/phrases to explore (AO1 and AO2) — ACTIVITY 2

Choose the line that you think best captures:
- the boy's enjoyment of rowing
- his mood at the end of the poem.

Compare the differences in the lines – not just the feelings, but how Wordsworth creates them by the ways he writes the lines.

4 GradeStudio

a Read the GradeStudio extract to the class. Ask students: How has the writer of the sample answer shown 'appreciation/consideration of effect(s) of writers' uses of language and/or structure and/or form and effects on readers'?
b Ask students: Where else in the poem is there an opportunity to comment on the poet's choice of language or structure? For example, the description of the boy rowing, or the effect the incident had on the boy.
c Ask students to select a short quotation that will allow them to explore the writer's use of language/structure and its effect on the reader. The students then write a paragraph about it using point-evidence-explanation.

GradeStudio
Sample answer B

To achieve a B on this AO2 descriptor, you need to show **appreciation/consideration of effect(s) of writers' uses of language and/or structure and/or form and effects on reader.** This is more than just explaining effect (C) – you have to find more to say when you've done it. The following extract from a sample answer would hit the grade B requirement.

Activity 1, question 5

Wordsworth builds up the terror of the mountain by giving the 'grim' shape a head, as though it were living, and describing his own panic, but the word 'strode' is really powerful. Not only does it make the mountain's movement seem rapid, but also the placing of the word at the beginning of the line makes the action seem very sudden.

5 Comparison activities, page 65

Note: In order to do these activities, students would need to have completed their work on 'Below the Green Corrie'.

a In pairs or independently, students complete **Worksheet 2.29**, linking their response to the poems with the relevant Assessment Objective. Take feedback on any areas which students found difficult to grasp or to comment on.

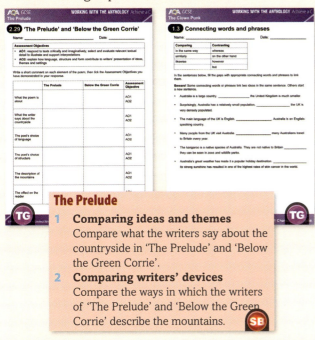

The Prelude

1. **Comparing ideas and themes**
   Compare what the writers say about the countryside in 'The Prelude' and 'Below the Green Corrie'.
2. **Comparing writers' devices**
   Compare the ways in which the writers of 'The Prelude' and 'Below the Green Corrie' describe the mountains.

b Students use their notes from **Worksheet 2.29** to write three or four key points comparing how the countryside is presented and the way in which the mountains are described in the two poems. They should write **in complete sentences using connectives**. Display Worksheet 1.3 to support them.

c Take feedback, compiling notes on the board. As a class, students find evidence from each poem to support each point.

d Students select three points with supporting evidence from those on the board.

e Students add a sentence or two to each point/piece of evidence, explaining and commenting on how the writers have presented their ideas.

6 Plenary

Take feedback on 'The Prelude', annotating the poem displayed on the whiteboard using Wordbox. Focus on relevant key features, e.g:
- content
- language
- tone.
- interpretation
- structure

If students have studied and compared 'Below the Green Corrie', take feedback on relevant key similarities and differences in content, interpretation, language, structure or tone.

Suggested answers

Activity 1

1. One summer evening, the boy finds 'a little boat' and rows it across a lake, aiming for a 'craggy ridge'. On the horizon, he sees a 'huge peak' which seems to grow 'in stature' until it seems to stride 'after me'. He turns the boat, returns it to its place and 'homeward went' but is haunted 'for many days' by the incident.

2. **a** 'It was an act of stealth/And troubled pleasure' suggests it was done in guilty secrecy.
   b When he returns the boat, he says he 'stole my way/Back to the covert of the willow tree' again suggesting his guilty secrecy.

3. The wake of the boat – the ripples it causes in the water – merge into a 'track' of disturbed water behind the boat, suggesting it stretching to the distance.

4. • 'Proud of his skill… unswerving… fixed… lustily… rose… heaving' suggest determination and pace.
   • 'summit… utmost… far above…' suggest the boy's enjoyment of this dramatic landscape.

5. **a** The mountains are personified through the choice of words: 'Upreared its head… stature… purpose of its own… measured motion like a living thing,/ Strode after me' suggest a living, malevolent being.
   b 'huge' is repeated to emphasise the mountain's size and threat; 'black' implies shadow and malevolence.

6. The boy's initial reaction is of fear: 'trembling oars'. Later the experience changes his response to nature itself, seeing fearful beings in all living things.

Activity 2

For example:

Went heaving through the water like a swan. Rowing described using natural imagery – a simile connecting him with nature; 'heaving' suggests power and effort and achievement.

O'er my thoughts/There hung a darkness. 'hung' suggests a threatening presence; metaphor of 'darkness' suggests absence of light and life.

Comparison activities

Key points for this activity are provided in **Worksheet 2.30**.

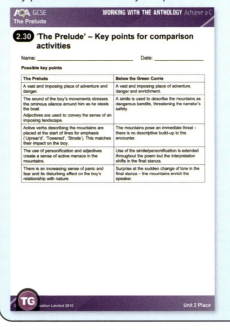

Chapter 2 Place

The Wild Swans at Coole by W. B. Yeats

Assessment Objectives
- **AO1:** respond to texts critically and imaginatively; select and evaluate relevant textual detail to illustrate and support interpretations
- **AO2:** explain how language, structure and form contribute to writers' presentation of ideas, themes and settings

Learning Objectives
- To develop students' responses to the poem
- To relate the Assessment Objectives to the poem

Required resources
- Poem text, available on CD-ROM and video/audio online at http://anthology.aqa.org.uk
- Student Book, page 48
- Worksheets 1.3, 2.31, 2.32, 2.33, 2.34

1 Starter

a Display **Worksheet 2.31** on the whiteboard, keeping the answers covered. Students decide whether the statements are true or false.
b Reveal the answers.
c What associations and ideas do swans prompt in the students?

2 Activity 1

a Using the Digital Anthology, listen to/watch/read the poem to the class. Clarify any points of understanding.
b Students complete questions 1–7 independently. Take feedback to share, ensure and develop understanding.
c Take students' initial response to the poem, commenting on the presentation of place in the poem.
d Ask students to write a sentence or two, summing up the content or meaning of the poem. They can begin: *'The Wild Swans at Coole' is about….*

Initial responses — ACTIVITY 1
1. a How long is it since the **speaker** first saw the swans?
   b What exactly does he see them do when he's watching them?
2. The first **stanza** seems very still. Which words make it seem still?
3. The second stanza seems very active. Which words make it seem active?
4. Lines 4 and 10 are both short.
   a How does line 4 add to the effect of stillness?
   b How does line 10 add to the sense of action?
5. In the third stanza, the speaker's heart is 'sore'.
   a Why, do you think? What do the swans make him think of?
   b What might have changed?
6. a In the fourth stanza, how do the swans seem unchanged?
   b How might the speaker have changed, unlike the swans?
7. Why does Yeats choose to end the poem with a question? Think about the effect.

3 Activity 2

a Display the poem using the Digital Anthology.
b Students discuss the task in pairs, expressing their response in complete sentences to ensure understanding and the ability to express it.
c Use Wordbox to highlight relevant quotations on the displayed poem, annotating with students' comments to ensure breadth of understanding for all.

4 GradeStudio

a Read the GradeStudio extract to the class. Ask: How has the writer of the sample answer shown 'thoughtful consideration of ideas and themes'?
b Students add a sentence or two to the sample answer, commenting on the poet's intended effect on the reader. For example: *In comparing the swans with himself, the narrator conveys his sadness without directly stating its cause, ending in the seeming hopelessness of the question on which the poem ends. It suggests that the narrator is unclear himself as to what he feels has changed in his life and what exactly he has lost.*
c Ask: Where else in the poem are we encouraged towards a particular response to ideas and themes? For example, the poem's setting or, to develop the point above, its final question.
d Ask students to select a short quotation that will allow them to explore the poet's ideas and themes and their effect on the reader. They then write a paragraph about it, using point-evidence-explanation.

64 © Pearson Education Limited 2010

5 Comparison activities, page 65

Note: In order to do these activities, students would need to have completed their work on 'Crossing the Loch' and 'Cold Knap Lake'.

1 a In pairs or independently, students complete **Worksheet 2.32**, linking their response to the poems with the relevant Assessment Objective. Take feedback on any areas which students found difficult to grasp or to comment on.

> **The Wild Swans at Coole**
> 1 **Comparing ideas and themes**
>   Compare the memories of the speakers about a place in 'The Wild Swans at Coole' and 'Crossing the Loch'.
> 2 **Comparing writers' devices**
>   Compare the ways in which the writers of 'The Wild Swans at Coole' and 'Cold Knap Lake' use swans in the poems.

b Students use their notes from **Worksheet 2.32** to write three or four key points comparing the presentation of memories in the poems. They should write **in complete sentences using connectives**. Display **Worksheet 1.3** to support them.

c Take feedback, compiling notes on the board. As a class, students find evidence from each poem to support each point.

d Students select three points with supporting evidence from those on the board.

e Students add a sentence or two to each point/piece of evidence, explaining and commenting on how the writers have presented their points of view.

2 Repeat the above sequence, using **Worksheet 2.33** to explore the use of swans in the poems.

6 Plenary

Take feedback on 'The Wild Swans at Coole', annotating the poem displayed on the whiteboard using Wordbox. Focus on relevant key features, e.g:
- content
- language
- tone.
- interpretation
- structure

If students have studied and compared 'Crossing the Loch' and/or 'Cold Knap Lake', take feedback on relevant key similarities and differences in content, interpretation, language, structure or tone.

Suggested answers

Activity 1

1 It has been nineteen years since the speaker first saw the swans. As he watches they first 'scatter' then 'drift on the still water'.

2 The verbs in the first stanza are static: 'are… mirrors… are'.

3 The verbs in the second stanza are, in contrast, active: 'has come… mount… scatter wheeling'.

4 **a/b** The short fourth line creates a pause for thought and (literally) reflection. The short tenth line creates an emphatic sense of movement.

5 **a/b** There is no direct or clear evidence; the line 'And now my heart is sore' suggests that the narrator has been at Coole before under different circumstances, perhaps with a loved one whom he has now lost. This is further suggested by the description of the swans as 'Unwearied still, lover by lover'.

6 **a** Swans select a mate for life: 'Their hearts have not grown old'.
  b This seems to return us to the third stanza: 'my heart is sore'.

7 This final question adds to the tone of uncertainty – about the narrator's life and experiences to date.

Activity 2

By comparison, the swans come to represent all that the narrator regrets he has lost: their constancy, vitality, beauty, passion, conquest. While he tells us nothing of his own experiences, his mood becomes clear through the comparison. Their beauty, strength and mystery are, to an extent, conveyed through sound: the silent stillness at the start, their sudden 'wheeling' on 'clamorous wings' and, in the third stanza, 'the bell-beat of their wings'.

Comparison activities

Key points for this activity are provided in **Worksheet 2.34**.

Chapter 2 Place

Spellbound
by Emily Brontë

Assessment Objectives
- **AO1:** respond to texts critically and imaginatively; select and evaluate relevant textual detail to illustrate and support interpretations
- **AO2:** explain how language, structure and form contribute to writers' presentation of ideas, themes and settings

Learning Objectives
- To develop students' responses to the poem
- To relate the Assessment Objectives to the poem

Required resources
- Poem text, available on CD-ROM and video/audio online at http://anthology.aqa.org.uk
- Student Book, page 49
- Worksheets 1.3, 2.35, 2.36, 2.37

1 Starter

a Ask students to contribute features to describe a storm in an empty landscape, e.g. rain, wind, thunder. You can compile the information as notes or visually on the whiteboard.

b For each feature, ask for a descriptive verb and adjective. Add these to the whiteboard.

c Now place a person in the middle of the storm. Ask: How might this person feel? Aim to elicit a range of responses from abject terror to high enjoyment!

d If time allows, give students a further 10 minutes to write a description of the storm from the perspective of the person caught in it.

2 Activity 1

a Using the Digital Anthology, listen to/watch/read the poem to the class. Clarify any points of understanding.

b Students complete questions 1–6 independently. Take feedback to share, ensure and develop understanding.

c Take students' initial response to the poem, commenting on the presentation of place in the poem.

d Ask students to write a sentence or two, summing up the content or meaning of the poem. They can begin: *'Spellbound' is about….*

Initial responses — ACTIVITY 1

1. **a** Looking at the poem as a whole, what can the **speaker** not do?
   b Why do you think she feels like this? Support what you think with some details from the poem.
2. The speaker thinks she is under a spell, and describes it as a 'tyrant' spell. Why does she use this word to describe it?
3. What is the effect of repeating 'cannot' at the end of the first **stanza**? What does it tell you about how the speaker feels?
4. Which words in the second stanza make the weather seem more threatening?
5. What do the first two lines of the last stanza say about how the speaker feels?
6. Look at the last line of the poem. Which words tell you that the speaker's determination not to move has strengthened from the first stanza.

3 Activity 2

a Display the poem using the Digital Anthology.

b Students record their response to the question in full sentences to ensure understanding and the ability to express it.

c Take feedback to share and develop thinking, annotating the poem with students' responses using Wordbox.

Words/phrases to explore (AO1 and AO2) — ACTIVITY 2

How does the writer make you realise what the speaker's mental state is? Look for repetitions of words and sounds in lines, between lines, and between stanzas.
You could start by working on 'wastes beyond wastes below'. Try writing a paragraph about her mental state and how it is shown, starting from this line.

4 GradeStudio

a Read the GradeStudio extract to the class. Ask: How has the writer of the sample answer shown a 'considered/qualified response to the text'?

b Where else in the poem are we encouraged towards a particular response? For example, the language of the second stanza in which danger is implied, or the more telling psychological picture that emerges in the first two lines of the third stanza.

c Ask students to select a short quotation that will allow them to explore their response to the text. They then write a paragraph about it, using point-evidence-explanation.

GradeStudio — Sample answer B

To achieve a B on this AO1 descriptor, you need to show **considered/qualified response to text**. The following extract from a sample answer would hit the grade B requirement.

Activity 1, question 6
The speaker in the poem seems terrified by the conditions, as shown by adjectives such as 'wild' and 'giant', so that she is unable to move; but 'I will not' in the last line suggests something else is going on in her mind beyond mere terror.

5 Comparison activities, page 65

Note: In order to do these activities, students would need to have completed their work on 'The Prelude' and 'Storm in the Black Forest'.

1 a In pairs or independently, students complete **Worksheet 2.35**, linking their response to the poems with the relevant Assessment Objective. Take feedback on any areas which students found difficult to grasp or to comment on.

Spellbound

1 Comparing ideas and themes
Compare the feelings of the speakers in 'Spellbound' and 'The Prelude'.

2 Comparing writers' devices
Compare how the writers of 'Spellbound' and 'Storm in the Black Forest' use repetitions to show feelings.

b Students use their notes from **Worksheet 2.35** to write three or four key points comparing the speakers' feelings in the poems. They should write **in complete sentences using connectives**. Display **Worksheet 1.3** to support them.

c Take feedback, compiling notes on the board. As a class, students find evidence from each poem to support each point.

d Students select three points with supporting evidence from those on the board.

e Students add a sentence or two to each point/piece of evidence, explaining and commenting on how the writers have presented their ideas.

2 Repeat the above sequence, using **Worksheet 2.36** to explore use of repetitions to show feelings in the poems.

6 Plenary

Take feedback on 'Spellbound', annotating the poem displayed on the whiteboard using Wordbox. Focus on relevant key features, e.g:
- content
- language
- tone.
- interpretation
- structure

If students have studied and compared 'The Prelude' and/or 'Storm in the Black Forest', take feedback on relevant key similarities and differences in content, interpretation, language, structure or tone.

Suggested answers

Activity 1

1 a/b The speaker 'cannot go' because 'a tyrant spell has bound me'. She is 'Spellbound' by the storm.

2 'tyrant' suggests an overpowering and uncaring ruler – implying that the spell has taken control of her.

3 It emphasises her inability to go, perhaps reinforcing the idea of a tyrant whose will is preventing her.

4 'giant', 'bending', 'weighed', 'snow', 'storm', 'fast descending' imply impending danger.

5 They suggest that she feels little connection with the world, and that she is lost in a kind of nothingness.

6 Not only is she not able to go, it seems that now she is refusing to do so. Perhaps this is the power of the spell taking effect.

Activity 2

- Repetition of 'clouds' and 'wastes' emphasises her isolation.
- Alliteration adds power to the forces of nature that constrain her: 'wild winds', bending… bare boughs'.
- Rhymed pattern of 'round me' and 'bound me' emphasises her imprisonment.
- Developed repetition of final line of each stanza suggests a growing resolve to remain 'spellbound'.

Comparison activities

Key points for this activity are provided in **Worksheet 2.37**.

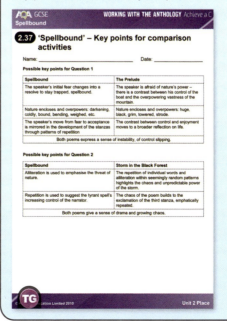

Chapter 2 Place

Below the Green Corrie
by Norman McCaig

Assessment Objectives
- **AO1:** respond to texts critically and imaginatively; select and evaluate relevant textual detail to illustrate and support interpretations
- **AO2:** explain how language, structure and form contribute to writers' presentation of ideas, themes and settings

Learning Objectives
- To develop students' responses to the poem
- To relate the Assessment Objectives to the poem

Required resources
- Poem text, available on CD-ROM and video/audio online at http://anthology.aqa.org.uk
- Student Book, page 50
- Worksheets 1.3, 2.38, 2.39, 2.40

1 Starter

a Ask students to review their notes on, and responses to, the poems they have studied so far which explore nature and the speaker's response to it.

b Display **Worksheet 2.38** on the whiteboard, then take feedback, compiling students' notes on it.

c Review and ask students: How have the poets in this cluster of poems presented and responded to the natural world? Collate responses on the board and leave them on display for reference during the lesson.

2 Activity 1

a Using the Digital Anthology, listen to/watch/read the poem to the class. Clarify any points of understanding.

b Students complete questions 1–7 independently. Take feedback to share, ensure and develop understanding.

c Take students' initial response to the poem, commenting on the presentation of place in the poem. Which other poems in the cluster, identified in the starter activity, could be effectively compared with 'Below the Green Corrie'? How?

d Ask students to write a sentence or two, summing up the content or meaning of the poem. They can begin: *'Below the Green Corrie' is about… .*

3 Activity 2

a Display the line using the Digital Anthology.

b Give students 3 minutes to work in pairs, recording their response in complete sentences to ensure understanding and the ability to express it.

c Take feedback, annotating the displayed poem using Wordbox.

Words/phrases to explore (AO1 and AO2) — ACTIVITY 2
1 'My life was enriched/with an infusion of theirs'. How do you think the poet's life has been 'enriched' by the experience?
2 Why do you think the first five words are on a line of their own?

4 GradeStudio

a Read the GradeStudio extract to the class. Ask: How has the writer of the sample answer shown 'thoughtful consideration of ideas/themes'?

b Students add a sentence to the sample answer, commenting on the poet's intended effect on the reader. For example: *This contrasting response to the mountains emphasises the substance and power of nature, and how powerful our connection with it can be.*

c Ask: Where else in the poem are we encouraged towards a particular response? For example, the threatening language of the first stanza, the final image of 'a bandolier of light'.

d Ask students to select a short quotation that will allow them to explore the poet's ideas and their effect on the reader. The students then write a paragraph about it, using point-evidence-explanation.

GradeStudio — Sample answer D
To achieve a D on this AO2 descriptor, you need to show **identification of effect(s) of writer's choices of language.** To do this, you need to identify the effect of a device, not simply name it. The following extract from a sample answer would hit the grade D requirement:

Activity 1, question 7b
The metaphor 'a bandolier of light' in the last line of the poem describes the shaft of sunlight hitting the mountain, so the speaker feels better about the experience at the end.

To move to C, you would have to explain exactly why the line gives 'a better feeling'.

5 Comparison activities, page 65

Note: In order to do these activities, students would need to have completed their work on 'Wind' and 'The Prelude'.

1 a In pairs or independently, students complete **Worksheet 2.38**, linking their response to the poems with the relevant Assessment Objective. Take feedback on any areas which students found difficult to grasp or to comment on.

> **Below the Green Corrie**
> 1 **Comparing ideas and themes**
> Compare the threats presented by the places in 'Below the Green Corrie' and 'Wind'.
> 2 **Comparing writers' devices**
> Compare the ways in which the writers of 'Below the Green Corrie' and 'The Prelude' present mountains. Think about the ways they write about mountains.

b Students use their notes from **Worksheet 2.38** to write three or four key points comparing the threats presented by the places in the poems. They should write **in complete sentences using connectives**. Display **Worksheet 1.3** to support them.

c Take feedback, compiling notes on the board. As a class, students find evidence from each poem to support each point.

d Students select three points with supporting evidence from those on the board.

e Students add a sentence or two to each point/piece of evidence, explaining and commenting on how the writers have presented their ideas.

2 Repeat the above sequence, using **Worksheet 2.39** to explore the writers' presentation of mountains.

6 Plenary

Take feedback on 'Below the Green Corrie', annotating the poem displayed on the whiteboard using Wordbox. Focus on relevant key features, e.g:
- content
- language
- tone.
- interpretation
- structure

If students have studied and compared 'Wind' and/or 'The Prelude', take feedback on relevant key similarities and differences in content, interpretation, language, structure or tone.

Suggested answers

Activity 1

1 The speaker is walking in the mountains. He finds himself surrounded by them as they 'gathered round me' and initially feels threatened. As he 'clambered downhill', the weather is 'ugly' but, when he turns to look back at the mountains, a shaft of sunlight has broken through.

2 'their leader', 'swaggered', 'stood and delivered', 'money', 'lives', 'prowlers', 'swashbuckling', 'wearing'.

3 • Mountains are compared to bandits, their leader personified.
  • Threatening vocabulary, e.g. 'swaggered… threats', and an image of confrontation.
  • Atmosphere of threat created with oxymoron of 'dark light'.

4 **a/b** For emphasis, and to connect the ideas of threats and thunders – perhaps the (actual) thunder is the (metaphorical) threat.

5 Highway robbery. The mountains are described as 'like bandits' in the first stanza – but they have not robbed him as threatened in the first stanza; they have benefited him.

6 **a** The weather is thundery with a 'dark light'.
  b A 'sunshaft' pierces the clouds.

7 **a** A bandolier is a cartridge or bullet belt worn over the shoulder; a metaphor for the shaft of sunlight falling across the mountain.
  b This last line connects to the simile/metaphor, established in the first stanza, of the mountains as bandits, 'armed' with weather.

Activity 2

1 The life of the mountains has given him life, filling him 'with mountains and thunders'.

2 Placing these five words on their own line makes the statement bolder, emphasising the transformation from threatening bandits to 'swashbuckling' heroes, wearing a 'bandolier of light'. The idea of enrichment is placed at the heart of the poem and further developed in the second half.

Comparison activities

Key points for this activity are provided in **Worksheet 2.40**.

AQA GCSE Working with the Anthology: Achieve a C 69

Chapter 2 Place

Storm in the Black Forest
by D. H. Lawrence

Assessment Objectives
- **AO1:** respond to texts critically and imaginatively; select and evaluate relevant textual detail to illustrate and support interpretations
- **AO2:** explain how language, structure and form contribute to writers' presentation of ideas, themes and settings

Learning Objectives
- To develop students' responses to the poem
- To relate the Assessment Objectives to the poem

Required resources
- Poem text, available on CD-ROM and video/audio online at http://anthology.aqa.org.uk
- Student Book, page 51
- Worksheets 1.3, 2.41, 2.42, 2.43

1 Starter

a Using Wordbox to export the first stanza of the poem to 'Magnets', or **Worksheet 2.41**, present students with all the words of the first stanza jumbled. Give them 5 minutes in pairs to use the vocabulary to construct a poem and give it a title.

b Listen to the students' poems, asking the class to comment on the decisions they made. How has this selection of language guided the title, subject and structure of their poem?

2 Activity 1

a Using the Digital Anthology, listen to/watch/read the poem to the class. Clarify any points of understanding.

b Students complete questions 1–6 independently. Take feedback to share, ensure and develop understanding.

c Take students' initial response to the poem, commenting on the presentation of place in the poem.

d Ask students to write a sentence or two, summing up the content or meaning of the poem. They can begin: *'Storm in the Black Forest' is about...*.

3 Activity 2

a Display the poem using Digital Anthology.

b Students work in pairs, recording their response to the question in complete sentences to ensure understanding and the ability to express it.

c Take feedback, recording students' responses as annotations on the displayed poem using Wordbox.

Words/phrases to explore (AO1 and AO2) — ACTIVITY 2

Do you think the speaker here admires the storm? Find specific evidence for what you think.

4 GradeStudio

a Read the GradeStudio extract to the class. Ask: How has the writer of the sample answer shown an 'explained response to element(s) of text'?

b How could this answer be added to or rewritten to show 'a sustained response to element(s) of text' and so achieve a C? For example: *He seems to admire the power of nature and mock man's stupidity for thinking he can control it.*

c Ask students: Where else in the poem are we encouraged towards a particular response? For example, the image of a snake, or the use of the word 'cackle'.

d Ask students to select a short quotation that will allow them to explore their response to the poem. Students then write a paragraph about it, using point-evidence-explanation.

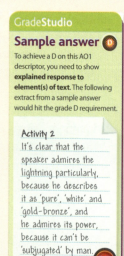

© Pearson Education Limited 2010

5 Comparison activities, page 65

Note: In order to do these activities, students would need to have completed their work on 'Wind'.

a In pairs or independently, students complete **Worksheet 2.42**, linking their response to the poems with the relevant Assessment Objective. Take feedback on any areas which students found difficult to grasp or to comment on.

Storm in the Black Forest

1. **Comparing ideas and themes**
Compare the violent weather in 'Storm in the Black Forest' and 'Wind'.
2. **Comparing writers' devices**
Compare the ways in which violent weather is presented in 'Storm in the Black Forest' and 'Wind' by the way the writers describe the weather.

b For each of the questions in the activity, students use their notes from **Worksheet 2.42** to write three or four key points comparing the presentation of weather in the poems. They should write **in complete sentences using connectives**. Display **Worksheet 1.3** to support them.

c Take feedback, compiling notes on the board. As a class, students find evidence from each poem to support each point.

d Students select three points with supporting evidence from those on the board.

e Students add a sentence or two to each point/piece of evidence, explaining and commenting on how the writers have presented their ideas.

6 Plenary

Take feedback on 'Storm in the Black Forest', annotating the poem displayed on the whiteboard using Wordbox. Focus on relevant key features, e.g:
- content
- language
- tone
- interpretation
- structure

If students have studied and compared 'Wind', take feedback on relevant key similarities and differences in content, interpretation, language, structure or tone.

Suggested answers

Activity 1

1. The speaker sees lightning in a storm, but no rain. It is 'almost night'.
'white liquid fire', 'tipples over and spills down', 'electric liquid pours out… spilled'.

2. **a** 'i': long (white) and short (liquid).
   b The almost tongue-twisterish pattern reflects the chaos and power of the lightning.
   c 'jugfull', 'white'.

3. **a/b** The chaotic pattern of repetition ends in a simple, monosyllabic statement, a sudden end to this sudden chaos.

4. 'wriggles'/'wriggling'.

5. 'cackle' is a word often associated with witches; it implies supernatural qualities.

6. It suggests a shift in tone; an increase in volume from the power of the lightning to the speaker's excitement, fear, even awe, almost as if shouting above its noise.

Activity 2

The speaker seems to admire the power of the lightning, suggested in his initial description of 'pure white liquid fire'. This is further emphasised in the final three lines: its power is such that man is not able to subjugate it.

Comparison activities

Key points for this activity are provided in **Worksheet 2.43**.

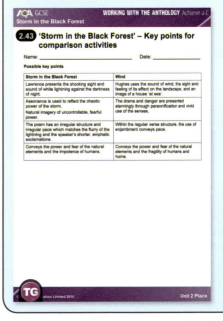

Chapter 2 Place

Wind by Ted Hughes

Assessment Objectives
- **AO1:** respond to texts critically and imaginatively; select and evaluate relevant textual detail to illustrate and support interpretations
- **AO2:** explain how language, structure and form contribute to writers' presentation of ideas, themes and settings

Learning Objectives
- To develop students' responses to the poem
- To relate the Assessment Objectives to the poem

Required resources
- Poem text, available on CD-ROM and video/audio online at http://anthology.aqa.org.uk
- Student Book, page 52
- Worksheets 1.3, 2.44, 2.45, 2.46

1 Starter

a Write the nouns 'breeze', 'gale', 'tornado' and 'hurricane' on the board. Give students 2 minutes to write down adjectives and verbs appropriate to each one. Take feedback to ensure and share understanding.

b Now give another 2 minutes to write down similes to describe each one, e.g. *A breeze is like…*.

c Take feedback. Note any patterns, such as positive or negative associations or personification, that are common to students' perceptions of these natural events.

2 Activity 1

a Using the Digital Anthology, listen to/watch/read the poem to the class. Clarify any points of understanding.

b Students complete questions 1–6 independently. Take feedback to share, ensure and develop understanding.

c Take students' initial response to the poem, commenting on the presentation of place in the poem.

d Ask students to write a sentence or two, summing up the content or meaning of the poem. They can begin: *'Wind' is about…*.

Initial responses — ACTIVITY 1

1. In the whole poem, how are the people aware of the power of the wind? Think about what they see and hear and feel.
2. **a** What is the house being compared to in the first line?
   b What other two things is it compared to in the last two **stanzas**?
3. Jot down all the action words in the first stanza, such as 'crashing'. What things here are made to seem alive, which aren't usually?
4. How does the writer suggest the strength of the wind in the third stanza? Look for at least three things.
5. Why do you think the fields seem to be 'quivering'? Remember that the **speaker** is looking at the view in front of him.
6. In the last stanza, inanimate things are **personified** again – given living qualities, as in the first stanza. How many can you find? Jot them down.

3 Activity 2

a Display the poem using the Digital Anthology.

b Give students, in pairs, 5 minutes to write their response to the question. They should write in complete sentences to ensure understanding and their ability to express it.

c Take feedback, annotating the displayed poem with students' responses using Wordbox.

Words/phrases to explore (AO1 and AO2) — ACTIVITY 2
Which line of the poem best shows the power of the storm? Look for a line which you can say at least two things about, including something about the way the line is written that makes it powerful.

4 GradeStudio

a Read the GradeStudio extract to the class. Ask: How has the writer of the sample answer shown an 'explanation of effect(s) of writer's uses of language and/or structure and/or form and effects on readers'?

b Where else in the poem can students find an opportunity to comment on the poet's choice of language? For example, the image of the hills as tents, or Hughes's description of the wind's impact on the speaker.

c Ask students to select a short quotation that will allow them to explore the poet's use of language and its effect on the reader. The students then write a paragraph about it, using point-evidence-explanation.

GradeStudio
Sample answer

To achieve a C on this AO2 descriptor, you need to show **explanation of effect(s) of writers' uses of language and/or structure and/or form and effects on reader**. To do this, you need to work hard on your view of the ideas in the poem. The following extract from a sample answer would hit the grade C requirement.

Activity 1, question 4
The word 'scaled' makes it sound like it's as difficult as climbing a mountain when the speaker just walks along the side of the house, so you realise how strong the wind was to make him struggle in that way.

5 Comparison activities, page 65

Note: In order to do these activities, students would need to have completed their work on 'The Prelude' and 'Below the Green Corrie'.

1 a In pairs or independently, students complete **Worksheet 2.44**, linking their response to the poems with the relevant Assessment Objective. Take feedback on any areas which students found difficult to grasp or to comment on.

> **Wind**
> 1 **Comparing ideas and themes**
> Compare the threats presented by nature in 'Wind' and 'The Prelude'.
> 2 **Comparing writers' devices**
> Compare the ways in which the weather is presented in 'Wind' and 'Below the Green Corrie'.

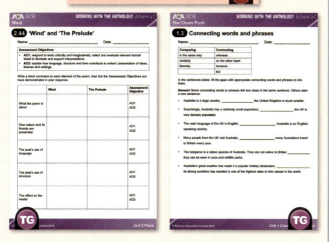

b Students use their notes from **Worksheet 2.44** to write three or four key points comparing the threats presented by nature in the poems. They should write **in complete sentences using connectives**. Display **Worksheet 1.3** to support them.

c Take feedback, compiling notes on the board. As a class, students find evidence from each poem to support each point.

d Students select three points with supporting evidence from those on the board.

e Students add a sentence or two to each point/piece of evidence, explaining and commenting on how the writers have presented their ideas.

2 Repeat the above sequence, using **Worksheet 2.45** to explore the presentation of weather in the two poems.

6 Plenary

Take feedback on 'Wind', annotating the poem displayed on the whiteboard using Wordbox. Focus on relevant key features, e.g:
- content
- language
- tone.
- interpretation
- structure

If students have studied and compared 'The Prelude' and/or 'Below the Green Corrie', take feedback on relevant key similarities and differences in content, interpretation, language, structure or tone.

Suggested answers

Activity 1

1 The woods are 'crashing', the hills are 'booming', the winds are 'stampeding'. The fields are 'quivering' and a bird is 'flung… away'. In the house, the 'windows tremble' and 'we grip our hearts' suggesting fear.

2 a A ship.
  b A 'green goblet', a tree.

3 'crashing', 'booming', 'stampeding', 'Floundering', 'astride'. The woods, hills, winds are made to seem alive.

4 The wind was so strong, the speaker 'scaled along the house-side', suggesting his position was as precarious as if he was rock-climbing; it 'dented the balls of my eyes', and threatened the stability of the hills.

5 The wind is making the grass or crops in the field quiver.

6 The house has roots; the window trembles, asking to come into the house; the stones cry out.

Activity 2

All answers are arguable.

Comparison activities

Key points for this activity are provided in **Worksheet 2.46**.

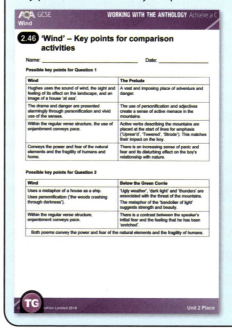

AQA GCSE Working with the Anthology: Achieve a C 73

Chapter 2 Place

Looking at the poems individually: what have you learned?

Assessment Objectives
- **AO1:** respond to texts critically and imaginatively; select and evaluate relevant textual detail to illustrate and support interpretations
- **AO2:** explain how language, structure and form contribute to writers' presentation of ideas, themes and settings

Learning Objectives
- To recap and explore students' responses to the poems

Required resources
- Student Book, page 53
- Worksheet 2.47, ideally enlarged to A3 size

1 Starter

a Explain to students that this lesson will consolidate, recap and explore their knowledge and understanding of, and response to, the 15 poems they have explored.

Looking at the poems individually: what have you learned?

b Give students 3 minutes to complete the following task in silence:
Without looking at their Anthology or any notes, how many of the poems can they remember from those they have explored over the last 15 lessons? They can either note down the titles (and poets, if possible) or give a brief description of the poem's content: *The one about…*.

c List the 15 poems aloud so students can check their answers. Ask students to add titles to the poems where the content but not the title had been remembered.

d Take feedback. How many poems could students remember? Based on the class's response as a whole, were some more memorable than others? Why?

The poems

The Blackbird of Glanmore *Seamus Heaney*	**Neighbours** *Gillian Clarke*	**The Wild Swans at Coole** *W. B. Yeats*
A Vision *Simon Armitage*	**Crossing the Loch** *Kathleen Jamie*	**Spellbound** *Emily Brontë*
The Moment *Margaret Atwood*	**Hard Water** *Jean Sprackland*	**Below the Green Corrie** *Norman McCaig*
Cold Knap Lake *Gillian Clarke*	**London** *William Blake*	**Storm in the Black Forest** *D. H. Lawrence*
Price We Pay for the Sun *Grace Nichols*	**The Prelude (extract)** *William Wordsworth*	**Wind** *Ted Hughes*

2 Activity 1

a Explain that Question 1 of the activity will consolidate students' thinking from the starter activity.

b Read Question 1 aloud, then ask students to choose the **five** poems which they responded to most strongly – it is likely that these will be the first five they listed in the Starter. Ask them to add a sentence explaining why they found this poem memorable: it may be an activity, a word, a line, an idea, a character, or a title which has sparked their engagement. Ask volunteers to share with the class.

c Read Question 2. Ask students: Are your answers to this question likely to feature the same poems as Question 1? Why?

d Give students 5 minutes to list the **five** poems they found it easiest to offer an interpretation about, using their notes from the last 15 lessons. Take feedback to ensure understanding. Ask: Is it easier to talk and write about poems that are simpler to understand? Or is there more to be said (and more marks to be gained!) by exploring a variety of different interpretations of more complex poems?

Assessment Objective 1 (AO1) — **ACTIVITY 1**

1. Which of these poems did you **respond** to most strongly? You may have liked it, or disliked it, or found it the most interesting, or horrible. You may have a number of things to say about it.
Working with a partner, or by yourself, display your responses as a spider diagram, and then compare it with someone else's, to see if you have responded to the poems in similar ways.

2. Which poems did you find it easiest to offer an **interpretation** about? In other words, you had an opinion about a poem's meaning that you could argue from the text and **select detail** to support your opinion. For instance, you might have found it easy to argue and support the view that the speaker in 'Spellbound' is suffering a breakdown.
Suggesting more than one interpretation of a poem, or parts of a poem, gives you opportunities to score more marks. For instance, there are several ways in which you could interpret the nature of the mountains in the excerpt from 'The Prelude'.

3 Activity 2

Give students 20 minutes to complete both questions 1 and 2 of the activity. They can record their responses on **Worksheet 2.47**. Point out that if they cannot think of anything significant in a particular area within, say, 30 seconds, then it does not suggest a ready understanding: they should move on to a new feature or poem. Take feedback to ensure and develop understanding.

Assessment Objective 2 (AO2) — ACTIVITY 2

1 Which features of **language**, **structure** or **form** did you understand best? The most promising ones to write about in the exam will be the ones where you have most to say. For instance, you might have found several things to say about:
- the effect of personification in 'Below the Green Corrie' (**language**)
- the way 'A Vision' changes at the end (**structure**)
- the effects of the change to full rhyme at the end of 'Cold Knap Lake' (**form**).

2 What **ideas** did you pick out in the poems? Again, the best answers will probably identify more than one idea in a poem, or several aspects of one idea. For instance, you might have identified or explored more than one idea about society in 'London'.

AQA GCSE — WORKING WITH THE ANTHOLOGY Achieve a C
Looking at the poems individually: what have you learned?

2.47 What have you learned?

Name: _____ Date: _____

Title	Language	Structure	Form	Ideas
The Blackbird of Glanmore – Seamus Heaney				
A Vision – Simon Armitage				
The Moment – Margaret Atwood				
Cold Knap Lake – Gillian Clarke				
Price We Pay for the Sun – Grace Nichols				
Neighbours – Gillian Clarke				
Crossing the Loch – Kathleen Jamie				
Hard Water – Jean Sprackland				
London – William Blake				
The Prelude (extract) – William Wordsworth				
The Wild Swans at Coole – W.B. Yeats				
Spellbound – Emily Brontë				
Below the Green Corrie – Norman McCaig				
Storm in the Black Forest – D.H. Lawrence				
Wind – Ted Hughes				

Unit 2 Place

4 Plenary

Ask students:
- Based on your exploration of content, interpretation, language, structure, form and ideas, which are the most memorable, exam-friendly poems in the 'Place' cluster? Do they have any significant links or points of comparison?
- Which poems are particularly difficult to write about?
- Which poems do you feel you need to give more (of your own) time to?

5 Further work

a Students identify the **five** poems that have the fewest entries on **Worksheet 2.47**.

b Students complete each column for each poem, using **Worksheet 2.47** and their notes.

AQA GCSE — WORKING WITH THE ANTHOLOGY Achieve a C
Looking at the poems individually: what have you learned?

2.47 What have you learned?

Name: _____ Date: _____

Title	Language	Structure	Form	Ideas
The Blackbird of Glanmore – Seamus Heaney				
A Vision – Simon Armitage				
The Moment – Margaret Atwood				
Cold Knap Lake – Gillian Clarke				
Price We Pay for the Sun – Grace Nichols				
Neighbours – Gillian Clarke				
Crossing the Loch – Kathleen Jamie				
Hard Water – Jean Sprackland				
London – William Blake				
The Prelude (extract) – William Wordsworth				
The Wild Swans at Coole – W.B. Yeats				
Spellbound – Emily Brontë				
Below the Green Corrie – Norman McCaig				
Storm in the Black Forest – D.H. Lawrence				
Wind – Ted Hughes				

Unit 2 Place

Chapter 2 Place

Comparing the 'Place' poems (1)

Assessment Objective
- **AO3:** make comparisons and explain links between texts, evaluating writers' different ways of expressing meaning and achieving effects.

Learning Objectives
- To develop students' abilities to compare the poems
- To relate the Assessment Objectives to the poems
- To develop students' writing skills for the exam

Required resources
- Poem texts, available on CD-ROM and video/audio online at http://anthology.aqa.org.uk
- Student Book, page 54
- Worksheet 2.48

1 Starter

a Read the explanation of the Assessment Objective on page 54 of the Student Book, clarifying understanding of the Assessment Objective's demands.
b Explain to students that in this lesson they are going to compare 'Hard Water' and 'London'.
c Display both poems on the whiteboard, side by side, using the Digital Anthology. Re-read the poems.
d Ask students to describe the content of each poem, providing evidence where appropriate. Draw the place and events on the board as they are described, annotating with quotations. Depending on your artistic skills, you may want to ask a volunteer student to take this role!

Assessment Objective:

The Assessment Objective you will be focusing on in this part of the chapter is:

AO3 make comparisons and explain links between texts, evaluating writers' different ways of expressing meaning and achieving effects.

2 Activity 1

a Using **Worksheet 2.48**, students record all the similarities and differences they can think of in the two poems in the first column on the worksheet. The second column is for their responses to Activity 2.
b Take feedback, ideally compiling students' responses on a copy of the worksheet projected onto the whiteboard.

ACTIVITY 1

Think about the ideas and themes in the two poems. List as many similarities and differences as you can. Both poems are about particular places. Think about:
- whether the places have anything in common
- whether the attitudes to the places in the poems are similar or diffe

76 © Pearson Education Limited 2010

3 Activity 2

Explain that this is an opportunity for students to develop their points of comparison, using **Worksheet 2.48**. Use the example in the Student Book and perhaps one other from the class' responses compiled on the whiteboard. Remind students of the need for evidence to support each point. Take feedback, again compiling notes on the whiteboard.

ACTIVITY 2

Using your list of similarities and differences from Activity 1, decide how different each of the poems are for each point you made. For example, the **speaker** in 'London' seems to dislike the place. How can you tell this from the details of the poem? The speaker in 'Hard Water', loved coming 'home'. What exactly does she love? Does she have any other emotions about it? Are any of them like anything in 'London'?

Use quotations or refer to specific parts of the poem to support what you think.

4 Activity 3

a Recap the key features of similarity/difference compiled on the whiteboard.

b Explain to students that this is an opportunity to explore the **effect** of the differences they noted in Activity 2.

c Clarify the three key areas outlined in the activity:
- the language of the poems
- the use of the five senses
- the structure of the poems.

d Using their notes from **Worksheet 2.48** and the notes compiled on the whiteboard, ask students, working in pairs, to select **one** of these three areas on which they feel they can comment and write a sentence or two explaining and commenting on the different effects achieved in the poems. If time allows, students can select a second area.

ACTIVITY 3

Compare the differences in the ways the poems are written. For example, the two poems are very different in the ways they are written, but they are both first person poems, which is a starting point in itself.
- The language of the two poems is very different, because they were written at different times. How is the language of one poem modern, and the other not? Be as exact as you can about this – don't just stop at "'London' has lots of old words'. Note down some exact details.
- Which of the five senses (seeing, hearing, touching, tasting and smelling) does each poem use? Remember you're looking for similarities and differences.
- 'London' uses lots of rhyme and repetition to create effects. What does 'Hard Water' use? Think about the sound of some of the words, and the breaks between lines.

5 Plenary

a Students swap their responses to Activity 3 with a partner, annotating to show where in their writing they have:
- identified a relevant detail
- commented on its effect on the reader.

b Ask volunteers for examples from their or their partner's writing which demonstrate the above bullet points. Allow 3 minutes in which students can add to their writing to ensure they have achieved both bullet points.

c Take feedback to share and develop thinking.

Suggested answers

Activities 1/2

Similarities:
- Both poems connect human experience and environment.
- Both describe place in negative terms.
- Both are written in the first person, suggesting reflection on actual experiences.

Differences:
- Hard Water is positive about 'home', about a sense of belonging; 'London' is relentlessly negative, suggesting alienation.
- A personal experience in 'Hard Water'; a personal view of the city in 'London'.
- 'London' has a regular rhyme scheme and structure; 'Hard Water' has none.

Comparison activities
- Language: 'London' refers to contemporary figures, e.g. chimney sweepers and harlots, and uses formal, archaic language; 'Hard Water' has similarly contemporary references to the bus and cooling towers, and uses slang ('the soft stuff') and local dialect ('hey up me duck').
- Senses: 'London' focuses on sight and sound: what the speaker sees and hears as he wanders through 'each charter'd street'; 'Hard Water' uses touch, sound, smell and taste but little visual description.
- Form/structure: stanza breaks, e.g. the first stanza break signifies the return from holiday to home; short sentences for emphasis.

Chapter 2 Place

Comparing the 'Place' poems (2)

Assessment Objective
- **AO3:** make comparisons and explain links between texts, evaluating writers' different ways of expressing meaning and achieving effects

Learning Objectives
- To develop students' abilities to compare the poems
- To relate the Assessment Objectives to the poems
- To develop students' writing skills for the exam

Required resources
- Poem texts, available on CD-ROM and video/audio online at http://anthology.aqa.org.uk
- Student Book, pages 54–57, 142–143

1 Starter

Assessment Objective:
The Assessment Objective you will be focusing on in this part of the chapter is:

AO3 make comparisons and explain links between texts, evaluating writers' different ways of expressing meaning and achieving effects.

a Recap the comparison process from the previous lesson.
b Read the explanation of the Assessment Objective on page 54 of the Student Book, clarifying understanding of the Assessment Objective's demands.
c Explain to students that in this lesson, they are going to continue to compare 'London' and 'Hard Water', then use this process to develop their comparison skills further.
d Display both poems on the whiteboard, side by side, using the Digital Anthology. Re-read the poems.

2 GradeStudio

a Read the GradeStudio E grade extract to the class. Ask: How has the writer of the sample answer made 'some comment(s) on similarities/differences, with detail'?
b Now read the GradeStudio D extract to the class. How do the additional sentences give 'structured comments on similarities/differences, with detail'?
c Looking at the grade descriptors on pages 142–143 of the Student Book, what would students have to do to raise this D to a C?

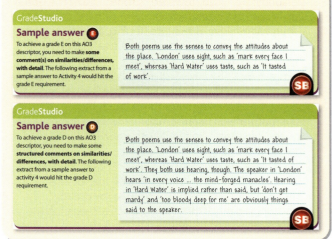

3 Activity 4

a Read the activity instructions, discussing each bullet point as a class. Point out the instruction to 'be careful' when writing about the senses in 'Hard Water': note that although the word 'taste' is used repeatedly, it does not necessarily refer to that sense literally.

ACTIVITY 4
One of the best ways to score well when comparing poems is to compare two details, one from each poem, that you can say a lot about when you put them together. Find a detail from each poem that you could compare directly. For example:

b Give students 10 minutes to note down their thoughts in bullet points. Take feedback to share, ensure and develop understanding.
c Based on their thoughts from the GradeStudio activity above, and their preparation in this activity, ask students to write a paragraph comparing the two poems, aiming to achieve a C.

4 Activity 5

a The students now move on to compare 'Below the Green Corrie' and 'The Prelude'. Display both poems on the whiteboard, side by side, using the Digital Anthology. Re-read the poems.
b What initial points of comparison, similarities and differences, can students suggest?
c Students work independently, recording their response to questions 1–4, one at a time. Encourage students to record as wide a range of responses as possible. Leave the final writing task of question 4 until after considering the GradeStudio exemplars.
d Take feedback after each question, discussing and developing a whole class response, then giving students a minute or two to add to their written response.

ACTIVITY 5
1 What ideas and themes can you find in the poems which are similar?
  a Both the poems are about people alone in a natural surrounding. What attitudes to nature can you find in the poems?
  b What similarities and differences are there in the type of threat that nature seems to make?
  c What are the effects on the **speakers** of their experiences? List similarities and differences as you can.

5 GradeStudio

a Read the GradeStudio exemplars on page 57 of the Student Book. Ask students to identify how the C has identified and explored similarities and differences.

b Ask students to identify which elements of the paragraph show 'sustained focus on similarities/differences with material for a range of comparisons', i.e. are key in achieving a C. Which are 'structured comments on similarities/differences, with detail', i.e. without the C elements and would achieve a D?

c Ask students to look at the B exemplar. How has this student further developed the comparison by making a 'developed comparison in terms of writers' uses of language and/or structure and/or form and/or structure and effects on readers, with detail'?

d Return to the final instruction of Activity 5, Question 4: give students 10 minutes to write a point-evidence-explanation paragraph comparing the two details from the poem.

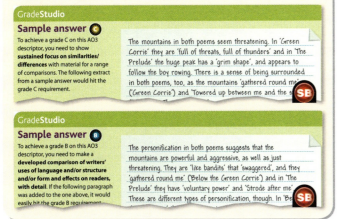

6 Plenary

a Students swap their written response to Activity 4 with a partner and, using the grade descriptors on pages 142–143 of the Student Book, decide what grade their partner's response should be awarded.

b Working together, students identify one way in which they could improve or add to their writing to aim for the next grade up.

c Take feedback, summarising those key areas which students have identified as targets to achieve in order to raise their grade.

Suggested answers

Activity 4
- London is more universally damning, note the use of 'every', the repetition of 'marks' and the alliterative pairing of 'weakness' and 'woe'. The oxymorons of 'Hard Water', e.g. 'fierce, lovely water' suggest a fondness for the harsher elements of home.
- Although people here are 'blunt' and confrontational ('don't get mardy'), they are a part of her sense of belonging.
- The sense of sight and hearing in 'London'; taste, touch and hearing in 'Hard Water'.

Activity 5
1 a 'Below the Green Corrie', although initially threatening, becomes a positive experience. The impact of the encounter on the speaker in 'The Prelude' seems much more far reaching than his initial fear.

b The mountains in 'Below the Green Corrie' are compared to swaggering bandits, full of threats. The 'huge peak' in 'The Prelude' is much more actively threatening, described as if some kind of monster: it 'upreared its head' and 'like a living thing, strode after me'.

c The speaker in 'Below the Green Corrie' is at first threatened, then 'enriched'. The speaker in 'The Prelude' at first regards nature as something to be challenged – he is 'proud of his skill' in rowing across the lake – then to fear; this fear dominates his mood 'for many days'.

2 a Personification: 'Below the Green Corrie': 'Their leader swaggered up close'; 'The Prelude': 'upreared its head'

b Change in mood: 'Below the Green Corrie': Threats/enriched; 'The Prelude': Proud/trembling

The change of moods is inverted in the two poems: from fear to happiness and from happiness to fear.

c The speaker in 'The Prelude' details his feelings clearly: 'in grave and serious mood'. The speaker in 'Below the Green Corrie' uses figurative language to express his feelings: an oxymoron – 'marvellous prowlers' to reflect his ambivalent respect for the mountains and the metaphor of 'a bandolier of light' to remind us of the bandits of his initial response and express the beauty he sees in them.

3 The threat in 'Below the Green Corrie' is expressed in the first four lines, then dispelled as the narrator describes his positive response. In 'The Prelude', the threat is introduced in the second half of the extract, contrasting sharply and suddenly, its disturbing effect on the speaker enduring beyond the poem's end.

Activity 6
- 'The Prelude' uses active and disturbing verbs to personify: 'upreared', 'towered', 'strode'; 'Below the Green Corrie' uses the extended metaphor of 'bandits' which, though aggressive, is less threatening, almost fairy-tale-like, further suggested in the use of 'swashbuckling'.
- The speaker in 'Below the Green Corrie' has a more human experience, implied in the albeit threatening character of the bandit; the speaker in 'The Prelude' seems threatened by something much more supernatural and unfathomable, blocking out all the rest of nature: 'No familiar shapes/Remained, no images of trees…'.
- The positive image of 'a bandolier of light' concludes 'Below the Green Corrie'; alarmingly, the speaker of 'The Prelude' is left with 'a trouble to my dreams', suggesting a much more invasive effect, verging on possession.

Chapter 2 Place

Writing in the exam

Assessment Objectives

- **AO1:** respond to texts critically and imaginatively; select and evaluate relevant textual detail to illustrate and support interpretations
- **AO2:** explain how language, structure and form contribute to writers' presentation of ideas, themes and settings
- **AO3:** make comparisons and explain links between texts, evaluating writers' different ways of expressing meaning and achieving effects

Learning Objectives

- To develop students' ability to structure a successful exam response

Required resources

- Poem text, available on CD-ROM and video/audio online at http://anthology.aqa.org.uk
- Student Book, pages 58–63, 142–143
- Worksheets 1.51, 2.49

1 Starter

a Write the word 'planning' on the board. Ask: What are the advantages and disadvantages of using the first 5 minutes of exam time to plan a written response? Give students 2 minutes to record their thoughts.

b Take feedback. Aim to refute the argument that planning takes up valuable writing time, and that your plan is not marked. Point out that your response **is** marked – and a well-planned response gets the best mark.

2 Writing your response – planning and structuring

Read the sequence of read-think-write-edit to the class, pausing to discuss whether the students agree or disagree that each of these stages is vital. Discuss with students whether anything can be cut out of this process to speed it up and still achieve the best possible grade. Conclude with students that all stages in the process are vital to getting the best possible grade.

3 Putting it into practice

a Read the material from the Student Book to the class, pausing to clarify understanding where needed.

b Do students think that this is a successful plan? How might they improve it? Point out that the task has to be completed in a limited time, so anything that is added may well mean that something else must be cut. Remind the class that this guide was written by the Chief Examiner – so it's good advice!

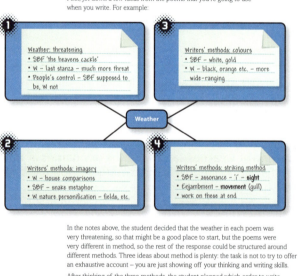

4 GradeStudio

a Close the Student Book and distribute or display **Worksheet 2.49**. Note that two of the paragraphs focus on specific Assessment Objectives, while the answer as a whole focuses on AO3: the comparison of the two poems.

b Using the grade descriptors on pages 142–143 of the Student Book (also available on **Worksheet 1.51**), ask students to work in pairs to decide which grade they would award Student A and Student B, matching specific features from the mark scheme to specific evidence from each response to justify their decision.

c Take feedback, continually aiming to re-affirm the Assessment Objectives: the importance of responding to, and comparing, the details, ideas, themes, language, structure and form of the poems.

d Return to the Student Book and read through the Examiner comments. Do the class's marks and justifications tally with the Chief Examiner's?

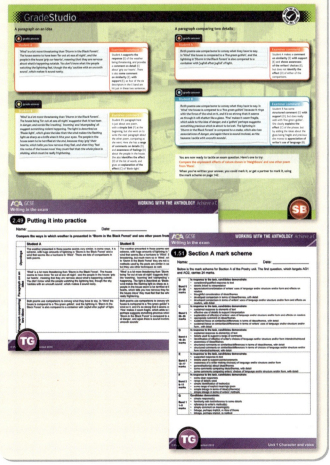

5 Sample exam question

Depending on the confidence of your class, this can be tackled as homework, as entirely independent work, or planned as a class prior to independent writing.

a Ask students to spend 2 minutes noting down the sequence of thinking they would follow before writing. For example:
1 Read the question **carefully**.
2 Identify which parts of the question relate to which Assessment Objective.
3 Consider which poem to compare 'Neighbours' with. Draw up a short list of two or three possibilities. Which will allow you to demonstrate your skill and understanding most fully? Choose one.
4 Note down points comparing the themes and ideas in the poems.
5 Note down points comparing details in the poems.
6 Note down points comparing the writer's choice of language, form and/or structure in the poems and its effect on the reader.

b Give students 10 minutes to follow this sequence, completing their essay plan. Point out that, although this should take 5 minutes in the exam, this is practice to help get students up to exam pace!

> You are now ready to tackle an exam question. Here's one to try:
> Compare the unpleasant effects of nature shown in 'Neighbours' and one other poem from 'Place'.
> When you've written your answer, you could mark it, or get a partner to mark it, using the mark scheme on page 142.

6 Plenary

Students swap plans. Does their partner's plan cover all the necessary Assessment Objectives and explore the poem in enough developed detail? What grade do they think the essay based on this plan will achieve? Why? Take feedback, focusing on the grade awarded and the peer marker's justification for that grade. Does the class agree that the grade is justified?

7 Further work

Students can write up their essay in their own time. The following lesson can then be spent peer-marking the essays using the grade descriptors on pages 142–143 of the Student Book – also available on **Worksheet 1.51** – then listening as a class to the peer-marker's choices of:
- the most successful point targeting AO1
- the most successful point targeting AO2
- the most successful point targeting AO3.

Chapter 3 Conflict

Getting to know the poems

Assessment Objectives
- **AO1:** respond to texts critically and imaginatively; select and evaluate relevant textual detail to illustrate and support interpretations
- **AO2:** explain how language, structure and form contribute to writers' presentation of ideas, themes and settings
- **AO3:** make comparisons and explain links between texts, evaluating writers' different ways of expressing meaning and achieving effects

Learning Objectives
- To become familiar with the cluster as a whole
- To start to make links between the poems

Required resources
- Student Book, pages 66–68
- Worksheet 3.1, ideally enlarged to A3 size
- A3 paper

1 Starter

a Focus on the title of this cluster.

b Ask students to consider what this title might suggest: List all the different types of conflict you can think of in 3 minutes. Ask volunteers to share with the class.

c Ask students which type of conflict they think would make the best subject matter for a poem, and why. In order to develop students' arguments and thinking, aim for a class consensus.

2 Introduction

a Read through and clarify with the class the focus and purpose of this and subsequent lessons.

b Draw students' attention to the Assessment Objectives which this lesson will support (an explanation of them is available on page 66 of the Student Book).

c Ask students to locate the cluster in their Anthology.

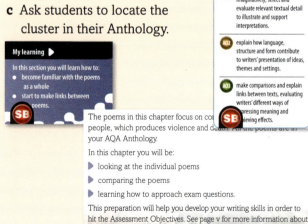

3 Activity 1

ACTIVITY 1

Read all the 'Conflict' poems in your AQA Anthology. Just notice what they seem to be about – don't worry about trying to make sense of every line.

a Divide the class into pairs according to ability, with poems allocated accordingly. For example:

More accessible
- Mametz Wood
- The Right Word
- The Charge of the Light Brigade
- At the Border
- The Falling Leaves

Intermediate
- Flag
- Cameo Appearance
- Out of the Blue (extract)
- Belfast Confetti
- The Yellow Palm

More challenging
- Futility
- Bayonet Charge
- Come On, Come Back
- next to of course god america
- Hawk Roosting

b Give pairs 5 minutes to read their allocated poem, giving clear prior warning that they will be asked to feed back information and comments to the whole class. Use the prompts below to focus discussion and feedback. (You may want to note these prompts on the board.)
- How difficult is the poem to understand?
- What is the poem about?
- What can you say about the presentation of conflict?

c Read each poem to the class, then take feedback from the relevant group. Encourage students to take notes in their Anthology or exercise book, recording their first impressions of each poem.

4 Preparation for Activity 2

Ask the class to think of different ways in which these or any poems can be compared. Note them on the whiteboard, e.g. a description of an event or experience, an impartial voice, a point to make, the use of descriptive language.

5 Activity 2

ACTIVITY 2

Write the headings listed below on a sheet of paper. Under each heading make notes of any links between poems. Include poems that have similarities and differences. Use the tips below to help you.

Headings	Tips
What the poems are about	All the poems are about conflict – but wh particular war or time, which one? Does t angry/regretful/accepting? Which poems

a Distribute copies of **Worksheet 3.1** and look at the comparison table in Activity 2 on page 67 of the Student Book. Clarify  the terms of comparison if necessary. As a class, decide which of the categories on the whiteboard (from the preparation) it will be most useful to focus on. Ask students to add them to the blank columns on the worksheet.

b Reshuffle students into groups of three or four. Clarify with them the precise requirements of this task. Depending on the ability of the class, there are a number of possible approaches. You could:
- set a clear timescale, e.g. 20 minutes, for the entire activity, or allow 3–5 minutes for each heading, taking feedback after each to ensure understanding
- group some of the headings, e.g.
  - titles
  - what the poems are about
  - beginnings and endings
  - length
  - language and imagery
  - rhythm and rhyme
- rather than trying to compare all 15 poems, ask students to put them into pairs, e.g. two with similar content or language choices, or two with very different structures or viewpoints.

Encourage students to note what leaps out at them rather than hunt for answers. This is very much an initial response to familiarise and demystify.

6 Activity 3

Get students to complete this activity in pairs or groups of three. Depending on the time available, ask a range of groups to show and explain their A3 paper to the rest of the class. Try to choose groups that have taken different approaches.

ACTIVITY 3

Now display your findings on a sheet of A3 in one of the following ways.

1 Spread the titles out on the sheet and draw links between them, labelling each one.

2 Draw a picture or symbol for each idea (such as death or nature) that appears in more than one poem, and group the poems around each – a poem can appear in more than one group.

3 Draw a picture, or pictures, for each poem on the sheet, and link similar ones with arrows.

In these activities you have started to tackle all three Assessment Objectives. Now you will be focusing on AO1 and AO2 as you look at the poems individually (pages 69–85). You will return to AO3 when you compare the poems (pages 86–89). Finally, you will look at how to turn your knowledge and skills into successful exam answers, before you attempt one yourself (pages 90–97).

7 Plenary

Take specific feedback on individual poems and points of comparison, then ask students:
- What are your first impressions of this cluster?
- What have you found easier or harder than they expected?
- What support do you feel you will need?

Chapter 3 Conflict

Flag by John Agard

Assessment Objectives
- **AO1:** respond to texts critically and imaginatively; select and evaluate relevant textual detail to illustrate and support interpretations
- **AO2:** explain how language, structure and form contribute to writers' presentation of ideas, themes and settings

Learning Objectives
- To develop students' responses to the poem
- To relate the Assessment Objectives to the poem

Required resources
- Poem text, available on CD-ROM and video/audio online at http://anthology.aqa.org.uk
- Student Book, page 70
- Worksheets 1.3, 3.2, 3.3, 3.4
- Image of Union Flag from the Internet (see starter activity)

1 Starter
If available from the Internet, or as clipart in a word-processing program, display the Union Flag (Union Jack) on the board. Ask students to write down the first five things that come to mind on looking at the flag. What does it represent to them? What else can it be/is it used to suggest or represent? Are these all positive representations? Why do nations have flags? Aim to record five statements about flags on the board.

2 Activity 1
a Using the Digital Anthology, listen to/watch/read the poem to the class. Clarify any points of understanding.

b Students complete questions 1–5 independently. Take feedback to share, ensure and develop understanding. Display the poem using the Digital Anthology, annotating the text with students' responses using Wordbox.

c Take students' initial response to the poem, commenting on the presentation of conflict in the poem.

d Ask students to write a sentence or two, summing up the content or meaning of the poem. They can begin: *'Flag' is about…* .

Initial responses — ACTIVITY 1
1. Why exactly is a flag an important 'piece of cloth' to write about? Find evidence from the poem to support your view.
2. Look at the first lines of each of the first four **stanzas**.
   a. Identify the active words in these lines. For example, in line 1 of the first stanza the active word is 'fluttering'.
   b. Why do you think Agard has chosen to make the flag seem like an active thing by doing this?
3. 'Just a piece of cloth' is a small thing that actually has great power. Look at the last lines of the stanzas. How does the writer show the power of this piece of cloth?
4. Look at the last lines of each of the stanzas. How do they portray war?
5. Why would the **speaker's** 'friend' want 'such a cloth'? What does he think the flag might give him?

3 Activity 2
a Display the poem on the whiteboard using the Digital Anthology.

b Students discuss the question in pairs, writing their response in full sentences to ensure clarity of thought and their ability to express it. Take feedback to share and develop understanding. Aim to validate all interpretations supported with evidence from the poem and/or explanation.

Words/phrases to explore (AO1) — ACTIVITY 2
Why do you think conscience has to be blinded 'to the end'? What might your conscience tell you not to do? Look at all the things that the flag is said to give in the poem.

4 GradeStudio
a Read the GradeStudio sample answer to the class. Ask: How has the writer of this answer made a 'considered/qualified response to text', thinking about more than one thing?

b Ask: Where else in the poem is there an opportunity to offer and explore a considered response? For example, the power of the flag explored in the final line of the first four stanzas.

c Ask students to select a short quotation that will allow them to explore their response to the poem. They then write a paragraph about it, using point-evidence-explanation.

GradeStudio
Sample answer
To achieve a C on this AO1 descriptor, you need to show **sustained response to elements of text.** To do this, you need to write several connected comments about what you think about the poem. The following extract from a sample answer would hit the grade C requirement:

> **Activity 2**
> The flag stands for danger throughout. It's hugely dangerous right from the start as it 'brings a nation to its knees.' It encourages men to fight (which is dangerous) because it 'makes the guts of men grow bold' and 'dares the coward to relent'. The danger is made clear in the fourth stanza, because 'the blood you bleed' is what the flag will cause, and go on causing.

© Pearson Education Limited 2010

5 Comparison activities, page 96

Note: In order to do these activities, students would need to have completed their work on 'Futility' and 'The Charge of the Light Brigade'.

1 a In pairs or independently, students complete **Worksheet 3.2**, linking their response to the poems with the relevant Assessment Objective. Take feedback on any areas which students found difficult to grasp or to comment on.

> **Flag**
> 1. **Comparing ideas and themes**
>   Compare the attitudes of the voices to conflict in 'Flag' and 'Futility'.
> 2. **Comparing writers' devices**
>   Compare the ways in which repeated words and phrases are used in 'Flag' and 'The Charge of the Light Brigade'.

b Students use their notes from **Worksheet 3.2** to write three or four key points comparing the two poems' attitudes to conflict. They should write **in complete sentences using connectives**. Display **Worksheet 1.3** to support them.

c Take feedback, compiling notes on the board. As a class, students find evidence from each poem to support each point.

d Students select three points with supporting evidence from those on the board.

e Students add a sentence or two to each point/piece of evidence, explaining and commenting on how the writers have presented their points of view.

2 Repeat the above sequence using **Worksheet 3.3**, looking at the use of repetition in the poems.

6 Plenary

Take feedback on 'Flag', annotating the poem displayed on the whiteboard using Wordbox. Focus on relevant key features, e.g:
- content
- language
- tone.
- interpretation
- structure

If students have studied and compared 'Futility' and/or 'The Charge of the Light Brigade', take feedback on relevant key similarities and differences in content, interpretation, language, structure or tone.

Suggested answers

Activity 1

1. A flag is a symbol that can represent a cause, a nation, and the associated aggression in a time of conflict. The poem explores the destructive power of this symbol.
2. **a** 'fluttering', 'unfurling', 'rising', 'flying'.
   b The active verbs give the symbol of the flag a movement and life which is in keeping with its power.
3. Agard's use of emotive language – and the powerful images themselves.
4. War is portrayed as 1) merciless, 2) violent and bloody, 3) empowering, 4) enduring and 5) immoral.
5. To obtain its power.

Activity 2

The final line suggests that in order to wage war, conscience must be 'blinded' – i.e. ignored. Your conscience might argue against war; the poem suggests that the power of a flag and its associated patriotism can overrule conscience.

Comparison activities

Key points for this activity are provided in **Worksheet 3.4**.

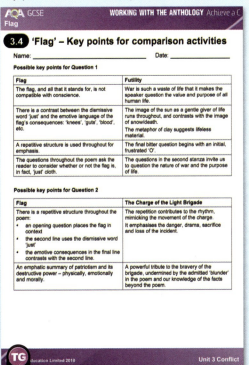

Chapter 3 Conflict

Out of the Blue (extract) by Simon Armitage

Assessment Objectives
- **AO1:** respond to texts critically and imaginatively; select and evaluate relevant textual detail to illustrate and support interpretations
- **AO2:** explain how language, structure and form contribute to writers' presentation of ideas, themes and settings

Learning Objectives
- To develop students' responses to the poem
- To relate the Assessment Objectives to the poem

Required resources
- Poem text, available on CD-ROM and video/audio online at http://anthology.aqa.org.uk
- Student Book, page 71
- Worksheets 1.3, 3.5, 3.6, 3.7

1 Starter
Find some news footage of 9/11 on the Internet and watch it together. Do students remember hearing about the attack on the Twin Towers?

2 Activity 1
a Using the Digital Anthology, listen to/watch/read the poem to the class. Clarify any points of understanding.
b Students complete questions 1–5 independently. Take feedback to share, ensure and develop understanding. Display the poem using the Digital Anthology, annotating the text with students' responses using Wordbox.
c Take students' initial response to the poem, commenting on the presentation of conflict in the poem.
d Ask students to write a sentence or two, summing up the content or meaning of the poem. They can begin: 'Out of the Blue' is about… .

Initial responses — ACTIVITY 1
1 What exactly is the man's situation in the poem?
2 The man in the building is waving a white shirt. What different things does he imagine the onlooker might see this as? Look at **stanzas** three and four.
3 There are lots of repetitions in this poem: of words, sentence forms and letters at the beginning of words (**alliteration**), like 'building burning'. Go through the poem and pick them all out. This will help you to notice where the patterns vary.
4 The man on the ledge is clearly desperate. Find places in the poem where you think that you can see or hear this. You could start with the **rhetorical question** at the end of the second stanza.
5 In the fourth stanza the heat of the flames is described as 'bullying, driving'. This is an example of **personification** (where something not human is given human characteristics).
   a Why do you think the writer has chosen to do this?
   b How does it make you feel the effect on the man on the ledge?

3 Activity 2
a Display the poem on the whiteboard, using the Digital Anthology, with the final line highlighted.
b Students discuss the questions in pairs, writing their response in full sentences to ensure clarity of thought and their ability to express it. Take feedback, annotating the displayed quotation using Wordbox. Aim to validate all points supported with evidence from elsewhere in the poem and/or explanation.

Words/phrases to explore (AO1 and AO2) — ACTIVITY 2
'My love' in the last line identifies the person the character is speaking to for the first time.
1 Why does Armitage wait until this moment to mention this?
2 What effect does it have on the feeling of the poem as a whole? Try to suggest more than one point.

4 GradeStudio
a Read the GradeStudio sample answer to the class. Ask: How has the writer of the sample answer given an 'explanation of effect(s) of writer's uses of language and/or form and/or structure and effects on readers'?
b Ask: Where else in the poem is there an opportunity to comment on the poet's choice of language or form or structure? For example, the repetition in the fifth or sixth stanzas, or the use of rhetorical questions in the second and third stanzas.
c Ask students to select a short quotation that will allow them to explore the poet's choices. They then write a paragraph about it, using point-evidence-explanation.

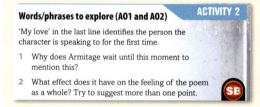

GradeStudio Sample answer
To achieve a C on this AO2 descriptor, you need to make an explanation of the effect(s) of writers' uses of language and/or form and/or structure. The following extract from a sample answer would hit the grade C requirement.

Activity 1, question 3
In the second line of the fifth stanza the writer makes the word 'appalling' stand out by repeating it, and putting a full stop between the two words before the end of the line. It makes the reader think about what comes next, what is 'appalling', and in this stanza it's 'Appalling' that lots of other people are falling to their deaths, not just the speaker.

5 Comparison activities, page 96

Note: In order to do these activities, students would need to have completed their work on 'The Right Word' and 'Bayonet Charge'.

1 a In pairs or independently, students complete **Worksheet 3.5**, linking their response to the poems with the relevant Assessment Objective. Take feedback on any areas which students found difficult to grasp or to comment on.

> **Out of the Blue**
> 1 **Comparing ideas and themes**
> Compare the ways in which the feelings of an individual in a desperate situation are shown in 'Out of the Blue' and 'Bayonet Charge'.
> 2 **Comparing writers' devices**
> Compare the ways in which danger is shown in 'Out of the Blue' and 'The Right Word'.

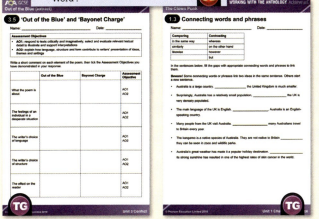

b Students use their notes from **Worksheet 3.5** to write three or four key points comparing the ways that the feelings of an individual in a desperate situation are shown in the two poems. They should write **in complete sentences using connectives**. Display **Worksheet 1.3** to support them.

c Take feedback, compiling notes on the board. As a class, students find evidence from each poem to support each point.

d Students select three points with supporting evidence from those on the board.

e Students add a sentence or two to each point/piece of evidence, explaining and commenting on how the writers have presented their points of view.

2 Repeat the above sequence using **Worksheet 3.6**, looking at the poems' presentation of danger.

6 Plenary

Take feedback on 'Out of the Blue', annotating the poem displayed on the whiteboard using Wordbox. Focus on relevant key features, e.g:
- content
- language
- tone
- interpretation
- structure

If students have studied and compared 'The Right Word' and/or 'Bayonet Charge', take feedback on relevant key similarities and differences in content, interpretation, language, structure or tone.

Suggested answers

Activity 1

1 He is trapped in a burning building – the World Trade Center following the September 11th terrorist attack. He is signalling for help by waving a white cotton shirt while others fall or jump from the building.

2 'waving', 'shaking crumbs', 'pegging out washing'.

3 'building burning', 'noticed now', 'twirling, turning', 'waving, waving' (twice), 'soul worth saving', 'watching, watching', 'trying and trying', 'appalling. Appalling', 'believing, believing', 'tiring, tiring', 'failing, flagging'. The pattern varies most obviously in the sixth stanza.

4 The rhetorical question in stanza 2; another two immediately after in stanza 3, implying sarcasm; the brevity of the lines in the sixth stanza; 'my nerves are sagging' in the final stanza.

5 **a** Suggests the fire is malevolently forcing him to his death.
   b It suggests not only the physical effect of the heat but the consequences it will inevitably have: forcing him to jump.

Activity 2

Initially it seems to be the reader who is being addressed, engaging us with the man's terrible situation. Revealing 'my love' at the end suddenly changes the poem's tone, broadening its ending to reflect on, not only the horror, but the emotional consequences of this event: this is not just a man in a hopeless situation facing death, but a man with loved ones who will also suffer. As we reach the end of the poem, we are forced to look again and reassess the poem entirely.

Comparison activities

Key points for this activity are provided in **Worksheet 3.7**.

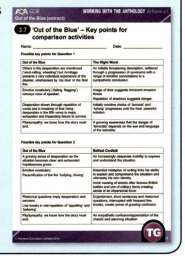

Chapter 3 Conflict

Mametz Wood by Owen Sheers

Assessment Objectives
- **AO1:** respond to texts critically and imaginatively; select and evaluate relevant textual detail to illustrate and support interpretations
- **AO2:** explain how language, structure and form contribute to writers' presentation of ideas, themes and settings

Learning Objectives
- To develop students' responses to the poem
- To relate the Assessment Objectives to the poem

Required resources
- Poem text, available on CD-ROM and video/audio online at http://anthology.aqa.org.uk
- Student Book, page 72
- Worksheets 1.3, 3.8, 3.9, 3.10

1 Starter
Display **only** stanzas 5 and 6 of the poem using the Digital Anthology. Tell students they must play 'forensic detective'. What can a close reading of the evidence tell them about these bodies? Who are they? What has happened? Give students 5 minutes to note their thoughts. Take feedback, focusing on the writer's choice of language, annotating the poem with students' thoughts using Wordbox.

2 Activity 1
a Using the Digital Anthology, listen to/watch/read the whole poem to the class. Clarify any points of understanding.

b Students complete questions 1–8 independently. Take feedback to share, ensure and develop understanding. Display the poem using the Digital Anthology, annotating the text with students' responses using Wordbox.

c Take students' initial response to the poem, commenting on the presentation of conflict in the poem.

d Ask students to write a sentence or two, summing up the content or meaning of the poem. They can begin: *'Mametz Wood' is about….*

Initial responses — ACTIVITY 1
1. Exactly what do farmers find in the field by Mametz Wood? List everything.
2. What happened to the soldiers? Look at the end of the third **stanza**.
3. What different times are mentioned in the poem?
4. How does Sheers make life seem fragile in the second stanza? Think about why he compares the skull to 'a blown and broken bird's egg'.
5. Why do you think Sheers describes the earth as 'standing sentinel'? What does it make the earth seem like?
6. Work out the idea that Sheers has about the earth in the fourth stanza. Think about what happens to a splinter in your finger.
7. In the last stanza, what do the skeletons appear to be doing? What effect does this have on the reader?
8. Find the **rhyme** in the last stanza. Why do you think Sheers u[ses] rhyme here? Think which two words are connected by the rh[yme].

3 Activity 2
a Display the poem using the Digital Anthology.

b Students discuss the question in pairs, writing their response in full sentences to ensure clarity of thought and their ability to express it. Take feedback, annotating the displayed poem using Wordbox. Aim to validate all interpretations supported with explanation.

4 GradeStudio
a Read the GradeStudio sample answer to the class. Ask: How has the writer of the sample answer made an 'appropriate comment on the ideas/themes' in the poem?

b Where else in the poem is there an opportunity for students to comment on its ideas/themes? For example, the image of the wound or the soldiers' dancing and singing.

c Ask students to select a short quotation that will allow them to explore their response to the poem. They then write a paragraph about it, using point-evidence-explanation.

GradeStudio
Sample answer
To achieve a C on this AO2 descriptor, you need to make a make an **appropriate comment on ideas/themes**. The following extract from a sample answer would hit the grade C requirement.

> Activity 1, question 6
> The earth, damaged by the war and the buried bodies, is gradually being restored. The farmers 'tended the land back into itself' and the earth is healing itself by slowly working the bones out onto the surface.

5 Comparison activities, page 96

Note: In order to do these activities, students would need to have completed their work on 'Futility' and 'The Falling Leaves'.

1. **a** In pairs or independently, students complete **Worksheet 3.8**, linking their response to the poems with the relevant Assessment Objective. Take feedback on any areas which students found difficult to grasp or to comment on.

> **Mametz Wood**
> 1 **Comparing ideas and themes**
>   Compare the attitudes of the **speakers** to dead soldiers in 'Mametz Wood' and 'Futility'.
> 2 **Comparing writers' devices**
>   Compare the ways in which death is presented in 'The Falling Leaves' and 'Mametz Wood'.

   b Students use their notes from **Worksheet 3.8** to write three or four key points comparing the attitudes of the speakers to dead soldiers in the two poems. They should write **in complete sentences using connectives**. Display **Worksheet 1.3** to support them.

   c Take feedback, compiling notes on the board. As a class, students find evidence from each poem to support each point.

   d Students select three points with supporting evidence from those on the board.

   e Students add a sentence or two to each point/piece of evidence, explaining and commenting on how the writers have presented their points of view.

2. Repeat the above sequence using **Worksheet 3.9**, looking at how death is presented in 'The Falling Leaves' and 'Mametz Wood'.

6 Plenary

Take feedback on 'Mametz Wood', annotating the poem displayed on the whiteboard using Wordbox. Focus on relevant key features, e.g:
- content
- language
- tone.
- interpretation
- structure

If students have studied and compared 'The Falling Leaves' and/or 'Futility', take feedback on relevant key similarities and differences in content, interpretation, language, structure or tone.

Suggested answers

Activity 1

1 Over the years, farmers found fragments of bone. This morning, they found the skeletons of twenty men in one long grave, still wearing boots.

2 They were killed during the war: they were told to 'walk, not run towards the wood' in which Germans and their machine guns were waiting.

3 The First World War, the years after the war, and the present day.

4 Images of bone as 'china' and a skull as an 'egg' emphasise the violence and vulnerability of these soldier's lives. The addition of 'blown and broken' further draws our attention to the emptiness of the skull: what it once contained and why it no longer does.

5 A military image suggesting that the earth is all that guards them, perhaps further implying their vulnerability – and their oblivion.

6 As the earth shifts and resettles, the bones rise to the surface. The image of a wound implies the earth is rejecting these foreign bodies' bones as if they do not belong there, perhaps suggesting that they should not have died or been buried in these circumstances.

7 The position of the skeletons suggests that they are singing in chorus and dancing. A shocking image.

8 'sung' and 'tongues' link the song and its source.

Activity 2

'Wasted' offers two meanings: decayed and pointlessly lost. The idea of decay, from a 'chit of bone' to 'their absent tongues', dominates the poem. The image of the soldiers being 'told to walk, not run' is the only reference to the events of 1916, but swiftly conveys the military's attitude to life and its loss.

Comparison activities

Key points for this activity are provided in **Worksheet 3.10**.

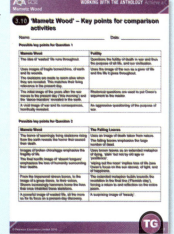

Chapter 3 Conflict

The Yellow Palm by Robert Minhinnick

Assessment Objectives
- **AO1:** respond to texts critically and imaginatively; select and evaluate relevant textual detail to illustrate and support interpretations
- **AO2:** explain how language, structure and form contribute to writers' presentation of ideas, themes and settings

Learning Objectives
- To develop students' responses to the poem
- To relate the Assessment Objectives to the poem

Required resources
- Poem text, available on CD-ROM and video/audio online at http://anthology.aqa.org.uk
- Student Book, page 73
- Worksheets 1.3, 3.11, 3.12, 3.13, 3.14

1 Starter
Display/distribute **Worksheet 3.11**, explaining that these are words and phrases taken from the poem which you will be exploring during the lesson. What can students say about these words and phrases, and what can they guess about the poem as a whole? Are there any words which seem out of place? Give pairs 3 minutes to note their thoughts. Take feedback to share responses with the class.

2 Activity 1

a Using the Digital Anthology, listen to/watch/read the poem to the class. Clarify any points of understanding.

b Students complete questions 1–6 independently. Take feedback to share, ensure and develop understanding. Display the poem using the Digital Anthology, annotating the text with students' responses using Wordbox.

c Take students' initial response to the poem, commenting on the presentation of conflict in the poem.

d Ask students to write a sentence or two, summing up the content or meaning of the poem. They can begin: *'The Yellow Palm' is about...*.

Initial responses — ACTIVITY 1
1 The **speaker** in the poem sees lots of unhappiness and danger as he walks down the street. Make a list of what he sees.
2 Each of the first five **stanzas** contains a contrast of some sort. For example, the first stanza mentions 'lilac stems', and then the face of a man killed by poison gas. Find and write down the contrasts in the other stanzas.
3 In the third stanza, the speaker meets two beggars.
   a What did these beggars used to be?
   b How does the writer show the difference between what they were and what they are?
4 In the fourth stanza, even nature seems to be part of the war. How does the writer suggest this? Look for the words he uses as well as ideas.
5 In the fifth stanza, how is something dangerous made to seem not dangerous? Think about what it is compared to and the words used.
6 In the last stanza the beggar child is given something he hasn't asked for. What is it, and how does he get it? Think about what is happening in the previous stanza, and what falls out of the...

3 Activity 2

a Display the poem on the whiteboard using the Digital Anthology.

b Students discuss the question in pairs, writing their response in full sentences to ensure clarity of thought and their ability to express it. Take feedback, to share and develop thinking. Aim to validate all interpretations supported with evidence from the poem and/or explanation.

Words/phrases to explore (AO1 and AO2) — ACTIVITY 2
Do you think there are any signs of hope in the poem, or is it just bleak and depressing? Write a paragraph on this, supporting what you think with details from the poem. You could start with 'in a city such as...

4 GradeStudio

a Read the GradeStudio sample answer to the class. Ask: How has the writer of the sample answer shown 'thoughtful consideration of ideas/themes' in the poem?

b Where else in the poem is there an opportunity for students to explore its ideas? For example, the description of the mosque, or the 'barbarian sun'.

c Ask students to select a short quotation that will allow them to explore their response to the poem. They then write a paragraph about it, using point-evidence-explanation.

GradeStudio
Sample answer B
To achieve a B on this AO2 descriptor, you need to show **thoughtful consideration of ideas/themes**. To do this, you need to think of more than one idea about the poem. The following extract from a sample answer would hit the grade B requirement.

Activity 1, question 3
The war has destroyed the soldiers' lives, making them into beggars; but this is made to seem sharper by the soldiers, who were not just guards but 'Imperial' Guards, being now blind, and ironically giving their soldiers' salutes in return for alms.

5 Comparison activities, page 96

Note: In order to do these activities, students would need to have completed their work on 'At the Border' and 'The Charge of the Light Brigade'.

1 a In pairs or independently, students complete **Worksheet 3.12**, linking their response to the poems with the relevant Assessment Objective. Take feedback on any areas which students found difficult to grasp or to comment on.

> **The Yellow Palm**
> 1 **Comparing ideas and themes**
>   Compare the effects of war on civilians in 'The Yellow Palm' and 'At the Border'.
> 2 **Comparing writers' devices**
>   Compare how the writers of 'The Yellow Palm' and 'The Charge of the Light Brigade' make the cities seem horrible places.

b Students use their notes from **Worksheet 3.12** to write three or four key points comparing the effects of war on civilians in the two poems. They should write **in complete sentences using connectives**. Display **Worksheet 1.3** to support them.

c Take feedback, compiling notes on the board. As a class, students find evidence from each poem to support each point.

d Students select three points with supporting evidence from those on the board.

e Students add a sentence or two to each point/piece of evidence, explaining and commenting on how the writers have presented their ideas.

2 Repeat the above sequence using **Worksheet 3.13**, looking at the effects of repetition in the two poems.

6 Plenary

Take feedback on 'The Yellow Palm', annotating the poem displayed on the whiteboard using Wordbox. Focus on relevant key features, e.g:
- content
- language
- tone.
- interpretation
- structure

If students have studied and compared 'At the Border' and/or 'The Charge of the Light Brigade', take feedback on relevant key similarities and differences in content, interpretation, language, structure or tone.

Suggested answers

Activity 1

1 The funeral of a man who has been gassed; blood on the walls of a mosque; blind beggars; a Cruise missile; a beggar child.

2 golden mosque contrasts with red blood on walls (stanza 2); beggars contrasts with Imperial Guard (stanza 3); the river smell lifting the air contrasts with the barbarian sun falling down on his head (stanza 4); Cruise missile contrasts with the child's smile (stanza 5).

3 **a/b** They are former members of Saddam's Imperial Guard, now forced to beg for money. The contrast is emphasised in their salute, presumably at the speaker for his generosity.

4 Suggests even the sun is aggressive: it is 'barbarian'; it falls 'down on my head', implying some kind of attack.

5 The Cruise missile is described in a positive terms: 'slow' and 'silver' implying grace and value; it is blessed 'with a smile' by the beggar child.

6 The beggar child reaches up to the yellow dates on the Yellow Palm and they fall into his arms. The significance of the fruit falling is not explicitly clear. Perhaps the child is being rewarded for his positive attitude to the Cruise missile which he should fear, implying acceptance of it, and the violence it represents. Or perhaps it is, more simply, a positive image countering the negativity earlier in the poem.

Activity 2

The final line seems to change the tone of the poem from one of cynicism and violence, to one of simple, natural generosity. Yet it forces us back to the image of the child blessing the Cruise missile and wondering whether one is a metaphorical consequence of the other.

Comparison activities

Key points for this activity are provided in **Worksheet 3.14**.

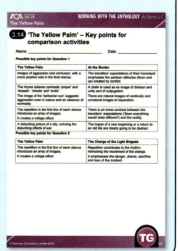

Chapter 3 Conflict

The Right Word by Imtiaz Dharker

Assessment Objectives
- **AO1:** respond to texts critically and imaginatively; select and evaluate relevant textual detail to illustrate and support interpretations
- **AO2:** explain how language, structure and form contribute to writers' presentation of ideas, themes and settings

Learning Objectives
- To develop students' responses to the poem
- To relate the Assessment Objectives to the poem

Required resources
- Poem text, available on CD-ROM and video/audio online at http://anthology.aqa.org.uk
- Student Book, page 74
- Worksheets 1.3, 3.15, 3.16, 3.17, 3.18

1 Starter

Display or distribute **Worksheet 3.15**. In pairs, students rank the terms from the most positive to the most negative. Take feedback, insisting on clear explanations for students' decisions. Aim for a class consensus in order to promote discussion.

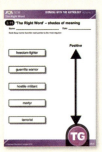

2 Activity 1

a Using the Digital Anthology, listen to/watch/read the poem to the class. Clarify any points of understanding.

b Students complete questions 1–7 independently. Take feedback to share, ensure and develop understanding. Display the poem using the Digital Anthology, annotating the text with students' responses using Wordbox.

c Take students' initial response to the poem, commenting on the presentation of conflict in the poem.

d Ask students to write a sentence or two, summing up the content or meaning of the poem. They can begin: 'The Right Word' is about… .

Initial responses — ACTIVITY 1

1 The woman in the poem is frightened of the figure outside. Why do you think she is frightened of him?

2 a Identify the different words used to describe the figure in the shadows, starting with 'terrorist'.
   b The word 'shadow' is repeated several times. Why do you think the writer does this?

3 Identify the different things the figure is doing in the shadows, beginning with 'lurking'.

4 The poem changes in the fifth **stanza**.
   a How does the first line of the stanza connect with 'a martyr'? Think about the use of the word 'God'.
   b How does the figure become clearer here, and more dangerous?

5 'No words can help me now.' What does this line show about how the **speaker** feels at this point?

6 Who do you think the 'you' might be at the beginning of the seventh stanza?

7 a How is the last stanza a surprise, after the rest of the poem? Think about the changes in the way the stanza is written as well as the change of feeling.
   b What is the effect of the last line?

3 Activity 2

a Display the poem using the Digital Anthology.

b Students discuss the question in pairs, writing their response in full sentences to ensure clarity of thought and their ability to express it. Take feedback, annotating the displayed poem using Wordbox. Aim to validate all interpretations supported with evidence from elsewhere in the poem and/or explanation.

Words/phrases to explore (AO1) — ACTIVITY 2

Words are very important in this poem. What sort of person does the woman think the figure might be, and what does he turn out to be? Write some sentences about this, using details from the poem. Try to include the lines 'Are words no more/Than waving, wavering flags'

4 GradeStudio

a Read the GradeStudio sample answer to the class. Ask: How has the writer of the sample answer shown 'details linked to interpretation' of the poem?

b Where else in the poem is there an opportunity for students to explore details linked to interpretation? For example, the progression of terms used to describe the 'terrorist', or the line 'No words can help me now'.

c Ask students to select a short quotation that will allow them to explore their response to the poem. The students then write a paragraph about it, using point-evidence-explanation

GradeStudio — Sample answer

To achieve a C on this AO1 descriptor, you need to show **effective use of details.** The following extract from a sample answer would hit the grade C requirement:

Activity 1, question 7
The feeling of the poem changes in the last stanza to one of respect and civilised, peaceful behaviour. The invitation 'Come in' is repeated and the frightening figure actually 'steps in' and 'carefully' removes his shoes.

5 Comparison activities, page 96

Note: In order to do these activities, students would need to have completed their work on 'At the Border' and 'Flag'.

1 **a** In pairs or independently, students complete **Worksheet 3.16**, linking their response to the poems with the relevant Assessment Objective. Take feedback on any areas which students found difficult to grasp or to comment on.

> **The Right Word**
> 1 **Comparing ideas and themes**
>   Compare how the two sides of conflict are shown in 'The Right Word' and 'At the Border'.
> 2 **Comparing writers' devices**
>   Compare the effects of the repetitions in 'The Right Word' and 'Flag'.

b Students use their notes from **Worksheet 3.16** to write three or four key points comparing how the writers explore the two sides of conflict. They should write **in complete sentences using connectives**. Display **Worksheet 1.3** to support them.

c Take feedback, compiling notes on the board. As a class, students find evidence from each poem to support each point.

d Students select three points with supporting evidence from those on the board.

e Students add a sentence or two to each point/piece of evidence, explaining and commenting on how the writers have presented their points of view.

2 Repeat the above sequence using **Worksheet 3.17**, looking at the use of repetition in the two poems.

6 Plenary

Take feedback on 'The Right Word', annotating the poem displayed on the whiteboard using Wordbox. Focus on relevant key features, e.g:
- content
- language
- tone.
- interpretation
- structure

If students have studied and compared 'At the Border' and/or 'Flag', take feedback on relevant key similarities and differences in content, interpretation, language, structure or tone.

Suggested answers

Activity 1

1 Her initial fear seems to come from her perception that this is a terrorist and that he is 'lurking' – a word implying negative intentions.

2 **a** 'terrorist', 'freedom fighter', 'hostile militant', 'guerrilla warrior', 'martyr', 'a child who looks like mine', 'a boy who looks like your son'.

  b It suggests that the figure is hiding and perhaps waiting for her.

3 'lurking', 'taking shelter', 'waiting', 'defying', 'lost'.

4 **a** A martyr is someone who dies for their, usually religious, beliefs.

  b The figure is not lurking in the shadows any more, he is 'defying' them: his face is visible.

5 It suggests a state of fear: this is a dangerous situation in which words will be of no use; however, reading on, it becomes clear that the speaker means that the terms she has used up to this point are meaningless now that she sees the face of a child: she can no longer dismiss this person as a 'terrorist'.

6 The reader: this could be anyone's child.

7 **a/b** After the rising terror of the earlier stanzas, this acceptance of hospitality is surprising. The structural repetition of the previous stanzas is not used here. Instead of lurking at the speaker's door, the boy removes his shoes at the door: a mark of respect. Suddenly the fear dissipates: this is a person, not a monster to be feared.

Activity 2

The words used to describe the 'terrorist' are increasingly positive, the context of each suggesting a shifting bias, until the final recognition of figure as a human being, as somebody's child. This seems to suggest that attitudes are not only reflected in, but created, by language. The image of the 'flags' implies a kind of patriotism, an alliance to a cause, and 'waving' further indicates the biased language associated with that cause.

Comparison activities

Key points for this activity are provided in **Worksheet 3.18**.

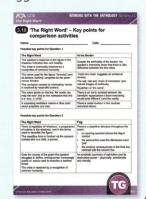

Chapter 3 Conflict

At the Border by Choman Hardi

Assessment Objectives
- **AO1:** respond to texts critically and imaginatively; select and evaluate relevant textual detail to illustrate and support interpretations
- **AO2:** explain how language, structure and form contribute to writers' presentation of ideas, themes and settings

Learning Objectives
- To develop students' responses to the poem
- To relate the Assessment Objectives to the poem

Required resources
- Poem text, available on CD-ROM and video/audio online at http://anthology.aqa.org.uk
- Student Book, page 75
- Worksheets 1.3, 3.19, 3.20, 3.21

1 Starter
Write the phrases 'Going away' and 'Coming home' on the whiteboard. Ask students to think of the longest and furthest they have been away from home. Aim to prompt them to consider visits abroad as well as within their home country. Ask: Which places were most similar or most different? What was it like coming home – good or bad? In what ways? What reminds you of home or makes you glad to return? Is home very different from everywhere else?

2 Activity 1

a Using the Digital Anthology, listen to/watch/read the poem to the class. Clarify any points of understanding.

b Students complete questions 1–8 independently. Take feedback to share, ensure and develop understanding. Display the poem using the Digital Anthology, annotating the text with students' responses using Wordbox.

c Take students' initial response to the poem, commenting on the presentation of conflict in the poem.

d Ask students to write a sentence or two, summing up the content or meaning of the poem. They can begin: 'At the Border' is about....

Initial responses — ACTIVITY 1
1. What is the situation of the people waiting at the check-in point? Why do they think things will be different on the other side?
2. 'It is your last check-in point in this country!' What do the words and punctuation suggest about the guard who says this line?
3. In lines 3–5, what is going to stay the same, and what will be different?
4. The two sides are divided by a 'thick iron chain'. Why do you think the writer uses the words 'thick' and 'iron'?
5. 'The border guards told her off'. Look for all the mentions of the guards in the poem.
6. a What do you think the writer wants you to think about the guards?
   b What does this make you think about the authorities behind the guards?
7. What does the child think when she compares the two sides of the border? Look at the sixth **stanza**.
8. It is autumn, and it is raining on both sides of the border. Apart from being a literal description, what else might these two details say about the situation of the people in the poem? Will they be better or worse off on the other side of the border?

3 Activity 2

a Display the line from the poem in close-up using the Digital Anthology.

b Students discuss the question in pairs, writing their response in full sentences to ensure clarity of thought and their ability to express it. Take feedback, annotating the displayed quotation using Wordbox. Aim to validate all interpretations supported with evidence from elsewhere in the poem and/or explanation.

Words/phrases to explore (AO1 and AO2) — ACTIVITY 2
'The same chain of mountains encompassed all of us.' This is the fourth time in the poem that the word 'chain' is used. The meaning of 'chain' seems very different here from the 'thick iron chain'.
1. Could they be the same in any way?
2. How might both sides still be 'chained'?

4 GradeStudio

a Read the GradeStudio sample answer to the class. Ask: How has the writer of the sample answer demonstrated an 'explained response to element(s) of text'?

b Ask students to improve the response and achieve a C by adding a sentence or two in which they select evidence to support the point and comment on the way the writer has written about the guards. For example, the blunt, monosyllabic language and exclamation mark of the poem's opening line.

c Ask students to select a short quotation that will allow them to explore their response to the poem. They then write a paragraph about it, using point-evidence-explanation.

GradeStudio Sample answer D
To achieve a D on this AO1 descriptor, you need to show **explained response to element(s) of text**. The following extract from a sample answer would hit the grade D requirement.

Activity 1, question 6a
The guards in the poem seem repressive and harsh, because they shout at the refugees in the first line, and tell off the speaker's sister, who is only a child, just for putting her leg over the chain.

© Pearson Education Limited 2010

5 Comparison activities, page 96

Note: In order to do these activities, students would need to have completed their work on 'Flag' and 'The Falling Leaves'.

1 a In pairs or independently, students complete **Worksheet 3.19**, linking their response to the poems with the relevant Assessment Objective. Take feedback on any areas which students found difficult to grasp or to comment on.

> **At the Border**
> 1 **Comparing ideas and themes**
> Compare how feelings about a country are shown in 'At the Border' and 'Flag'.
> 2 **Comparing writers' devices**
> Compare the effects of the uses of the chain in 'At the Border' and the leaves in 'The Falling Leaves'.

b Students use their notes from **Worksheet 3.19** to write three or four key points comparing how the two poems present feelings about a country. They should write **in complete sentences using connectives**. Display **Worksheet 1.3** to support them.

c Take feedback, compiling notes on the board. As a class, students find evidence from each poem to support each point.

d Students select three points with supporting evidence from those on the board.

e Students add a sentence or two to each point/piece of evidence, explaining and commenting on how the writers have presented their points of view.

2 Repeat the above sequence using **Worksheet 3.20**, looking at the two images in the poems.

6 Plenary

Take feedback on 'At the Border', annotating the poem displayed on the whiteboard using Wordbox. Focus on relevant key features, e.g:
- content
- language
- tone.
- interpretation
- structure

If students have studied and compared 'Flag' and/or 'The Falling Leaves', take feedback on relevant key similarities and differences in content, interpretation, language, structure or tone.

Suggested answers

Activity 1

1. They are crossing the border to return to their homeland. Their expectations suggest their unhappiness while in exile, and their love of 'home'.
2. Blunt, monosyllabic language and exclamation mark suggest an abrupt and officious guard.
3. The land continues but, beyond the chain, the speaker believes that everything will taste different once they have crossed the border to their homeland.
4. Emphasises the strength and power of this artificial division.
5. The border guards 'appear' throughout the poem: their exclamation in stanza 1; they tell the narrator's sister off in stanza 3; they check papers and inspect the families in stanza 7.
6. **a** As above, they seem abrupt, officious and invasive, checking papers and inspecting faces thoroughly.
   b It suggests that this country is ruled with a strong, perhaps dictatorial force.
7. They are the same.
8. The dark, rainy autumn day seems an ironic contrast with the family's bright – and perhaps misplaced – hope for their homeland and suggests that the homeland may not be as marvellous as he is expecting.

Activity 2

Both meanings suggest restrictions. A chain, however, can be seen as an image of connection and co-operation: a series of interconnected links, the individual parts combining to create something much greater. Both sides are inextricably linked, by their border, by the mountains and, perhaps, by their situation.

Comparison activities

Key points for this activity are provided in **Worksheet 3.21**.

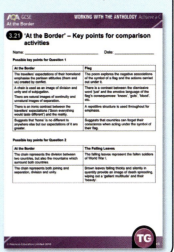

AQA GCSE Working with the Anthology: Achieve a C 95

Chapter 3 Conflict

Belfast Confetti
by Ciaran Carson

Assessment Objectives
- **AO1:** respond to texts critically and imaginatively; select and evaluate relevant textual detail to illustrate and support interpretations
- **AO2:** explain how language, structure and form contribute to writers' presentation of ideas, themes and settings

Learning Objectives
- To develop students' responses to the poem
- To relate the Assessment Objectives to the poem

Required resources
- Poem text, available on CD-ROM and video/audio online at http://anthology.aqa.org.uk
- Student Book, page 76
- Worksheets 1.3, 3.22, 3.23, 3.24

1 Starter
Display **Worksheet 3.22**, posing the question 'What is it?' Give students 3 minutes to record their thoughts, then take feedback. Leave the worksheet on display.

2 Activity 1

a Using the Digital Anthology, listen to/watch/read the poem to the class. Clarify any points of understanding. Return to **Worksheet 3.22**, looking again in the light of the poem. What is it?

b Students complete questions 1–5 independently. Take feedback to share, ensure and develop understanding. Display the poem using the Digital Anthology, annotating the text with students' responses using Wordbox.

c Take students' initial response to the poem, commenting on the presentation of conflict in the poem.

d Ask students to write a sentence or two, summing up the content or meaning of the poem. They can begin: *'Belfast Confetti' is about….*

Initial responses — ACTIVITY 1
1. List all the references you can find to weapons and ammunition in the poem.
2. What is ironic about the term 'Belfast confetti'? Think what occasion confetti is usually associated with, and what is happening in the poem.
3. To get into this poem, imagine a writer in the battle area trying to write. He uses punctuation marks as **metaphors** for the events and feelings that occur.
   a. Why do you think the objects listed in line 2 are described as 'exclamation marks'? Remember what sort of feeling an exclamation mark usually shows.
   b. Why is the explosion like an 'asterisk on the map'?
   c. Why is the burst of rapid fire like 'a hyphenated line'? (Think about how you would draw bullets being fired.)
   d. Why do you think the sentence 'kept stuttering'? Think of more than one reason here, if you can.
4. From lines 5–7, what do you think the **speaker** is trying to do and what is he feeling about his situation? Base your ideas on details in the text.
5. Line 8 lists items used by the troops. Why do you think the writer presents the troops like this, rather than saying 'The troops had…'? How does it make them appear to the reader? What does it say about the way the people in the city think about the troops?

3 Activity 2

Words/phrases to explore (AO1 and AO2) — ACTIVITY 2
'Dead end again'. How does the writer show that the speaker in the poem feels trapped? Starting from this phrase, write a couple of sentences on this.

a Display lines 6–8 ('I know this labyrinth… Dead end again') in close-up on the whiteboard using the Digital Anthology.

b Students discuss the question in pairs, writing their response in full sentences to ensure clarity of thought and their ability to express it. Take feedback, annotating the displayed quotation using Wordbox. Aim to validate all interpretations supported with evidence from elsewhere in the poem and/or explanation.

4 GradeStudio

a Read the GradeStudio sample answer to the class. Ask: How has the writer of the sample answer shown a 'supported response to text'?

b How could students add to the sentence to achieve the 'explained response' needed for a D? For example: *He is being intimidated by the soldiers and their military equipment.*

c How could students add to this to achieve the 'sustained response' needed for a C? For example: *This is one of lots of questions at the end of the poem, showing how confused he is.*

d Where else in the poem is there an opportunity for students to offer an exploratory response? For example, the punctuation metaphor, or the poem's title.

e Ask students to select a short quotation that will allow them to explore their response to the poem. The students then write a paragraph about it, using point-evidence-explanation.

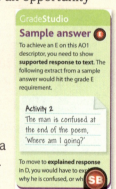

GradeStudio Sample answer
To achieve an E on this AO1 descriptor, you need to show **supported response to text**. The following extract from a sample answer would hit the grade E requirement.

Activity 2
The man is confused at the end of the poem, 'Where am I going?'

To move to **explained response** in D, you would have to explain why he is confused, or why…

5 Comparison activities, page 96

Note: In order to do these activities, students would need to have completed their work on 'Bayonet Charge'.

a In pairs or independently, students complete **Worksheet 3.23**, linking their response to the poems with the relevant Assessment Objective. Take feedback on any areas which students found difficult to grasp or to comment on.

Belfast Confetti

1 **Comparing ideas and themes**
Compare how individual people caught up in war are shown in 'Belfast Confetti' and 'Bayonet Charge'.
2 **Comparing writers' devices**
Compare the ways in which similes and metaphors are used in 'Belfast Confetti' and 'Bayonet Charge'.

b Students use their notes from **Worksheet 3.23** to write three or four key points comparing how individuals caught up in war are shown and the use of similes and metaphors in the two poems. They should write **in complete sentences using connectives**. Display **Worksheet 1.3** to support them.
c Take feedback, compiling notes on the board. As a class, students find evidence from each poem to support each point.
d Students select three points with supporting evidence from those on the board.
e Students add a sentence or two to each point/piece of evidence, explaining and commenting on how the writers have presented their points of view.

6 Plenary

Take feedback on 'Belfast Confetti', annotating the poem displayed on the whiteboard using Wordbox. Focus on relevant key features, e.g:
- content
- language
- tone.
- interpretation
- structure

If students have studied and compared 'Bayonet Charge', take feedback on relevant key similarities and differences in content, interpretation, language, structure or tone.

Suggested answers

Activity 1

1 'Nuts', 'bolts', 'nails', 'car-keys', 'explosion', 'burst of rapid fire', 'fusillade'.

2 Confetti is small scraps of coloured paper, usually thrown at a wedding in celebration. This 'confetti' consists of nuts and bolts and nails and is thrown aggressively.

3 a An exclamation mark suggests loud surprise – it is, perhaps, the most 'aggressive' punctuation mark.
  b A visual representation of an explosion.
  c Each hyphen represents a bullet, tracing its way across the page/through the air.
  d Stuttering suggests an inability to get to the end of the sentence, perhaps due to the violent interruptions, perhaps due to fear.

4 He seems to be looking for a way out, to escape from the violence. The rhetorical question ('Why can't I escape?') suggests frustration and perhaps fear.

5 This list of military items presents the troops in terms of their armoury, their protection. It suggests that the troops are seen as something inhuman, something to be challenged.

Activity 2

'Dead end' literally refers to the streets from which he is trying to escape, but perhaps also refers to the battles after which the streets are named: famous British battles which, like this one, he considers to be historical dead ends – paths which led nowhere – and ended in death.

Comparison activities

Key points for this activity are provided in **Worksheet 3.24**.

AQA GCSE Working with the Anthology: Achieve a C 97

Chapter 3 Conflict

Poppies by Jane Weir

Assessment Objectives
- **AO1:** respond to texts critically and imaginatively; select and evaluate relevant textual detail to illustrate and support interpretations
- **AO2:** explain how language, structure and form contribute to writers' presentation of ideas, themes and settings

Learning Objectives
- To develop students' responses to the poem
- To relate the Assessment Objectives to the poem

Required resources
- Poem text, available on CD-ROM and video/audio online at http://anthology.aqa.org.uk
- Student Book, page 77
- Worksheets 1.3, 3.25, 3.26, 3.27

1 Starter

Look at the image of the poppy in the Student Book or source and display one from the Internet. What does the poppy symbolise? Why? Look for responses which recognise that poppies filled the battlefields of World War I; also the red symbolising blood and the black symbolising death.

2 Activity 1

a Using the Digital Anthology, listen to/watch/read the poem to the class. Clarify any points of understanding.

b Students complete questions 1–6 independently. Take feedback to share, ensure and develop understanding. Display the poem using the Digital Anthology, annotating the text with students' responses using Wordbox.

c Take students' initial response to the poem, commenting on the presentation of conflict in the poem.

d Ask students to write a sentence or two, summing up the content or meaning of the poem. They can begin: *'Poppies' is about…* .

Initial responses — ACTIVITY 1

1. What does the mother do before her son leaves, and then after he leaves?
2. 'Spasms of paper red, disrupting a blockade' describes the poppy on the blazer, but the writer uses words that make the reader think of war or injury. Find as many examples as you can of this technique in the rest of the poem.
3. In the second **stanza**, the **speaker** 'steeled the softening of her face'.
   a. Why do you think her face softens, and why does she 'steel' it?
   b. Why does the writer use the word 'steel'? What effect does it have?
4. Why do you think the mother finds her words 'slowly melting'? These words appear immediately after a pause. What effect does this pause have on the reader?
5. When the front door is opened, the world is 'overflowing like a treasure chest'. Why does this seem an unusual comparison in this poem? Do you think this is the mother's point of view or the son's?
6. Look at the last line. The mother hopes to hear 'your playground voice catching on the wind'. What is the effect of the last line on the reader? How many other references to the son's childhood can you find?

3 Activity 2

a Display the last few lines of the poem in close-up using the Digital Anthology.

b Students should discuss the question in pairs, writing their response in full sentences to ensure clarity of thought and their ability to express it. Take feedback, annotating the displayed quotation using Wordbox. Aim to validate all interpretations supported with evidence from elsewhere in the poem and/or explanation.

Words/phrases to explore (AO1 and AO2) — ACTIVITY 2

The writer describes herself leaning against the war memorial 'like a wishbone'. Find as many things to say about this comparison as you can. Think about what she looks like and what she is feeling.

4 GradeStudio

a Read the GradeStudio extract to the class. How has the writer shown 'details linked to interpretation'?

b Where else in the poem is there an opportunity to explore the writer's use of language or structure linked to interpretation? For example, the use of war imagery or the image of a treasure chest.

c Ask students to select a short quotation which will allow them to explore their response to the poem; then write a paragraph about it using point-evidence-explanation.

GradeStudio

Sample answer B

To achieve a B on this AO1 descriptor, you need to show **details linked to interpretation**. The following extract from a sample answer would hit the grade B requirement:

> Death is never far from the mother's thoughts. The information about the poppies being placed on graves that opens the poem has nothing to do with the son's departure, except for her fear, and when at the end of the poem the dove 'has led me' to the church yard and the war memorial, it has only led her here because they represent the death that she thinks about constantly, and fears.

5 Comparison activities, page 96

Note: In order to do these activities, students would need to have completed their work on 'The Right Word' and 'At the Border'.

1 a In pairs or independently, students complete **Worksheet 3.25**, linking their response to the poems with the relevant Assessment Objective. Take feedback on any areas which students found difficult to grasp or to comment on.

> **Poppies**
> 1 **Comparing ideas and themes**
>   Compare the feelings shown by the speakers in 'Poppies' and 'At the Border'.
> 2 **Comparing writers' devices**
>   Compare how feelings are shown in 'Poppies' and 'The Right Word'.

b Students use their notes from **Worksheet 3.25** to write three or four key points comparing the feelings shown by the speakers. They should write **in complete sentences using connectives**. Display **Worksheet 1.3** to support them.

c Take feedback, compiling notes on the board. As a class, students find evidence from each poem to support each point.

d Students select three points with supporting evidence from those on the board.

e Students add a sentence or two to each point/piece of evidence, explaining and commenting on how the writers have presented their points of view.

2 Repeat the above sequence using **Worksheet 3.26**, looking at the ways feelings are shown in the two poems.

6 Plenary

Take feedback on 'Poppies', annotating the poem displayed on the whiteboard using Wordbox. Focus on relevant key features, e.g:
- content
- language
- tone.
- interpretation
- structure

If students have studied and compared 'The Right Word' and/or 'At the Border', take feedback on relevant key similarities and differences in content, interpretation, language, structure or tone.

Suggested answers

Activity 1

1 Before he leaves, she pins a poppy to his jacket and smartens him up. After he leaves, she goes to his bedroom and then to the war memorial in the churchyard.

2 For example, 'Sellotape <u>bandaged</u> around my hand... <u>reinforcements</u> of scarf, gloves'.

3 a/b 'Softening' suggests a failing of her 'brave' face; 'steeling' suggests she wants to hide her feelings. It suggests cold hardness, not the soft warmth of emotion.

4 It suggests she is not able to speak. The word 'melt' suggests liquid, perhaps implying that her words have become tears. The pause of the stanza break reflects her halting words prompting the reader's sympathy.

5 The comparison seems incongruously positive. It suggests the son's perspective: going out into the wide world by himself for the first time.

6 Our sympathy is encouraged for the mother. We are reminded of the image of her son when much younger, e.g. I wanted to... /... play at/being Eskimos like we did when/you were little', 'run my fingers through... your hair'.

Activity 2

A wishbone is forked. The image suggests together the mother and memorial form this shape, implying her affinity with its sentiment, and her wishes for her son: presumably that he does not follow the same fate as the names on the memorial.

Comparison activities

Key points for this activity are provided in **Worksheet 3.27**.

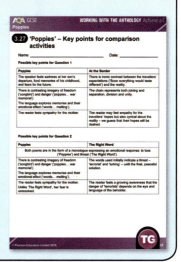

Chapter 3 Conflict

Futility by Wilfred Owen

Assessment Objectives
- **AO1:** respond to texts critically and imaginatively; select and evaluate relevant textual detail to illustrate and support interpretations
- **AO2:** explain how language, structure and form contribute to writers' presentation of ideas, themes and settings

Learning Objectives
- To develop students' responses to the poem
- To relate the Assessment Objectives to the poem

Required resources
- Poem text, available on CD-ROM and video/audio online at http://anthology.aqa.org.uk
- Student Book, page 78
- Worksheets 1.3, 3.28, 3.29

1 Starter

a Write the word 'futile' on the whiteboard. Give students 3 minutes to record their definitions, associations and thoughts on the word.

b Take feedback, recording students' thoughts as a spider diagram.

c Give students a further 2 minutes to write two or three sentences, using the word correctly. Take feedback to share and ensure understanding. Leave the spider diagram on the whiteboard for further reference in Activity 1.

2 Activity 1

a Using the Digital Anthology, listen to/watch/read the poem to the class. Clarify any points of understanding.

b Students complete questions 1–7 independently. Take feedback to share, ensure and develop understanding. Display the poem using the Digital Anthology, annotating the text with students' responses using Wordbox.

c Take students' initial response to the poem, commenting on the presentation of conflict in the poem.

d Referring back to the starter activity, ask: Why did Owen call this poem 'Futility'?

e Ask students to write a sentence or two, summing up the content or meaning of the poem. They can begin: *'Futility' is about....*

Initial responses — ACTIVITY 1
1. Look at line 3. What was the occupation of the dead soldier in peace time?
2. At the end of the first **stanza**, the sun is described as 'kind'. What other words in this stanza suggest that the sun is 'kind'?
3. The other adjective about the sun in that line is 'old'. How is the idea of the sun being 'old' used at the beginning of the second stanza?
4. There are three questions in the second stanza. Why does Owen choose to use questions here, do you think? What does he not understand?
5. The man's sides are 'still warm'. Look for the other references to warmth and cold in the poem, starting with the first line. Jot them down.
6. The sun once 'woke the clays of a cold star' and began life on our planet. What do you think the line beginning 'Was it for this' means? Remember what the **speaker** is looking at.
7. The poem is written in **half-rhyme** rather than full **rhyme**, as in 'seeds/sides': the consonants are the same, but the vowels change. Why do you think Owen has chosen this form for this poem about death? Think about the different sound this makes compared to full rhyme.

3 Activity 2

a Display the poem on the whiteboard, using the Digital Anthology, with the final line highlighted.

b Students discuss the questions in pairs, writing their response in full sentences to ensure clarity of thought and their ability to express it. Take feedback, annotating the displayed quotation using Wordbox and establishing connections to the rest of the poem. Aim to validate all interpretations supported with evidence and/or explanation.

Words/phrases to explore (AO1 and AO2) — ACTIVITY 2
The last line is about breaking sleep.
1. How is this idea used elsewhere in the poem, starting in line 2?
2. How is it a suitable ending for this poem, and what is the speaker saying?

4 GradeStudio

a Read the GradeStudio sample answer to the class. Ask: How has the writer of the sample answer shown 'details used to support a range of comments'?

b How could students add to this response to show 'effective use of details to support interpretation' and so achieve a C? For example: *Owen is questioning whether the sun's efforts were worthwhile if all we do is fight wars and kill each other.*

c Where else in the poem is there an opportunity for students to select details from the poem and explore their significance? For example, the comparison of the farmer's old life, when woken by the sun, with his death.

d Ask students to select a short quotation that will allow them to explore their response to the poem. They then write a paragraph about it using point-evidence-explanation.

GradeStudio Sample answer
To achieve a D on this AO1 descriptor, you need to show **details used to support a range of comments**. The following extract from a sample answer would hit the grade D requirement.

Activity 1, question 2
The sun is very important in the poem. It used to 'rouse' the farmer in the mornings, not roughly but 'gently', and it is benevolent, 'the kind old sun'. It 'wakes the seeds' too, and brought life to 'the clays of a cold star'.

© Pearson Education Limited 2010

5 Comparison activities, page 97

Note: In order to do these activities, students would need to have completed their work on 'The Falling Leaves'.

a In pairs or independently, students complete **Worksheet 3.28**, linking their response to the poems with the relevant Assessment Objective. Take feedback on any areas which students found difficult to grasp or to comment on.

Futility

1. **Comparing ideas and themes**
   Compare the attitudes to death in war in 'Futility' and 'The Falling Leaves'.
2. **Comparing writers' devices**
   Compare the endings of 'Futility' and 'The Falling Leaves' – what effects they have, and how the writers make them work.

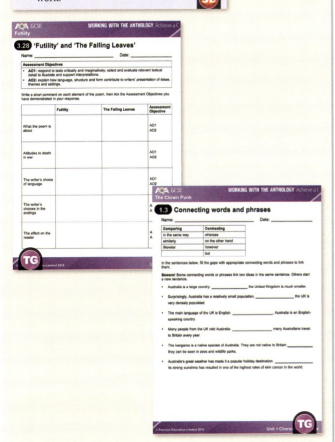

b Students use their notes from **Worksheet 3.28** to write three or four key points comparing the two writer's attitudes to death and the two poems' endings. They should write **in complete sentences using connectives**. Display **Worksheet 1.3** to support them.

c Take feedback, compiling notes on the board. As a class, students find evidence from each poem to support each point.

d Students select three points with supporting evidence from those on the board.

e Students add a sentence or two to each point/piece of evidence, explaining and commenting on how the writers have presented their points of view.

6 Plenary

Take feedback on 'Futility', annotating the poem displayed on the whiteboard using Wordbox. Focus on relevant key features, e.g:
- content
- language
- tone.
- interpretation
- structure

If students have studied and compared 'The Falling Leaves', take feedback on relevant key similarities and differences in content, interpretation, language, structure or tone.

Suggested answers

Activity 1

1. A farmer.
2. 'Gently its touch awoke him… whispering'.
3. It refers to the birth of life on earth as having woken 'the clays of a cold star'.
4. Owen is asking us to question the purpose of life in the face of Man's destruction.
5. Warmth: 'the sun… its touch awoke him'. Cold: 'snow', 'the clays of a cold star'.
6. Was life created only so that it could be destroyed by war? Is this brutality the highest purpose of our existence?
7. While full rhyme can be used to create a sense of finality and conclusion, half-rhyme can disturb and unsettle, in keeping with the bitter and questioning tone of the poem.

Activity 2

1. The poem begins by looking at this farmer/soldier being woken by the sun in peacetime; it then progresses to his death, to the image of the sun waking our planet and our species.
2. The final line links the soldier's sleep with the state in which (Owen suggests) the sun should have left our planet: unwoken.

Comparison activities

Key points for this activity are provided in **Worksheet 3.29**.

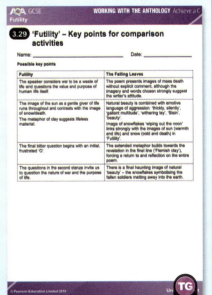

Chapter 3 Conflict

The Charge of the Light Brigade
by Alfred, Lord Tennyson

Assessment Objectives
- **AO1:** respond to texts critically and imaginatively; select and evaluate relevant textual detail to illustrate and support interpretations
- **AO2:** explain how language, structure and form contribute to writers' presentation of ideas, themes and settings

Learning Objectives
- To develop students' responses to the poem
- To relate the Assessment Objectives to the poem

Required resources
- Poem text, available on CD-ROM and video/audio online at http://anthology.aqa.org.uk
- Student Book, page 79
- Worksheets 1.3, 3.30, 3.31, 3.32, 3.33

1 Starter

Display or distribute **Worksheet 3.30**, which shows the nursery rhyme 'The Grand Old Duke of York'. Ask students to perform a class reading of the rhyme while you, or a musical volunteer, beat time. Students need to identify the **syllable** on which each beat falls. Underline those stressed syllables on the displayed worksheet. Why is the rhythm of this rhyme so effective? Look for responses that indicate awareness of the marching rhythm.

2 Activity 1

a Using the Digital Anthology, listen to/watch/read the poem to the class. Clarify any points of understanding.

b Students complete questions 1–7 independently. Take feedback to share, ensure and develop understanding. Display the poem using the Digital Anthology, annotating the text with students' responses using Wordbox.

c Take students' initial response to the poem, commenting on the presentation of conflict in the poem.

d Ask students to write a sentence or two, summing up the content or meaning of the poem. They can begin: *'The Charge of the Light Brigade' is about… .*

Initial responses — ACTIVITY 1
1. What do the cavalrymen do during the course of the charge, and what happens to them? Be as exact as you can.
2. Read the first two lines out loud. How does Tennyson make the feeling of the charge on the horses come alive in these lines? Think about the use of repetition and **rhythm**.
3. All of the first five **stanzas** start with repeated words and phrases except one stanza.
   a Find this stanza.
   b Which line in this stanza suggests that going into battle is a huge mistake?
4. 'Was there a man dismay'd?' suggests the courage of the s…

3 Activity 2

a Display the poem in close-up using the Digital Anthology.

b Students discuss the question in pairs, writing their response in full sentences to ensure clarity of thought and their ability to express it. Take feedback, annotating the displayed poem using Wordbox.

Words/phrases to explore (AO1 and AO2) — ACTIVITY 2
'Some one had blundered'. Although the writer praises the soldiers who charge, what are the effects of the 'blunder' that 'some one' had made? Gather together the details from the poem that show the effects, and write a paragraph showing the effects of the mistake.

4 GradeStudio

a Read the GradeStudio sample answer to the class. Ask: How has the writer of the sample answer shown 'explanation of effect(s) of writer's uses of language and/or form and/or structure and effects on readers'?

b Where else in the poem is there an opportunity for students to explore the effect of the writer's choices? For example, the use of rhythm or the language used to describe the charge.

c Ask students to select a short quotation that will allow them to explore their response to the poem. They then write a paragraph about it, using point-evidence-explanation.

GradeStudio
Sample answer
To achieve a C on this AO2 descriptor, you need to show **explanation of the effect(s) of writers' uses of language and/or structure and/or form.** The following extract from a sample answer would hit the grade C requirement.

The repetition of 'not' at the end of the fourth stanza is very striking, because it's the only time that the writer repeats a word like this, at the end of one line and the beginning of the next. 'Not' emphasises the loss – six hundred did not come back.

5 Comparison activities, page 97

Note: In order to do these activities, students would need to have completed their work on 'Futility' and 'Bayonet Charge'.

1. **a** In pairs or independently, students complete **Worksheet 3.31**, linking their response to the poems with the relevant Assessment Objective. Take feedback on any areas which students found difficult to grasp or to comment on.

> **The Charge of the Light Brigade**
> 1. **Comparing ideas and themes**
>   Compare the attitudes to death in battle in 'The Charge of the Light Brigade' and 'Futility'.
> 2. **Comparing writers' devices**
>   Compare the ways in which battle is shown in 'The Charge of the Light Brigade' and 'Bayonet Charge'.

   b Students use their notes from **Worksheet 3.31** to write three or four key points comparing the two writers' attitudes to death. They should write **in complete sentences using connectives**. Display **Worksheet 1.3** to support them.

   c Take feedback, compiling notes on the board. As a class, students find evidence from each poem to support each point.

   d Students select three points with supporting evidence from those on the board.

   e Students add a sentence or two to each point/piece of evidence, explaining and commenting on how the writers have presented their points of view.

2. Repeat the above sequence using **Worksheet 3.32**, looking at the ways that battle is shown in the two poems.

6 Plenary

Take feedback on 'The Charge of the Light Brigade', annotating the poem displayed on the whiteboard using Wordbox. Focus on relevant key features, e.g:
- content
- language
- tone.
- interpretation
- structure

If students have studied and compared 'Futility' and/or 'Bayonet Charge', take feedback on relevant key similarities and differences in content, interpretation, language, structure or tone.

Suggested answers

Activity 1

1. They charge into battle, surrounded by cannon fire, and, though they fought bravely and broke through the Russian line, many of them were killed.

2. The repetition and rhythm create a sense of pace, reflecting the galloping rhythm of the cavalry horses.

3. **a** The second stanza.
   b 'Someone had blundered': the charge was a fatal error made by the brigade's senior officers.

4. 'Theirs but to do and die', 'Boldly they rode and well', 'They that had fought so well', 'glory'.

5. The repetition in the first three lines emphasises that they face cannon in every direction.

6. The fifth stanza echoes the third stanza with some changes, e.g. cannon are now 'behind' not 'in front' of them; they have come 'through the jaws of Death/Back from the mouth of Hell'.

7. 'glory', 'Honour', 'Noble'.

Activity 2

For example:

'Cannon to right… left… in front of them'. They were surrounded and faced massive firepower.

'Charging an army, while/All the world wondered'. They were vastly outnumbered.

'the jaws of death'. They were riding to almost certain death.

'the wild charge'. Suggests its recklessness.

'All that was left of them'. Suggests many died.

Comparison activities

Key points for this activity are provided in **Worksheet 3.33**.

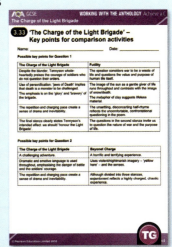

AQA GCSE Working with the Anthology: Achieve a C   103

Chapter 3 Conflict

Bayonet Charge
by Ted Hughes

Assessment Objectives
- **AO1:** respond to texts critically and imaginatively; select and evaluate relevant textual detail to illustrate and support interpretations
- **AO2:** explain how language, structure and form contribute to writers' presentation of ideas, themes and settings

Learning Objectives
- To develop students' responses to the poem
- To relate the Assessment Objectives to the poem

Required resources
- Poem text, available on CD-ROM and video/audio online at http://anthology.aqa.org.uk
- Student Book, page 80
- Worksheets 1.3, 3.34, 3.35

1 Starter

a Write the letters '-ing' on the board. Explain that verbs ending in '-ing' are (usually) present participles and can be used to create a sense of movement.

b Ask students to list ten or fifteen action verbs which they can use to write a short poem using **only** present participles to describe a journey, event or experience. Take feedback to share and ensure understanding.

2 Activity 1

a Using the Digital Anthology, listen to/watch/read the poem to the class. Clarify any points of understanding.

b Students complete questions 1–6 independently. Take feedback to share, ensure and develop understanding. Display the poem using the Digital Anthology, annotating the text with students' responses using Wordbox.

c Take students' initial response to the poem, commenting on the presentation of conflict in the poem.

d Ask students to write a sentence or two, summing up the content or meaning of the poem. They can begin: *'Bayonet Charge' is about... .*

Initial responses — ACTIVITY 1

1. Where is the soldier in the poem, what does he have, and what happens around him?
2. 'Suddenly' sets off the active feeling of the whole poem. Beginning with 'running', find as many words of action in the poem as you can.
3. Hughes uses the senses a lot in this poem – seeing, hearing, smelling, tasting, touching.
   a. Beginning with 'raw', find as many examples as you can of the senses being used.
   b. What overall effect do you think this creates for the reader?
4. A lot of the **imagery** in the poem is violent, such as 'smacking the belly out of the air'. Find some more examples of violent imagery, and think what effect each of them has – more than one effect, if you can.
5. Before the action in the poem began, the soldier had a 'patriotic tear' in his eye. What happened to his feeling of patriotism, do you think? Find evidence from the poem for what you think.
6. a. What is there about the 'yellow hare' which seems nightmarish?
   b. What else in the poem seems to belong to a nightmare?

3 Activity 2

a Display the poem using the Digital Anthology.

b Students discuss the question in pairs, writing their response in full sentences to ensure clarity of thought and their ability to express it. Take feedback, annotating the displayed poem using Wordbox.

Words/phrases to explore (AO1 and AO2) — ACTIVITY 2

How is the soldier's 'terror' made clear? You could write a paragraph beginning with the last line of the poem, 'His terror's touchy dynamite'.

4 GradeStudio

a Read the GradeStudio sample answer to the class. Ask: How has the writer of the sample answer shown 'appropriate comment on ideas/themes' in the poem?

b Where else in the poem is there an opportunity for students to comment on the ideas in the poem? For example, the use of active present participles or the image of the yellow hare in conveying the soldier's terror.

c Ask students to select a short quotation that will allow them to explore their response to the poem. They then write a paragraph about it, using point-evidence-explanation.

GradeStudio
Sample answer
To achieve a C on this AO1 descriptor, you need to show **appropriate comment on ideas/themes**. The following extract from a sample answer would hit the grade C requirement.

> Activity 1, question 5
> In the heat of the action, the soldier has no time for patriotic ideas. The 'patriotic tear' has turned to hot, dangerous metal, 'molten iron', like bullets, and 'King' and 'honour' have no value in the face of abject terror.

5 Comparison activities, page 97

Note: In order to do these activities, students would need to have completed their work on 'The Charge of the Light Brigade'.

a In pairs or independently, students complete **Worksheet 3.34**, linking their response to the poems with the relevant Assessment Objective. Take feedback on any areas which students found difficult to grasp or to comment on.

> **Bayonet Charge**
> 1 **Comparing ideas and themes**
>   Compare the way conflict is presented in 'Bayonet Charge' and 'The Charge of the Light Brigade'.
> 2 **Comparing writers' devices**
>   Compare the presentation of danger in 'Bayonet Charge' and 'The Charge of the Light Brigade'.

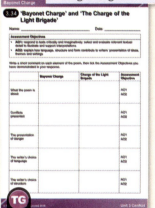
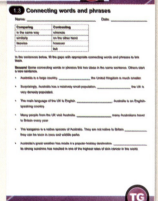

b Students use their notes from **Worksheet 3.34** to write three or four key points comparing the conflicts and the presentation of danger in the poems. They should write **in complete sentences using connectives**. Display **Worksheet 1.3** to support them.

c Take feedback, compiling notes on the board. As a class, students find evidence from each poem to support each point.

d Students select three points with supporting evidence from those on the board.

e Students add a sentence or two to each point/piece of evidence, explaining and commenting on how the writers have presented their points of view.

6 Plenary

Take feedback on 'Bayonet Charge', annotating the poem displayed on the whiteboard using Wordbox. Focus on relevant key features, e.g:
- content
- language
- tone.
- interpretation
- structure

If students have studied and compared 'The Charge of the Light Brigade', take feedback on relevant key similarities and differences in content, interpretation, language, structure or tone.

Suggested answers

Activity 1

1 The soldier is taking part in a bayonet charge across a battlefield. He has a rifle. He is charging through rifle fire and bomb blasts.

2 'running', 'stumbling', 'dazzled', 'smacking', 'lugged', 'sweating', 'stopped', 'pointing', 'running', 'jumped', 'Threw up', 'rolled', 'crawled', 'plunged', 'dropped', 'yelling'.

3 **a**
 - Touch: raw, heavy, numb, cold
 - Sight: dazzled
 - Sound: hearing, listening, footfalls, silent, yelling, crackling.

 b A vivid account of the experience is created.

4
 - 'numb as a smashed arm'
 - 'Sweating like molten iron'
 - 'shot-slashed furrows'
 - 'His terror's touchy dynamite'

The images are consistently linked to the equipment and consequences of war. Each creates an image of pain, destruction, or volatility.

5 The implication is that his patriotism has been blown away by his 'terror's touchy dynamite' – forgotten and lost in fear: 'King, honour… dropped like luxuries in a yelling alarm'.

6 **a** Its sudden, almost surreal, appearance ('threw up'), its movement ('rolled like a flame/And crawled… threshing'), its appearance ('mouth wide/Open silent, its eyes standing out'). It seems to reflect the movement and terror of the soldier.

 b 'Suddenly he awoke and was running' suggests a nightmare. Hughes presents the terror of battle as horrific enough to be unreal, unbelievable: the kind of thing that could only happen in a bad dream.

Activity 2

Several details suggest his fear: 'his sweat heavy', sweating like molten iron'. 'His terror's touchy dynamite' reflects the soldier's experience in the face of this violence. Dynamite is clearly linked to the violence of war; being 'touchy' implies the volatility of his emotions under these circumstances.

Comparison activities

Key points for this activity are provided in **Worksheet 3.35**.

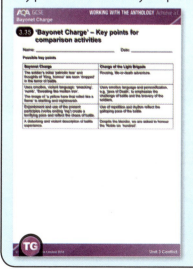

Chapter 3 Conflict

The Falling Leaves by Margaret Postgate Cole

Assessment Objectives
- **AO1:** respond to texts critically and imaginatively; select and evaluate relevant textual detail to illustrate and support interpretations
- **AO2:** explain how language, structure and form contribute to writers' presentation of ideas, themes and settings

Learning Objectives
- To develop students' responses to the poem
- To relate the Assessment Objectives to the poem

Required resources
- Poem text, available on CD-ROM and video/audio online at http://anthology.aqa.org.uk
- Student Book, page 81
- Worksheets 1.3, 3.36, 3.37, 3.38, 3.39

1 Starter

a Display or distribute **Worksheet 3.36**. Remind students of the definition and purpose of simile and metaphor.

b Give students 5 minutes in pairs to think of similes or metaphors. Take feedback to share and ensure understanding. Discuss: Which are most effective/evocative? Why?

2 Activity 1

a Using the Digital Anthology, listen to/watch/read the poem to the class. Clarify any points of understanding. Compare the extended metaphor of the poem to those considered in the starter activity. Is it used effectively here?

b Students complete questions 1–7 independently. Take feedback to share, ensure and develop understanding. Display the poem using the Digital Anthology, annotating the text with students' responses using Wordbox.

c Take students' initial response to the poem, commenting on the presentation of conflict in the poem.

d Ask students to write a sentence or two, summing up the content or meaning of the poem. They can begin: *'The Falling Leaves' is about...*

3 Activity 2

a Display the last four lines of the poem in close-up using the Digital Anthology.

b Students discuss the question in pairs, writing their response in full sentences to ensure clarity of thought and their ability to express it. Take feedback, annotating the displayed quotation using Wordbox. Aim to validate all interpretations supported with evidence from elsewhere in the poem and/or explanation.

Words/phrases to explore (AO1 and AO2) — ACTIVITY 2

The last word of the poem is 'clay', forming a **full rhyme** with 'lay', the only one in the poem. Why does the poet choose to use rhyme here and not elsewhere? Think about the two words that are joined together by the rhyme.

'Clay' means a type of earth. Look at the way the word is used in 'Futility', and it might add something to the meaning of this poem.

4 GradeStudio

a Read the GradeStudio sample answer to the class. Ask: How has the writer of the sample answer shown 'details linked to interpretation'?

b Where else in the poem is there an opportunity for students to explore details which can be linked to interpretation? For example, the image of 'snowflakes wiping out the noon', or the final full rhyme.

c Ask students to select a short quotation that will allow them to explore their response to the poem. They then write a paragraph about it, using point-evidence-explanation.

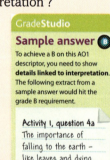

GradeStudio Sample answer B
To achieve a B on this AO1 descriptor, you need to show **details linked to interpretation**. The following extract from a sample answer would hit the grade B requirement.

Activity 1, question 4a
The importance of falling to the earth – like leaves and dying soldiers – is obvious from the title onwards. The leaves are 'dropping' to the earth 'thickly', showing the numbers involved as 'they fell', and 'falling' in the last line completes the circle begun with 'The Falling Leaves'.

5 Comparison activities, page 97

Note: In order to do these activities, students would need to have completed their work on 'Futility' and 'The Charge of the Light Brigade'.

1 a In pairs or independently, students complete **Worksheet 3.37**, linking their response to the poems with the relevant Assessment Objective. Take feedback on any areas which students found difficult to grasp or to comment on.

> **The Falling Leaves**
> 1 **Comparing ideas and themes**
>   Compare the attitudes to death in 'The Falling Leaves' and 'Futility'.
> 2 **Comparing writers' devices**
>   Compare the ways in which the feelings of the poems are created in 'The Falling Leaves' and 'The Charge of the Light Brigade'.

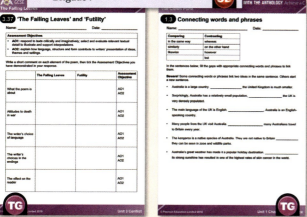

b Students use their notes from **Worksheet 3.37** to write three or four key points comparing the two writers' attitudes to death in war. They should write **in complete sentences using connectives**. Display **Worksheet 1.3** to support them.

c Take feedback, compiling notes on the board. As a class, students find evidence from each poem to support each point.

d Students select three points with supporting evidence from those on the board.

e Students add a sentence or two to each point/piece of evidence, explaining and commenting on how the writers have presented their points of view.

2 Repeat the above sequence using **Worksheet 3.38**, looking at the ways in which the feelings of the two poems are created.

6 Plenary

Take feedback on 'The Falling Leaves', annotating the poem displayed on the whiteboard using Wordbox. Focus on relevant key features, e.g:
- content
- language
- tone.
- interpretation
- structure

If students have studied and compared 'Futility' and/or 'The Charge of the Light Brigade', take feedback on relevant key similarities and differences in content, interpretation, language, structure or tone.

Suggested answers

Activity 1

1 Leaves falling from a tree; soldiers dying.

2 **a** Falling leaves.
  b Leaves die and fall in great quantity in autumn – like soldiers on the WW1 battlefields; snowflakes fall and melt into the ground, again suggesting the soldiers falling and dying in such quantity that the individuals merge and become a mass. Both are images of natural beauty, creating both irony in contrast with the horror of battle, but emphasising the 'beauty' of this 'gallant multitude', now 'Slain'.

3 'brown' immediately suggests the season of autumn, in which the leaves fall and die; it could also be a reference to the soldiers' khaki uniforms.

4 **a** 'thickly' emphasises the quantity of falling leaves and – through the metaphor – of soldiers.
  b The silence creates an eerie, still image of death, adding further to the effect of the 'still afternoon'.

5 'noon' is a metaphor for the soldiers' youth – it was as unnatural for them to die so young as for the daylight to be obscured at noon. The loss of light and warmth suggests the loss of life – and perhaps the effect of war on all humanity.

6 The soldiers who fought in battle. 'multitude' emphasises the numbers involved.

7 To emphasise the beauty of their young lives compared to their 'withering' in death.

Activity 2

The imagery of the poem up to this point is of leaves, snowflakes and wind. Clay forms a harsh, heavy contrast. The rhyme with 'lay' emphasises their death, creating a sense of sonorous finality. Clay suggests the earth from which, according to the Bible, all people came and to which they will return (see 'clays of a cold star' in 'Futility').

Comparison activities

Key points for this activity are provided in **Worksheet 3.39**.

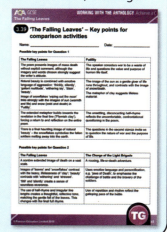

Chapter 3 Conflict

Come On, Come Back
by Stevie Smith

Learning Objectives
- To develop students' responses to the poem
- To relate the Assessment Objectives to the poem

Assessment Objectives
- **AO1:** respond to texts critically and imaginatively; select and evaluate relevant textual detail to illustrate and support interpretations
- **AO2:** explain how language, structure and form contribute to writers' presentation of ideas, themes and settings

Required resources
- Poem text, available on CD-ROM and video/audio online at http://anthology.aqa.org.uk
- Student Book, page 82
- Worksheets 1.3, 3.40, 3.41, 3.42, 3.43

1 Starter
Read the poem aloud to the class. Ask students to produce a storyboard, either showing in pictures or describing in words, a series of images to accompany and support a reading of the poem. Each frame in the storyboard should be captioned with a short, apt quotation from the poem. A storyboard frame is available on **Worksheet 3.40**.

2 Activity 1
a Using the Digital Anthology, listen to/watch/read the poem to the class again. Clarify any points of understanding.
b Students complete questions 1–7 independently. Take feedback to share, ensure and develop understanding. Display the poem using the Digital Anthology, annotating the text with students' responses using Wordbox.
c Take students' initial response to the poem, commenting on the presentation of conflict in the poem.
d Ask students to write a sentence or two, summing up the content or meaning of the poem. They can begin: *'Come On, Come Back' is about… .*

Initial responses — ACTIVITY 1
1 What has happened to Vaudevue, and what does she do?
2 Vaudevue's mind has been affected. How is this made clear in the first **stanza**? Think about what she is doing?
3 The reader is told at the beginning that this is 'an incident in a future war'. How does the writer suggest that this is happening in the future at the beginning of the second stanza?
4 The movement of the poem is quite uneven in the first three stanzas, but the two lines beginning 'The sand beneath' have a much livelier sound. Say them aloud to hear this.
    a What makes them lively and even? Think about **rhythm** and **rhyme**, and how it is different from what has gone before.
    b Why has Vaudevue now got a sense of purpose?
5 The pace is still quick at the beginning of the next stanza. Look at the first two lines, and decide how the writer makes this happen. Try to think of more than one thing.
6 The lake is described as 'adorable'. See if you can find other examples of Vaudevue loving the water. Why do you think she is attracted to it?
7 Look at the last stanza. What has happened to Vaudevue?

3 Activity 2
a Display the poem using the Digital Anthology.
b Students discuss the question in pairs, writing their response in full sentences to ensure clarity of thought and their ability to express it. Take feedback, annotating the displayed poem using Wordbox. Aim to validate all interpretations supported with evidence and/or explanation.

4 GradeStudio
a Read the GradeStudio sample answer to the class. Ask: How has the writer of this answer shown an 'awareness of writer making choice(s) of language and/or structure and/or form' in the poem?
b How could students add to the sample answer to show 'structured comment' on the writer's choices and so achieve a D? For example: *She is getting ready to dive into the lake and these three verbs show how quickly she is doing it.*
c How could students further develop the sample answer to show 'sustained focus' on the writer's choices and so achieve a C? For example: *This pattern of three verbs suggests sudden movement after stillness, suggesting that she has suddenly realised what she must do.*
d Where else in the poem is there an opportunity for students to explore the writer's choice of language or structure? For example, the image of the 'ribbon of white moonlight' or the change of tone/pace as Vaudevue prepares to dive into the lake.
e Ask students to select a short quotation that will allow them to explore their response to the poem. They then write a paragraph about it, using point-evidence-explanation.

5 Comparison activities, page 97

Note: In order to do these activities, students would need to have completed their work on 'Out of the Blue' and 'Bayonet Charge'.

1 a In pairs or independently, students complete **Worksheet 3.41**, linking their response to the poems with the relevant Assessment Objective. Take feedback on any areas which students found difficult to grasp or to comment on.

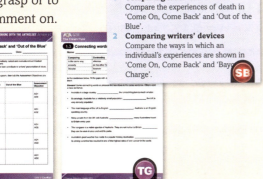

b Students use their notes from **Worksheet 3.41** to write three or four key points comparing the experiences of death in the poems. They should write **in complete sentences using connectives**. Display **Worksheet 1.3** to support them.

c Take feedback, compiling notes on the board. As a class, students find evidence from each poem to support each point.

d Students select three points with supporting evidence from those on the board.

e Students add a sentence or two to each point/ piece of evidence, explaining and commenting on how the writers have presented their points of view.

2 Repeat the above sequence using **Worksheet 3.42**, looking at the presentation of individuals' experiences in the two poems.

6 Plenary

Take feedback on 'Come On, Come Back', annotating the poem displayed on the whiteboard using Wordbox. Focus on relevant key features, e.g:
- content
- language
- tone
- interpretation
- structure

If students have studied and compared 'Out of the Blue' and/or 'Bayonet Charge', take feedback on relevant key similarities and differences in content, interpretation, language, structure or tone.

Suggested answers

Activity 1

1 Left behind after the battle of Austerlitz, she sits alone. Her memory is gone. She dives into an icy lake and drowns.

2 The image of the girl soldier, left behind on the battlefield while her 'fingers tap the ground' suggests some kind of mental disorientation.

3 In addition to the subtitle, the reference to 'M L 5', the 'first/Of all human exterminators' suggests some kind of mechanised soldier, reminiscent of science-fiction writing.

4 **a/b** In contrast to the jagged irregularity and imagery of the first 15 lines, this couplet combines simple sentence structure and enjambment to produce a sudden rhythmic rise in pace, further enhanced by the repetition of 'and', and the conclusive rhyme of 'feet' and 'beat'. Her sense of purpose is sparked by the sight of the lake.

5 Following the initial 'Quickly', the rhythm of the verse reflects her pace through longer line and sentence length, and repeated used of patterns of three, e.g. 'as a child, an idiot, as one without memory' and 'strips, stands and lunges'.

6 The 'ribbon of white moonlight' suggests a kind of path through the water's 'black' darkness which seems to reflect the mental darkness from which she is suffering.

7 She has drowned.

Activity 2

Either response is arguable, depending on interpretation. The death of Vaudevue's memory 'for evermore', caused by 'M L 5', has reduced her to a creature of instinct, drawn towards the lake in which she swims until an 'undercurrent' seizes her and 'the waters… close above her head'. Perhaps this is a welcome release from her mental state.

In the context of the final line, the poem's title becomes a song title, perhaps reminiscent of well known World War One songs – 'It's a Long Way to Tipperary' or 'Pack Up Your Troubles'. The song is Vaudevue's favourite and also the favourite of 'all the troops of all the armies'. Perhaps the song (and poem) title is not addressed to Vaudevue herself, but to her memory.

Comparison activities

Key points for this activity are provided in **Worksheet 3.43**.

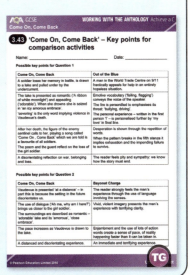

AQA GCSE Working with the Anthology: Achieve a C 109

Chapter 3 Conflict

next to of course god america
by e. e. cummings

Assessment Objectives
- **AO1:** respond to texts critically and imaginatively; select and evaluate relevant textual detail to illustrate and support interpretations
- **AO2:** explain how language, structure and form contribute to writers' presentation of ideas, themes and settings

Learning Objectives
- To develop students' responses to the poem
- To relate the Assessment Objectives to the poem

Required resources
- Poem text, available on CD-ROM and video/audio online at http://anthology.aqa.org.uk
- Student Book, page 83
- Worksheets 1.3, 3.44, 3.45, 3.46, 3.47, 3.48, 3.49

1 Starter

a Display or distribute **Worksheet 3.44**. Alternatively, using Wordbox on the Digital Anthology, export the poem text to 'Choptalk'. Explain to students that this is a poem, cut up into bits.

b Give students 5–10 minutes to try to put the poem back together again. Take feedback. What difficulties did they encounter?

2 Activity 1

a Using the Digital Anthology, listen to/watch/read the poem to the class. Clarify any points of understanding. How does it compare to students' versions, compiled in the starter activity?

b A quick look at, and discussion of, Cummings' poem 'A politician is an arse upon' will help students identify the poet's attitude to politicians. The poem is provided on **Worksheet 3.45**.

c Display the lyrics of two Patriotic American songs on **Worksheet 3.46**, to support students' work on questions 1–6. Take feedback.

d Take students' initial response to the poem, commenting on its presentation of conflict.

e Ask students to write two sentences, summing up the content or meaning of the poem. They can begin: 'next to of course god america' is about…

3 Activity 2

a Display the last line of the poem in close-up using the Digital Anthology.

b Students discuss the questions in pairs, writing their response in full sentences to ensure clarity of thought and their ability to express it. Take feedback, annotating the displayed quotation using Wordbox. Aim to validate all interpretations supported with evidence from elsewhere in the poem and/or explanation.

4 GradeStudio

a Read the GradeStudio sample answer to the class. Ask: How has the writer of this answer shown 'identification of effects of writer's choice(s) of language and/or structure and/or form intended/achieved'?

b How could students further develop the sample answer to achieve a C? For example: *It suggests that the speaker does not mean what he is saying, he is just using these words to sound patriotic.*

c Where else in the poem is there an opportunity for students to explore the poet's choices of language and structure? For example, the contrast of rhetorical and colloquial language, or the final line.

d Ask students to select a short quotation that will allow them to explore their response to the poem. They then write a paragraph about it, using point-evidence-explanation.

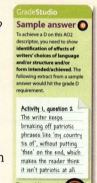

5 Comparison activities, page 97

Note: In order to do these activities, students would need to have completed their work on 'The Charge of the Light Brigade' and 'Flag'.

1 a In pairs or independently, students complete **Worksheet 3.47**, linking their response to the poems with the relevant Assessment Objective. Take feedback on any areas which students found difficult to grasp or to comment on.

> **next to of course god america**
> 1. **Comparing ideas and themes**
>   Compare the attitudes to death in 'next to of course god america' and 'The Charge of the Light Brigade'.
> 2. **Comparing writers' devices**
>   Compare the ways in which the writers attack the idea of patriotism in 'next to of course god america' and 'Flag'.

b Students use their notes from **Worksheet 3.47** to write three or four key points comparing the attitudes to death in the two poems. They should write **in complete sentences using connectives**. Display **Worksheet 1.3** to support them.

c Take feedback, compiling notes on the board. As a class, students find evidence from each poem to support each point.

d Students select three points with supporting evidence from those on the board.

e Students add a sentence or two to each point/piece of evidence, explaining and commenting on how the writers have presented their points of view.

2 Repeat the above sequence using **Worksheet 3.48**, looking at the ways the writers attack patriotism in the two poems.

6 Plenary

Take feedback on 'next to of course god america', annotating the poem displayed on the whiteboard using Wordbox. Focus on relevant key features, e.g:
- content
- language
- tone.
- interpretation
- structure

If students have studied and compared 'The Charge of the Light Brigade' and/or 'Flag', take feedback on relevant key similarities and differences in content, interpretation, language, structure or tone.

Suggested answers

Activity 1

1. Almost every line runs into the next – and, in a poem which makes little sense, we are constantly encouraged to move on to find meaning. In one case, a word is split between two lines, exaggerating this effect still further. Between the two sets of speech marks, there is no other punctuation. Again, this encourages movement to find meaning.

2. It further weakens any sense of conviction in his speech – see also 'etcetera' in 'Bayonet Charge'.

3. It suggests a blasé attitude.

4. There is a clear contrast between the highly rhetorical, almost biblical tone of 'thy sons…' and the American idioms 'by jingo' and 'by gee'.

5. 'Slaughter' is an emotive, negative choice in this description of war, undermining the Tennyson-like fervour of the previous two lines. It is in stark contrast to the (again, Tennyson-esque) imagery of the previous two lines: 'heroic happy dead who rushed like lions'. 'Roaring' is linked to lions which, in conjunction with 'slaughter', creates a negative, chaotic and brutal image of war.

6. Based on the subsequent description of the 'roaring slaughter', we can assume that the dead died neither heroically nor happily. Yes, it seems the 'voice of liberty' is mute, despite the patriotic soundbites of this speech. These soldiers have been sent to their death without stopping to think, while those who sent them regard it as 'beautiful'.

Activity 2

1. It emphasises that the speech does not give the views of the poet: that this is, for the most part, a reported speech.

2. The writer seems to be mocking the speaker.

3. The pace and content of these patriotic soundbites suggests the poet thinks such speeches are hollow and meaningless, delivered hurriedly to avoid closer investigation.

Comparison activities

Key points for this activity are provided in **Worksheet 3.49**.

AQA GCSE Working with the Anthology: Achieve a C   111

Chapter 3 Conflict

Hawk Roosting by Ted Hughes

Assessment Objectives
- **AO1:** respond to texts critically and imaginatively; select and evaluate relevant textual detail to illustrate and support interpretations
- **AO2:** explain how language, structure and form contribute to writers' presentation of ideas, themes and settings

Learning Objectives
- To develop students' responses to the poem
- To relate the Assessment Objectives to the poem

Required resources
- Poem text, available on CD-ROM and video/audio online at http://anthology.aqa.org.uk
- Student Book, page 84
- Worksheets 1.3, 3.50, 3.51, 3.52

1 Starter

a Write the word 'elephant' on the whiteboard. Ask students to imagine elephants as talking, thinking, feeling characters, e.g.
- the kinds of things they might talk about
- the way they see themselves
- two or three words to describe their personalities.

For example: constantly talks about childhood memories and the good old days; thinks he's enormously clever; loud and self-opinionated.

b Now get the students thinking about the hawk: How would a hawk talk, think, feel? Take feedback: what qualities might students expect the hawk to have?

2 Activity 1

a Using the Digital Anthology, listen to/watch/read the poem to the class. Clarify any points of understanding.

b Students complete questions 1–8 independently. Take feedback to share, ensure and develop understanding. Display the poem using the Digital Anthology, annotating the text with students' responses using Wordbox.

c Take students' initial response to the poem, commenting on the presentation of conflict in the poem.

d Ask students to write a sentence or two, summing up the content or meaning of the poem. They can begin: '*Hawk Roosting*' is about... .

3 Activity 2

a Display this line in close-up using the Digital Anthology.

b Students discuss the question in pairs, writing their response in full sentences to ensure clarity of thought and their ability to express it. Take feedback, annotating the displayed quotation using Wordbox. Aim to validate all interpretations supported with evidence from elsewhere in the poem and/or explanation.

Words/phrases to explore (AO1) — ACTIVITY 2
'Now I hold Creation in my foot'. How exactly is it true that he controls Creation? Think of as many reasons as you can, and write a paragraph about the hawk's control, beginning with this sentence from the poem.

4 GradeStudio

a Read the GradeStudio sample answer to the class. Ask: How has the writer of this answer shown a 'sustained response to element(s) of text'?

b Where else in the poem is there an opportunity for students to explore the poet's choices? For example, the use of the first person or references to power.

c Ask students to select a short quotation that will allow them to explore their response to the poem. They then write a paragraph about it, using point-evidence-explanation.

GradeStudio Sample answer
To achieve a C on this AO1 descriptor, you need to show a **sustained response to element(s) of text**. The following extract from a sample answer would hit the grade C requirement.

Activity 1, question 4
The hawk seems like a dictator as he sits in 'the top of the wood'. Everything seems to be working for him – the 'high trees', the air and the sun. Like a dictator, everything is below him, 'for my inspection'. 'No arguments assert my right' shows that he feels he can do anything without having to justify it.

5 Comparison activities, page 97

Note: In order to do these activities, students would need to have completed their work on 'Bayonet Charge' and 'The Falling Leaves'.

1 a In pairs or independently, students complete **Worksheet 3.50**, linking their response to the poems with the relevant Assessment Objective. Take feedback on any areas which students found difficult to grasp or to comment on.

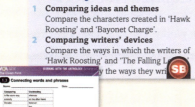

b Students use their notes from **Worksheet 3.50** to write three or four key points comparing the characters created in the two poems. They should write **in complete sentences using connectives**. Display **Worksheet 1.3** to support them.

c Take feedback, compiling notes on the board. As a class, students find evidence from each poem to support each point.

d Students select three points with supporting evidence from those on the board.

e Students add a sentence or two to each point/piece of evidence, explaining and commenting on how the writers have presented their points of view.

2 Repeat the above sequence, using **Worksheet 3.51** and looking at the way death is presented in the two poems.

6 Plenary

Take feedback on 'Hawk Roosting', annotating the poem displayed on the whiteboard using Wordbox. Focus on relevant key features, e.g:

- content
- language
- tone.
- interpretation
- structure

If students have studied and compared 'Bayonet Charge' and/or 'The Falling Leaves', take feedback on relevant key similarities and differences in content, interpretation, language, structure or tone.

Suggested answers

Activity 1

1 He can sit in high trees surveying the land around him; he has hooked feet and a beak with which to kill; he has no qualms ('manners') about killing.

2 **a** (line 1) 'I sit', 'my eyes closed'; (line 3) 'my hooked head'; (line 7) 'Are of advantage to me'; (line 8) 'my inspection'; (line 9) 'My feet'; (line 11) 'my foot, my each feather'; (line 12) 'my foot'; (line 14) 'I kill where I please', 'it is all mine'; (line 15) 'my body'; (line 16) 'My manners'; (line 18) 'my flight'; (line 20) 'my right'; (line 21) 'behind me'; (line 22) 'since I began'; (line 23) 'My eye'; (line 24) 'I am going to…'.

b The hawk seems to be a very egocentric character.

3 'rehearse perfect kills and eat', 'the earth's face upward for my inspection', 'I hold Creation in my foot', 'I kill where I please because it is all mine', 'The allotment of death', 'No arguments assert my right', 'My eye has permitted no change./I am going to keep things like this.'

4 The egocentrism, delight in power and killing suggest a psychopath, perhaps.

5 It seems that the earth has been made to suit him perfectly: the trees are tall, the sun shines, the air is buoyant, and the earth faces upward. Everything is suited to his hunting.

6 The word 'locked' implies strength and security. The internal alliteration of lo<u>ck</u>ed and bar<u>k</u>, and the use of monosyllables, suggests the hard, blunt strength of the hawk.

7 His right (to allot death) is not taken or given, it is not for discussion. The following stanza suggests that the sun being behind him is what asserts his right: his ability to exploit nature is what gives him power.

8 A series of hard, blunt statements of power, of control. The end-stopped lines add to the tone of control and power, and of absolute surety of that power.

Activity 2

The initial implication is that all the power of creation which went into creating his foot is contained within that foot; it further suggests an image of another creature caught and killed in the hawk's claws; and perhaps resembles a stereotypical villain's claim that 'your life is in my hands'.

Comparison activities

Key points for this activity are provided in **Worksheet 3.52**.

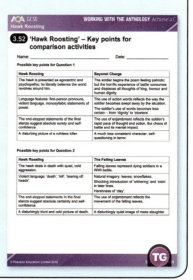

Chapter 3 Conflict

Looking at the poems individually: what have you learned?

Assessment Objectives
- **AO1:** respond to texts critically and imaginatively; select and evaluate relevant textual detail to illustrate and support interpretations
- **AO2:** explain how language, structure and form contribute to writers' presentation of ideas, themes and settings

Learning Objectives
- To recap and explore students' responses to the poems

Required resources
- Student Book, page 85
- Worksheet 3.53, ideally enlarged to A3 size

1 Starter

Looking at the poems individually: what have you learned?

a Explain to students that this lesson will consolidate, recap and explore their knowledge and understanding of, and response to, the 15 poems they have explored.

b Give students 3 minutes to complete the following task in silence:
Without looking at their Anthology or any notes, how many of the poems can they remember from those they have explored over the last 15 lessons? They can either note down the titles (and poets, if possible) or give a brief description of the poem's content: *The one about…* .

c List the 15 poems aloud so students can check their answers. Ask students to add titles to the poems where the content but not the title had been remembered.

d Take feedback. How many poems could students remember? Based on the class's response as a whole, were some more memorable than others? Why?

The poems

Flag *John Agard*	**At the Border** *Choman Hardi*	**Bayonet Charge** *Ted Hughes*
Out of the Blue (extract) *Simon Armitage*	**Belfast Confetti** *Ciaran Carson*	**The Falling Leaves** *Margaret Postgate Cole*
Mametz Wood *Owen Sheers*	**Poppies** *Jane Weir*	**Come On, Come Back** *Stevie Smith*
The Yellow Palm *Robert Minhinnick*	**Futility** *Wilfred Owen*	**next to of course god america** *e. e. cummings*
The Right Word *Imtiaz Dharker*	**The Charge of the Light Brigade** *Alfred, Lord Tennyson*	**Hawk Roosting** *Ted Hughes*

2 Activity 1

a Explain that Question 1 of the activity will consolidate students' thinking from the starter activity.

b Read Question 1 aloud, then ask students to choose the **five** poems which they responded to most strongly – it is likely that these will be the first five they listed in the Starter. Ask them to add a sentence explaining why they found this poem memorable: it may be an activity, a word, a line, an idea, a character, or a title which has sparked their engagement. Ask volunteers to share with the class.

c Read Question 2. Ask students: Are your answers to this question likely to feature the same poems as Question 1? Why?

d Give students 5 minutes to list the **five** poems they found it easiest to offer an interpretation about, using their notes from the last 15 lessons. Take feedback to ensure understanding. Ask: Is it easier to talk and write about poems that are simpler to understand? Or is there more to be said (and more marks to be gained!) by exploring a variety of different interpretations of more complex poems?

Assessment Objective 1 (AO1) — ACTIVITY 1

1 Which of these poems did you **respond** to most strongly? You may have liked it, or disliked it, or found it the most interesting, or horrible. You may have a number of things to say about it.

Working with a partner, or by yourself, display your responses as a spider diagram, and then compare it with someone else's, to see if you have responded to the poems in similar ways.

2 Which poems did you find it easiest to offer an **interpretation** about? In other words, you had an opinion about a poem's meaning that you could argue from the text and **select detail** to support your opinion. For instance, you might have found it easy to argue and support the idea that 'The Charge of the Light Brigade' is a poem about bravery.

Suggesting more than one interpretation of a poem, or parts of a poem, gives you opportunities to score more marks. For instance, you could respond to the final stanza of 'The Yellow Palm' as either a life-giving moment or a moment of destruction.

3 Activity 2

Give students 20 minutes to complete both questions 1 and 2 of the activity. Students can record their responses on **Worksheet 3.53**. Point out that if they cannot think of anything significant in a particular area within, say, 30 seconds, then it does not suggest a ready understanding; they should move on to a new feature or poem. Take feedback to ensure and develop understanding.

Assessment Objective 2 (AO2) — ACTIVITY 2

1 Which features of **language**, **structure** or **form** did you understand best? The most promising ones to write about in the exam will be the ones where you have most to say. For instance, you might have found several things to say about:
- the effect of the repetitions of words in 'Flag' (**language**)
- the effects of language and stanza at the end of 'The Right Word' (**structure**)
- the effects of the rhymes in 'The Charge of the Light Brigade' (**form**).

2 What **ideas** did you pick out in the poems? Again, the best answers will probably identify more than one in a poem, or several aspects of one idea. For instance, you might have identified or explored more than one idea about war in 'The Charge of the Light Brigade'.

4 Plenary

Ask students:
- Based on your exploration of content, interpretation, language, structure, form and ideas, which are the most memorable, exam-friendly poems in the 'Conflict' cluster? Do they have any significant links or points of comparison?
- Which poems are particularly difficult to write about?
- Which poems do you feel you need to give more (of your own) time to?

5 Further work

a Students identify the **five** poems which have the fewest entries on **Worksheet 3.53**.

b Students complete each column for each poem, using **Worksheet 3.53** and their notes.

AQA GCSE — WORKING WITH THE ANTHOLOGY Achieve a C
Looking at the poems individually: what have you learned?

3.53 What have you learned?

Name: _____ Date: _____

Title	Language	Structure	Form	Ideas
Flag – John Agard				
Out of the Blue – Simon Armitage				
Mametz Wood – Owen Sheers				
The Yellow Palm – Robert Minhinnick				
The Right Word – Imtiaz Dharker				
At the Border – Choman Hardi				
Belfast Confetti – Ciaran Carson				
Poppies – Jane Weir				
Futility – Wilfred Owen				
The Charge of the Light Brigade – Alfred, Lord Tennyson				
Bayonet Charge – Ted Hughes				
The Falling Leaves – Margaret Postgate Cole				
Come On, Come Back – Stevie Smith				
next to of course god america – e.e. cummings				
Hawk Roosting – Ted Hughes				

Unit 3 Conflict

Chapter 3 Conflict

Comparing the 'Conflict' poems (1)

Assessment Objectives
- **AO3:** make comparisons and explain links between texts, evaluating writers' different ways of expressing meaning and achieving effects

Required resources
- Poem texts, available on CD-ROM and video/audio online at http://anthology.aqa.org.uk
- Student Book, page 86
- Worksheet 3.54

Learning Objectives
- To develop students' abilities to compare the poems
- To relate the Assessment Objectives to the poems
- To develop students' writing skills for the exam

1 Starter

a Read the explanation of the Assessment Objective on page 86 of the Student Book, clarifying understanding of the Assessment Objective's demands.
b Explain to students that in this lesson they are going to compare 'The Falling Leaves' and 'Futility'.
c Display both poems on the whiteboard, side by side, using the Digital Anthology. Re-read the poems.
d Ask students to describe the content of each poem, providing evidence where appropriate. Draw the events in the poem on the board as they are described, annotating with quotations. Depending on your artistic skills, you may want to ask a volunteer student to take this role!

Assessment Objective:

The Assessment Objective you will be focusing on in this part of the chapter is:

 make comparisons and explain links between texts, evaluating writers' different ways of expressing meaning and achieving effects.

2 Activity 1

a Using **Worksheet 3.54**, students record all the similarities and differences they can think of in the two poems in the first column on the worksheet. The second column is for their responses to Activity 2.
b Take feedback, ideally compiling students' responses on a copy of the worksheet projected onto the whiteboard.

ACTIVITY 1

Think about the ideas and themes in the two poems.
List as many similarities and differences as you can. For example:
- Both poems are about the deaths of soldiers in war. Are the attitudes to death similar, or different?
- Both poems use nature a lot. What differences are there in the ways nature is used in each?

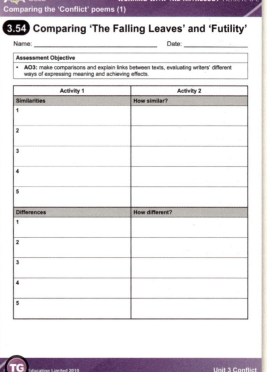

3 Activity 2

Explain that this is an opportunity for students to develop their points of comparison, using **Worksheet 3.54**. Read and discuss the examples in the Student Book and, using this as a model, explore one other example from the class' responses on the whiteboard. Remind students of the need for evidence to support each point. Give students 5 minutes working in pairs to identify another similarity or difference and explore how similar or different it is.

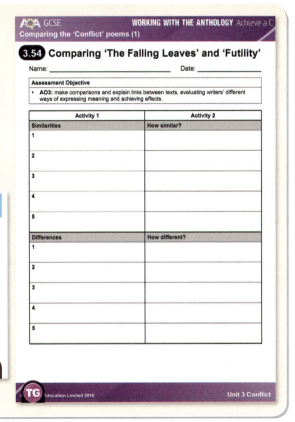

ACTIVITY 2

Using your list of similarities and differences from Activity 1, decide how different each of the poems are for each point you made.

For example, both of these poems are mourning the deaths of soldiers, but there are some differences in the ways the **speakers** seem to feel about the deaths. Think which words you would use to describe how they feel, and then find the words in the poems to support what you think. You could choose some of these words, for instance, and decide whether they apply to either of the poems, or to both of them: sad, angry, resigned, despairing, thoughtful.

4 Plenary

a Take feedback from Activity 2, compiling notes on the whiteboard.

b Which do students feel are the most valid or useful comparisons which will allow them to fully explore the language, structure, tone, etc of the two poems? Use this discussion to develop students' awareness of the level at which the two poems can be compared.

Suggested answers

Activities 1/2
Similarities:
- Both poems are about death in war.
- Both poems speak negatively of death in war.
- Both poems use natural imagery.

Differences:
- 'Futility' focuses on the death of one soldier, representing all humanity; 'Falling Leaves' reflects on the vast numbers of death in war.
- The tone of 'Futility' is much more bitter.
- 'Falling Leaves' indirectly questions the loss of life; 'Futility' directly questions the very purpose of life.

Chapter 3 Conflict

Comparing the 'Conflict' poems (2)

Assessment Objective
- **AO3:** make comparisons and explain links between texts, evaluating writers' different ways of expressing meaning and achieving effects

Learning Objectives
- To develop students' abilities to compare the poems
- To relate the Assessment Objectives to the poem
- To develop students' writing skills for the exam

Required resources
- Poem texts, available on CD-ROM and video/audio online at http://anthology.aqa.org.uk
- Student Book, pages 86–89, 142–143

1 Starter

a Recap the comparison process from the previous lesson.

b Read the explanation of the Assessment Objective on page 86 of the Student Book, clarifying understanding of the Assessment Objective's demands.

c Explain to students that in this lesson, they are going to continue to compare 'The Falling Leaves' and 'Futility', then use this process to develop their comparison skills further.

d Display both poems on the whiteboard, side by side, using the Digital Anthology. Re-read the poems.

2 Comparing writer's methods

a Discuss the bullet pointed questions as a whole class.

b Give students 2 minutes in between each question to note their own, independent response to the questions.

c Take feedback to ensure understanding and accurate expression of it.

3 GradeStudio

a Read the GradeStudio E grade extract on page 86 to the class. Ask: How has the writer of the sample answer made a 'supported response to the text'?

b Read the GradeStudio D extract on page 87 to the class. How do the additional sentences give 'structured comments on similarities/differences, with detail'?

c Looking at the grade descriptors on pages 142–143 of the Student Book, what would students have to do to raise this D to a C?

d Give students 5 minutes to add a sentence or two – or rewrite those in the exemplar – in order to show 'sustained focus on similarities and differences' and achieve a C.

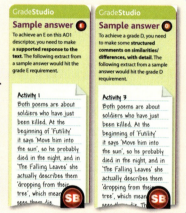

4 Activity 3

a Read the activity instructions, discussing each bullet point as a class.

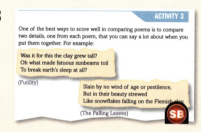

b Give students 5 minutes to note their own thoughts on the four bullet points.

c Take feedback to ensure and develop understanding.

d Give students 10 minutes to write a paragraph comparing these two details.

e Remind students of their recent work on the GradeStudio extracts. Students swap paragraphs with a partner. Using the grade descriptors on pages 142–143, what grade would they award their partner's paragraph? How would they suggest it could be improved to achieve a higher grade?

5 Activity 4

a The students now move on to compare 'Bayonet Charge' and 'Charge of the Light Brigade'. Display both poems on the whiteboard, side by side, using Wordbox. Re-read the poems.

118 © Pearson Education Limited 2010

b What initial points of comparison, similarities and differences, can students suggest?

c Students work independently, recording their response to questions 1–4, one at a time. Encourage students to record as wide a range of responses as possible. Leave the final writing task of question 4 until after considering the GradeStudio exemplars.

d Take feedback after each question, discussing and developing a whole class response, then giving students a minute or two to add to their written response.

6 GradeStudio

a Read the GradeStudio exemplars on page 89 of the Student Book. Ask students to identify how the C has identified and explored similarities and differences.

b Ask students to identify which elements of the paragraph show 'sustained focus on similarities/differences, with detail', i.e. are key in achieving a C. Which are 'structured comments on similarities/differences, with detail', i.e. without the C elements and so achieving a D?

c Ask students to look at the B exemplar. How has this writer further developed the comparison by making a 'developed comparison of writers' uses of language and/or structure and/or form and/or structure and effects on readers, with detail'?

d Return to the final instruction of Activity 4, Question 4: give students 10 minutes to write a point-evidence-explanation paragraph comparing the two details from the poem.

7 Plenary

a Students swap their written response to Activity 4 with a partner and, using the grade descriptors on pages 142–143 of the Student Book, decide what grade their partner's response should be awarded.

b Working together, students identify one way in which they could improve or add to their writing to aim for the next grade up.

c Take feedback, summarising those key areas which students have identified as targets to achieve in order to raise their grade.

Suggested answers

Activity 3

The Falling Leaves	Futility
Cole regrets the loss of life and beauty. She seems to see their beauty even in their death, comparing them to an image of strewn snowflakes.	Owen questions the purpose of life if all we do is destroy it. His rhetorical questions invite a response from the reader, engaging them in his argument.
E.g. 'beauty'	E.g. 'fatuous'
'clay' refers to the ground on which these bodies have fallen. Here 'clay' is descriptive as well as reminding us of the ground in which these bodies will be buried.	'clay' refers to the earth from which life rose and was created. Here 'clay' suggests the life of all humanity.
Irregular line length creates a reflective tone.	The exclamatory 'O' and the rhetorical questions create an aggressive, embittered tone.

Activity 4

1
- Both are about a military charge and use emotive language to reflect their perceived experience of battle.
- In 'The Charge of the Light Brigade', honour is regarded as something earned in unthinking bravery; in 'Bayonet Charge', honour is meaningless, something forgotten in the terror of battle.

2
- 'Bayonet Charge' uses a range of active verbs suggesting chaotic movement, e.g. 'running… stumbling…'. 'The Charge of the Light Brigade' in its rhythm and language – 'charged… stormed' – suggests a bolder and more determined pace.
- 'Bayonet Charge' is, perhaps, a much more realistic and personal depiction of terror in battle: compare the euphemistic personification of 'into the jaws of Death' with the graphically sensory detail of 'Bullets smacking the belly out of the air'.

3
- 'The Charge of the Light Brigade' uses rhythm and repetition to convey pace; 'Bayonet Charge' uses enjambment to convey chaos.
- In 'Bayonet Charge', the absence of rhyme creates uncertainty and inconclusiveness, reflected in the dense, alliterative final violent image; Tennyson's use of rhyme – and meaning – is much more ordered, delivered in emphatic end-stopped exclamations.
- In 'Bayonet Charge', we are left with the noise and colour of battle and its effect on the soldier's mental condition; 'The Charge of the Light Brigade' emphasises how 'noble' these soldiers are, and orders us to 'honour' them.

4
- 'sabres' in the plural suggests a formidable and glamorous weapon. The single 'rifle' seems useless in, and overwhelmed by, the horror of battle.
- The visual description suggests the power of the sabre as it 'flashes'. The description in 'Bayonet Charge' emphasises its weight, as though a burden.
- 'turned' suggests the active danger these sabres present to the enemy. 'lugged' and 'smashed' emphasise the weight and uselessness of the rifle.
- Tennyson presents a much more romantic, adventurous attitude to war.

Chapter 3 Conflict

Writing in the exam

Assessment Objectives
- **AO1:** respond to texts critically and imaginatively; select and evaluate relevant textual detail to illustrate and support interpretations
- **AO2:** explain how language, structure and form contribute to writers' presentation of ideas, themes and settings
- **AO3:** make comparisons and explain links between texts, evaluating writers' different ways of expressing meaning and achieving effects

Learning Objectives
- To develop students' ability to structure a successful exam response

Required resources
- Poem text, available on CD-ROM and video/audio online at http://anthology.aqa.org.uk
- Student Book, pages 90–95, 142–143
- Worksheets 1.51, 3.55

1 Starter

a Write the word 'planning' on the board. Ask: What are the advantages and disadvantages of using the first 5 minutes of exam time to plan a written response? Give students 2 minutes to record their thoughts.

b Take feedback. Aim to refute the argument that planning takes up valuable writing time, and that your plan is not marked. Point out that your response **is** marked – and a well-planned response gets the best mark.

2 Writing your response – planning and structuring

Read the sequence of read-think-write-edit to the class, pausing to discuss whether the students agree or disagree that each of these stages is vital. Discuss with students whether anything can be cut out of this process to speed it up and still achieve the best possible grade. Conclude with students that all stages in the process are vital to getting the best possible grade.

3 Putting it into practice

a Read the material from the Student Book to the class, pausing to clarify understanding where needed.

b Do students think that this is a successful plan? How might they improve it? Point out that the task has to be completed in a limited time, so anything that is added may well mean that something else must be cut. Remind the class that this guide was written by the Chief Examiner – so it's good advice!

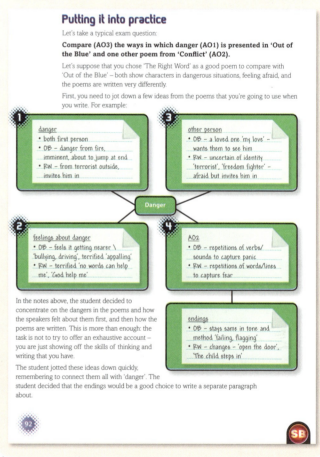

120 © Pearson Education Limited 2010

4 GradeStudio

a Close the Student Book and distribute or display **Worksheet 3.55**.

b Using the grade descriptors on pages 142–143 of the Student Book (also available on **Worksheet 1.51**), ask students to work in pairs to decide which grade they would award Student A and Student B, matching specific features from the mark scheme to specific evidence from each response to justify their decision.

c Take feedback, continually aiming to re-affirm the Assessment Objectives: the importance of responding to, and comparing, the details, ideas, themes, language, structure and form of the poems.

d Return to the Student Book and read through the Examiner's Comments. Do the class's marks and justifications tally with the Chief Examiner's?

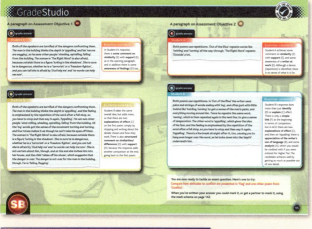

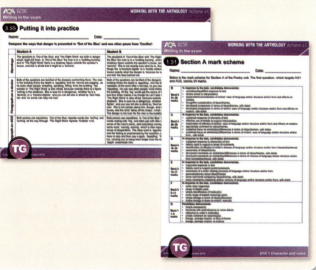

5 Sample exam question

Depending on the confidence of your class, this can be tackled as homework, as entirely independent work, or planned as a class prior to independent writing.

a Ask students to spend 2 minutes noting down the sequence of thinking they would follow before writing. For example:
 1 Read the question **carefully**.
 2 Identify which parts of the question relate to which Assessment Objective.
 3 Consider which poem to compare with 'Flag'. Draw up a shortlist of two or three possibilities. Which will allow you to demonstrate your skill and understanding most fully? Choose one.
 4 Note down points comparing the themes and ideas in the poems.
 5 Note down points comparing details in the poems.
 6 Note down points comparing the choice of language, form and/or structure in the poems and its effect on the reader.

b Give students 10 minutes to follow this sequence, completing their essay plan. Point out that, although this should take 5 minutes in the exam, this is practice to help get students up to exam pace!

> You are now ready to tackle an exam question. Here's one to try:
> Compare how attitudes to conflict are presented in 'Flag' and one other poem from 'Conflict'.
> When you've written your answer you could mark it, or get a partner to mark it, using the mark scheme on page 142.

6 Plenary

Students swap plans. Does their partner's plan cover all the necessary Assessment Objectives and explore the poem in enough developed detail? What grade do they think the essay based on this plan will achieve? Why? Take feedback, focusing on the grade awarded and the peer marker's justification for that grade. Does the class agree that the grade is justified?

7 Further work

Students can write up their essay in their own time. The following lesson can then be spent peer-marking the essays using the grade descriptors on pages 142–143 of the Student Book – also available on **Worksheet 1.51** – then listening as a class to the peer-marker's choices of:
- the most successful point targeting AO1
- the most successful point targeting AO2
- the most successful point targeting AO3.

Chapter 4 Relationships

Getting to know the poems

Assessment Objectives
- **AO1:** respond to texts critically and imaginatively; select and evaluate relevant textual detail to illustrate and support interpretations
- **AO2:** explain how language, structure and form contribute to writers' presentation of ideas, themes and settings
- **AO3:** make comparisons and explain links between texts, evaluating writers' different ways of expressing meaning and achieving effects

Learning Objectives
- To become familiar with the cluster as a whole
- To start to make links between the poems

Required resources
- Student Book, pages 98–100
- Worksheet 4.1, ideally enlarged to A3 size
- A3 paper

1 Starter

a Focus on the title of this cluster.

b Ask students to consider what this title might suggest: List all the different types of relationship you can think of in 3 minutes. Ask volunteers to share with the class.

c Ask students which type of relationship they think would make the best subject matter for a poem, and why. In order to develop students' arguments and thinking, aim for a class consensus.

2 Introduction

a Read through and clarify with the class the focus and purpose of this and subsequent lessons.

b Draw students' attention to the Assessment Objectives which this lesson will support (an explanation of them is available on page 98 of the Student Book).

c Ask students to locate the cluster in their Anthology.

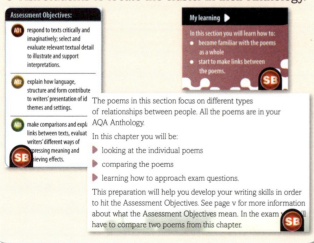

3 Activity 1

> **ACTIVITY 1**
>
> Read all the 'Relationships' poems in your AQA Anthology. Just notice what they seem to be about – don't worry about trying to make sense of every line.

a Divide the class into pairs according to ability, with poems allocated accordingly. For example:

More accessible
- Hour
- Praise Song for My Mother
- Harmonium
- Nettles
- Born Yesterday

Intermediate
- The Manhunt
- In Paris with You
- Quickdraw
- The Farmer's Bride
- Sister Maude

More challenging
- Sonnet 116
- Sonnet 43
- To His Coy Mistress
- Ghazal
- Brothers

b Give pairs 5 minutes to read their allocated poem, giving clear prior warning that they will be asked to feed back information and comments to the whole class. Use the prompts below to focus discussion and feedback. (You may want to note these prompts on the board.)
- How difficult is the poem to understand?
- What is the poem about?
- What can you say about the presentation of relationships?

c Read each poem to the class, then take feedback from the relevant group. Encourage students to take notes in their Anthology or exercise book, recording their first impressions of each poem.

4 Preparation for Activity 2

Ask the class to think of different ways in which these or any poems can be compared. Note them on the whiteboard, e.g. an exploration of a relationship, an event or experience, a point to make, the use of descriptive language.

5 Activity 2

ACTIVITY 2

Write the headings listed below on a sheet of paper. Under each heading make notes of any links between poems. Include poems that have similarities and differences. Use the tips below to help you.

Headings	Tips
What the poems are about	All the poems are about relationships but relationships here, and different fe...

a Distribute copies of **Worksheet 4.1** and look at the comparison table in Activity 2 on page 99 of the Student Book. Clarify the terms of comparison if necessary. As a class, decide which of the categories on the whiteboard (from the preparation) it will be most useful to focus on. Ask students to add them to the blank columns on the worksheet.

b Reshuffle students into groups of three or four. Clarify with them your precise requirements in this task. Depending on the ability of the class, there are a number of possible approaches. You could:
- give a clear timescale, e.g. 20 minutes, for the entire activity, or allow 3–5 minutes for each heading, taking feedback after each to ensure understanding
- group some of the headings, e.g.
  - titles
  - what the poems are about
  - beginnings and endings
  - length
  - language and imagery
  - rhythm and rhyme
- rather than trying to compare all 15 poems, ask students to put them into pairs, e.g. two with similar content or language choices, or two with very different structures or viewpoints.

Encourage students to note what leaps out at them rather than hunt for answers. This is very much an initial response to familiarise and demystify.

6 Activity 3

Get students to complete this activity in pairs or groups of three. Depending on the time available, ask a range of groups to show and explain their A3 paper to the rest of the class. Try to choose groups that have taken different approaches.

ACTIVITY 3

Now display your findings on a sheet of A3 in one of the following ways.

1 Spread the titles out on the sheet and draw links between them, labelling each one.

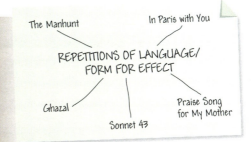

2 Draw a picture or symbol for each idea (such as death or nature) that appears in more than one poem, and group the poems around each – a poem can appear in more than one group.

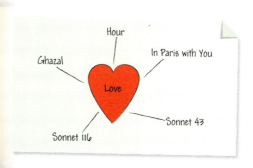

3 Draw a picture, or pictures, for each poem on the sheet, and link similar ones with arrows.

In these activities you have started to tackle all three Assessment Objectives. Now you will be focusing on AO1 and AO2 as you look at the poems individually (pages 101–117). You will return to AO3 when you compare the poems (pages 118–122). Finally, you will look at how to turn your knowledge and skills into successful exam answers, before you attempt one yourself (pages 123–129).

7 Plenary

Take specific feedback on individual poems and points of comparison, then ask students:
- What are your first impressions of this cluster?
- What have you found easier or harder than they expected?
- What support do you feel you will need?

Chapter 4 Relationships

The Manhunt by Simon Armitage

Assessment Objectives
- **AO1:** respond to texts critically and imaginatively; select and evaluate relevant textual detail to illustrate and support interpretations
- **AO2:** explain how language, structure and form contribute to writers' presentation of ideas, themes and settings

Learning Objectives
- To develop students' responses to the poem
- To relate the Assessment Objectives to the poem

Required resources
- Poem text, available on CD-ROM and video/audio online at http://anthology.aqa.org.uk
- Student Book, page 102
- Worksheets 1.3, 4.2, 4.3, 4.4, 4.5

1 Starter
Display **Worksheet 4.2**. Explain to students that the words and phrases on the sheet are metaphors taken from the poem they are looking at in this lesson. Ask them to match the two elements of each metaphor, writing a sentence or two explaining their decision. Take feedback to share and ensure understanding.

2 Activity 1
a Using the Digital Anthology, listen to/watch/read the poem to the class.
b Students complete questions 1–6 independently. Take feedback to share, ensure and develop understanding. Display the poem using the Digital Anthology, annotating the text with students' responses using Wordbox.
c Take students' initial response to the poem, commenting on the presentation of the relationship in the poem.
d Students write a sentence or two, summing up the content or meaning of the poem. They can begin: *'The Manhunt' is about…*.

3 Activity 2
a Display the poem title in close-up using the Digital Anthology.
b Students discuss the questions in pairs, writing their response in full sentences to ensure clarity of thought and their ability to express it. Take feedback, annotating the displayed title using Wordbox. Aim to validate all interpretations supported with evidence from elsewhere in the poem and/or explanation, 'zooming out' to display the whole poem and recording annotations on it.

Words/phrases to explore (AO1 and AO2) — ACTIVITY 2
Why do you think the poem is called 'The Manhunt'? Think of as many reasons as you can and write them down.

4 GradeStudio
a Read the GradeStudio sample answer to the class. Ask: How has the writer of this answer shown an 'explanation of effect(s) of writer's uses of language and/or form and/or structure and effects on readers'?
b Where else in the poem is there an opportunity for students to explore the poet's uses of language or structure? For example, the repetitions of 'and…and', or another metaphor.
c Ask students to select a short quotation that will allow them to explore their response to the poem. They then write a paragraph about it, using point-evidence-explanation.

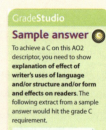

GradeStudio Sample answer
To achieve a C on this AO2 descriptor, you need to show **explanation of effect of writer's uses of language and/or structure and/or form and effects on readers**. The following extract from a sample answer would hit the grade C requirement.

Activity 1, question 5
The bullet is described as a 'foetus of metal' because it is buried within him, and it is also the beginning – like the birth – of his troubl[e]

124 © Pearson Education Limited 2010

5 Comparison activities, page 128

Note: In order to do these activities, students would need to have completed their work on 'Quickdraw' and 'Hour'.

1 a In pairs or independently, students complete **Worksheet 4.3**, linking their response to the poems with the relevant Assessment Objective. Take feedback on any areas which students found difficult to grasp or to comment on.

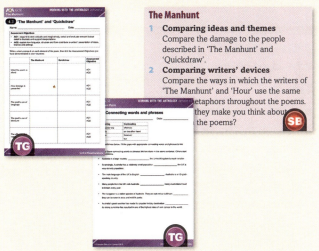

b Students use their notes from **Worksheet 4.3** to write three or four key points comparing how the two writers show damage in the poems. They should write **in complete sentences using connectives**. Display **Worksheet 1.3** to support them.

c Take feedback, compiling notes on the board. As a class, students find evidence from each poem to support each point.

d Students select three points with supporting evidence from those on the board.

e Students add a sentence or two to each point/piece of evidence, explaining and commenting on how the writers have presented their points of view.

2 Repeat the above sequence using **Worksheet 4.4**, looking at the two poets' use of metaphor.

6 Plenary

Take feedback on 'The Manhunt', annotating the poem displayed on the whiteboard using Wordbox. Focus on relevant key features, e.g:
- content
- language
- tone.
- interpretation
- structure

If students have studied and compared 'Quickdraw' and/or 'Hour', take feedback on relevant key similarities and differences in content, interpretation, language, structure or tone.

Suggested answers

Activity 1

1 a 'face', 'lower jaw', 'collar-bone', 'shoulder-blade', 'lung', 'ribs', 'heart', 'chest'.
  b They progress from his face, down to his heart.

2 a 'trace', 'explore', 'handle and hold', 'mind and attend', 'finger and thumb', 'bind', 'climb', 'feel', 'skirting'. These verbs suggest gentle and careful movement.
  b The first lines of the third to fifth stanzas.
  c They create a sense of movement.

3
- face: frozen river
- jaw: blown hinge
- collar-bone: damaged porcelain
- shoulder-blade: fractured rudder
- lung: parachute silk
- ribs: struts, rungs.

All suggest appearance but with connotations of damage, both emotional and physical.

4 a A metaphor might, perhaps, have clouded the many physical and, more importantly, emotional connotations of 'heart', used figuratively as well as literally.
  b This creates a similar effect to the sudden use of more literal language: a blunt and perhaps shocking moment in the poem.

5 Applying this term to a bullet, lodged in a man, is a shocking and disturbing image, implying growth and life which seem contradictory to its purpose.

6 The poem strongly suggests emotional as well as physical scarring. The image of the mine 'buried' suggests that the source of this scarring is intentionally hidden; the 'mine' suggests the metaphorical use of 'minefield' implying danger for the narrator as well as the victim; 'sweating' strongly implies that this is not a literal but a human 'mine'.

Activity 2

- The title suggests the aggression of war and the emotional search for the man within the damaged body.
- It could also refer to an event in the war which caused the damage or the rehabilitation which the narrator is undertaking.
- It could also refer to the speaker's hunt, seeking out the good that remains after the horror of war.

Comparison activities

Key points for this activity are provided in **Worksheet 4.5**.

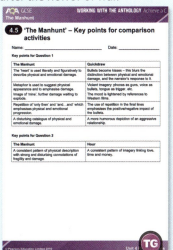

AQA GCSE Working with the Anthology: Achieve a C   125

Chapter 4 Relationships

Hour by Carol Ann Duffy

Assessment Objectives
- **AO1:** respond to texts critically and imaginatively; select and evaluate relevant textual detail to illustrate and support interpretations
- **AO2:** explain how language, structure and form contribute to writers' presentation of ideas, themes and settings

Learning Objectives
- To develop students' responses to the poem
- To relate the Assessment Objectives to the poem

Required resources
- Poem text, available on CD-ROM and video/audio online at http://anthology.aqa.org.uk
- Student Book, page 103
- Worksheets 1.3, 4.6, 4.7, 4.8, 4.9

1 Starter
Read the class the story of Rumpelstiltskin, on **Worksheet 4.6**. Ask: What connections does the story suggest between love and wealth? What connections do you see between the two ideas in your own lives/society?

2 Activity 1
a Using the Digital Anthology, listen to/watch/read the poem to the class.
b Students complete questions 1–6 independently. Take feedback to share, ensure and develop understanding. Display the poem using the Digital Anthology, annotating the text with students' responses using Wordbox.
c Take students' initial response to the poem, commenting on the presentation of the relationship in the poem.
d Ask students to write a sentence or two, summing up the content or meaning of the poem. They can begin: *'Hour' is about… .*

Initial responses — ACTIVITY 1
1 The phrase 'Love's time's beggar' sets up ideas about time and money. Pick out all the words about time and all the words about money in the poem.
2 A single hour 'makes love rich'. What things in the second **stanza** are described in terms of wealth?
3 'Flowers' and 'wine' are associated with things given to lovers, but these lovers prefer something simpler. In the first and third stanzas, what simple things are as good as the usual things that lovers give to each other?
4 Find all the references to light in the poem. What sort of light is there?
5 The lovers seem to bribe ('backhanding') the night to come more slowly ('Time slows').
  a How do they do this?
  b What word implies that this takes a lot of doing?
6 Look at the last two lines. Why do you think Duffy picks out 'Now' as a single word, by putting full stops on each side of it?

3 Activity 2
a Display the poem using the Digital Anthology.
b Students discuss the questions in pairs, writing their response in full sentences to ensure clarity of thought and their ability to express it. Take feedback, annotating the poem displayed on the whiteboard using Wordbox. Aim to validate all interpretations supported with evidence and/or explanation.

Words/phrases to explore (AO1 and AO2) — ACTIVITY 2
In the fairy tale 'Rumpelstiltskin' gold is spun from straw.
1 How do the lovers spin gold (something worth a lot) from straw (something simple and cheap) in the whole poem?
2 Why do you think Duffy repeats the word 'gold' three times in the final line?

4 GradeStudio
a Read the GradeStudio sample answer to the class. Ask: How has the writer of this answer shown an 'explained response to element(s) of text'?
b How could students add to or rewrite this response to show a 'sustained response to elements of text' and achieve a C? For example: *It seems that their love can triumph over time and money: it can even make something precious out of nothing because their love 'spins gold, gold, gold from straw'.*
c Where else in the poem is there an opportunity for students to explore their response to the poem? For example, the speaker's description of her lover, or the things which these lovers find valuable.
d Ask students to select a short quotation that will allow them to explore their response to the poem. They then write a paragraph about it, using point-evidence-explanation.

GradeStudio Sample answer
To achieve a D on this AO1 descriptor, you need to give an **explained response to element(s) of text**. The following extract from a sample answer would hit the grade D requirement.

Activity 1, question 1
The lovers seem to be at the mercy of time, but they are not really, because they manage to slow time down, spending 'thousands of seconds' together, so that they make an hour 'shining', and time doesn't make love 'poor' at all.

5 Comparison activities, page 128

Note: In order to do these activities, students would need to have completed their work on 'In Paris with You':

1 a In pairs or independently, students complete **Worksheet 4.7**, linking their response to the poems with the relevant Assessment Objective. Take feedback on any areas which students found difficult to grasp or to comment on.

> **Hour**
> **1 Comparing ideas and themes**
> Compare the ideas about love in 'Hour' and 'In Paris with You'.
> **2 Comparing writers' devices**
> Compare the ways in which the writers present love in 'Hour' and 'In Paris with You' by the ways they write about it.

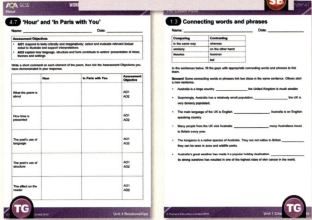

b Students use their notes from **Worksheet 4.7** to write three or four key points comparing the presentation of time in the two poems. They should write **in complete sentences using connectives**. Display **Worksheet 1.3** to support them.

c Take feedback, compiling notes on the board. As a class, students find evidence from each poem to support each point.

d Students select three points with supporting evidence from those on the board.

e Students add a sentence or two to each point/piece of evidence, explaining and commenting on how the writers have presented their points of view.

2 Repeat the above sequence using **Worksheet 4.8**, looking at the two poets' presentation of love.

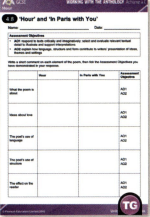

6 Plenary

Take feedback on 'Hour', annotating the poem displayed on the whiteboard using Wordbox. Focus on relevant key features, e.g:
- content
- language
- tone.
- interpretation
- structure

If students have studied and compared 'In Paris with You', take feedback on relevant key similarities and differences in content, interpretation, language, structure or tone.

Suggested answers

Activity 1

1 **Time:** 'a single hour', 'an hour', 'summer', 'thousands of seconds', 'Time slows', 'the night', 'our shining hour'.

Money: 'a dropped coin', 'rich', 'spend', 'treasure', 'Midas', 'gold', 'millionaires', 'jewel', 'poor', 'gold, gold, gold'. Note the dual use of 'spend': to spend time, to spend money.

2 'your hair', 'your limbs', 'we are millionaires': the narrator's physical attraction to her lover, and their relationship.

3 The whole of the summer sky and a grass ditch.

4 'summer sky', 'Midas light', 'our shining hour', 'a candle', 'chandelier', 'spotlight'. The 'light' of their love transforming the world, lighting it far more brightly than artificial light.

5 **a** It seems to be their love which gives them the wealth to bribe the night.
  b 'millionaires' suggests that the night will require a great deal of money.

6 The word emphasises this moment in time, a kind of freezing of time, in which love conquers it.

Activity 2

1 The implication is that love emotionally enriches both people in the relationship.

2 To emphasise the value and extent of her love, and the strength of her feeling.

Comparison activities

Key points for this activity are provided in **Worksheet 4.9**.

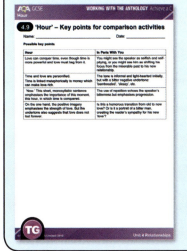

Chapter 4 Relationships

In Paris with You by James Fenton

Assessment Objectives
- **AO1:** respond to texts critically and imaginatively; select and evaluate relevant textual detail to illustrate and support interpretations
- **AO2:** explain how language, structure and form contribute to writers' presentation of ideas, themes and settings

Learning Objectives
- To develop students' responses to the poem
- To relate the Assessment Objectives to the poem

Required resources
- Poem text, available on CD-ROM and video/audio online at http://anthology.aqa.org.uk
- Student Book, page 104
- Worksheets 1.3, 4.10, 4.11, 4.12, 4.13

1 Starter

a Explain to students that:
  - **Worksheet 4.10** features some words and phrases from the poem.
  - They should use these to compile a poem or monologue of 30–40 words.
  - Their topic or focus is an entirely free choice.
  - They can add as many or as few words or phrases of their own as they wish.

b Allow 5 minutes to complete the task.

c Take feedback. Ask volunteers to:
  - share their writing with the class
  - comment on how the poet's choice of vocabulary has affected the mood or tone of their writing. Look for comments that recognise the bitter and, perhaps, lascivious tone of the poem.

2 Activity 1

a Using the Digital Anthology, listen to/watch/read the poem to the class.

b Students complete questions 1–7 independently. Take feedback to share, ensure and develop understanding. Display the poem using the Digital Anthology, annotating the text with students' responses using Wordbox.

c Take students' initial response to the poem, commenting on the presentation of the relationship in the poem.

d Ask students to write a sentence or two, summing up the content or meaning of the poem. They can begin: '*In Paris with You*' is about… .

3 Activity 2

a Display the first and last stanzas of the poem in close-up using the Digital Anthology.

b Students discuss the questions in pairs, writing their response in full sentences to ensure clarity of thought and their ability to express it. Take feedback, annotating the displayed stanzas using Wordbox. Aim to validate all interpretations supported with evidence and/or explanation, 'zooming out' to display the whole poem and recording annotations on it.

4 GradeStudio

a Read the GradeStudio sample answer to the class. Ask: How has the writer of this answer shown use of 'details linked to interpretation'?

b Does this writer's interpretation of the poem match the students' interpretation? Add a further sentence to the sample answer, focusing on the writer's negative interpretation. For example: *By the end of the poem, we are left with an image of a selfish, self-pitying man who talks constantly of his own miseries and failures. We feel pity for the poor woman he is with.*

c Ask students to use the same details to write a more positive interpretation, following the same structure.

d How do students respond to this speaker? Take feedback, insisting on quotation to support interpretation.

e Students write a point-evidence-explanation paragraph exploring their own interpretation of the poem, using appropriate quotation.

5 Comparison activities, page 128

Note: In order to do these activities, students would need to have completed their work on 'To His Coy Mistress' and 'Praise Song for My Mother'.

1 a In pairs or independently, students complete **Worksheet 4.11**, linking their response to the poems with the relevant Assessment Objective. Take feedback on any areas which students found difficult to grasp or to comment on.

In Paris with You

1 Comparing ideas and themes
Compare the attitudes of the speakers in 'In Paris with You' and 'To His Coy Mistress'.

2 Comparing writers' devices
Compare the ways in which the writers use repetitions in 'In Paris with You' and 'Praise Song for My Mother'.

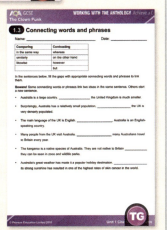

b Students use their notes from **Worksheet 4.11** to write three or four key points comparing the attitudes of the speakers in the two poems. They should write **in complete sentences using connectives**. Display **Worksheet 1.3** to support them.

c Take feedback, compiling notes on the board. As a class, students find evidence from each poem to support each point.

d Students select three points with supporting evidence from those on the board.

e Students add a sentence or two to each point/piece of evidence, explaining and commenting on how the writers have presented their points of view.

2 Repeat the above sequence using **Worksheet 4.12**, looking at the two poets' use of repetition.

6 Plenary

Take feedback on 'In Paris with You', annotating the poem displayed on the whiteboard using Wordbox. Focus on relevant key features, e.g:
- content
- language
- tone.
- interpretation
- structure

If students have studied and compared 'To His Coy Mistress' and/or 'Praise Song for My Mother', take feedback on relevant key similarities and differences in content, interpretation, language, structure or tone.

Suggested answers

Activity 1

1 The mood at the start of the poem is bitter: he is 'tearful' and 'angry'. However, the mood becomes more positive, particularly in the final stanza which suggest that his lover's 'slightest thing you do… eyes… mouth… all points south' can create all the romance of Paris in a 'sleazy Old hotel room'.

2 The first two stanzas imply that the speaker has had a bad experience in a relationship: he does not want to talk about love, he gets 'tearful', he is 'wounded', he is 'angry' that he has been 'bamboozled' and 'resentful at the mess' he has been through.

3 a/b Use of informal ('earful', 'a drink or two') and playful, childish language ('maroonded') to rhyme with 'wounded'.

4 'But' suggests that this visit could mark a change in the speaker's fortunes.

5 Use of first person and conversational informal language, e.g. 'Yes, I'm angry… Do you mind if…'.

6 'Learning who you are' suggests for the first time some interest in the person he is with, rather than his own bitter thoughts. It suggests progression rather than reflection on the past.

7 The speaker finally talks to the other person ('you') – and considers <u>their</u> feelings – suggesting a shift from self-pity to his new relationship.

Activity 2

1 By the end of the poem, the speaker seems to be more focused on the future, his new lover and his new relationship.

2 The progression is emphasised, paradoxically, by the similarity in the openings of stanzas 1, 5 and 6, contrasted with: his self-pity (stanzas 1/2); the 'sleazy' hotel room (stanzas 3/4); his new lover (stanzas 5/6).

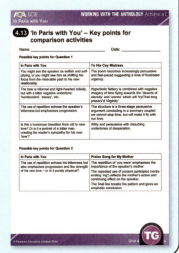

Comparison activities

Key points for this activity are provided in **Worksheet 4.13**.

Chapter 4 Relationships

Quickdraw by Carol Ann Duffy

Assessment Objectives
- **AO1:** respond to texts critically and imaginatively; select and evaluate relevant textual detail to illustrate and support interpretations
- **AO2:** explain how language, structure and form contribute to writers' presentation of ideas, themes and settings

Learning Objectives
- To develop students' responses to the poem
- To relate the Assessment Objectives to the poem

Required resources
- Poem text, available on CD-ROM and video/audio online at http://anthology.aqa.org.uk
- Student Book, page 105
- Worksheets 1.3, 4.14, 4.15, 4.16

1 Starter

a How are love and relationships presented in modern music? Ask students to list different songs in which love and relationships are explored in different ways from the most positive to the most negative. Ask volunteers to share.

b Ask students to think more closely about song lyrics. Ask: What is love compared to? Aim for as broad a range of responses as possible, from the clichéd to the bizarre.

2 Activity 1

a Using the Digital Anthology, listen to/watch/read the poem to the class. Refer back to the starter activity. Does this poem's presentation of love have any connection with any of the songs that were discussed?

b Students complete questions 1–7 independently. Take feedback to share, ensure and develop understanding. Display the poem using the Digital Anthology, annotating the text with students' responses using Wordbox.

c Take students' initial response to the poem, commenting on the presentation of the relationship in the poem.

d Ask students to write a sentence or two, summing up the content or meaning of the poem. They can begin: 'Quickdraw' is about….

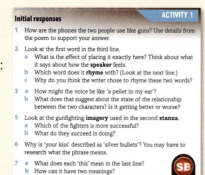

3 Activity 2

a Display the poem using the Digital Anthology.

b Students discuss the question in pairs, writing their response in full sentences to ensure clarity of thought and their ability to express it. Take feedback, annotating the poem displayed on the whiteboard using Wordbox. Aim to validate all interpretations supported with evidence and/or explanation.

Words/phrases to explore (AO1 and AO2) — ACTIVITY 2

How would you describe the state of the relationship in the poem? Write a paragraph about it. You could start with 'You've wounded

4 GradeStudio

a Read the GradeStudio sample answer to the class. Ask: How has the writer of this answer shown an 'appreciation/consideration of writers' uses of language and/or form and/or structure and effects on readers'?

b Where else in the poem is there an opportunity for students to explore the poet's uses of language and structure? For example, the use of images drawn from Westerns, or the repetition and ambiguity of the final line.

c Ask students to select a short quotation that will allow them to explore their response to the poem. The students then write a paragraph about it, using point-evidence-explanation.

GradeStudio
Sample answer

To achieve a C on this AO2 descriptor, you need to show **explanation of effects of writer's use of language.** To do this, you need to explain clearly what the effect is on you as the reader, not just say what the device is. The following extract from a sample answer would hit the grade C requirement:

Activity 2
The relationship is an unhealthy one. The state of loneliness of the speaker is stressed by placing 'alone' at the beginning of a line, after the slight pause that the line break makes when you read it.

5 Comparison activities, page 128

Note: In order to do these activities, students would need to have completed their work on 'In Paris with You' and 'The Manhunt'.

1 a In pairs or independently, students complete **Worksheet 4.14**, linking their response to the poems with the relevant Assessment Objective. Take feedback on any areas which students found difficult to grasp or to comment on.

Quickdraw

1 **Comparing ideas and themes**
   Compare the relationships shown in 'Quickdraw' and 'In Paris with You'.
2 **Comparing writers' devices**
   Compare the ways in which the writers use **metaphors** about fighting in 'Quickdraw' and 'The Manhunt'.

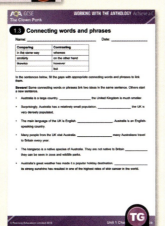

b Students use their notes from **Worksheet 4.14** to write three or four key points comparing how the two writers present relationships in the poems. They should write **in complete sentences using connectives**. Display **Worksheet 1.3** to support them.

c Take feedback, compiling notes on the board. As a class, students find evidence from each poem to support each point.

d Students select three points with supporting evidence from those on the board.

e Students add a sentence or two to each point/piece of evidence, explaining and commenting on how the writers have presented their points of view.

2 Repeat the above sequence using **Worksheet 4.15**, looking at the two poets' use of metaphor.

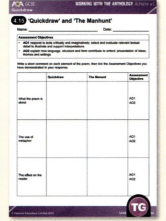

6 Plenary

Take feedback on 'Quickdraw', annotating the poem displayed on the whiteboard using Wordbox. Focus on relevant key features, e.g:
- content
- language
- tone.
- interpretation
- structure

If students have studied and compared 'In Paris with You' and/or 'The Manhunt', take feedback on relevant key similarities and differences in content, interpretation, language, structure or tone.

Suggested answers

Activity 1

1 The phones are 'slung from the pockets on my hips' suggesting guns in holsters; 'your voice' is compared to a 'pellet' which 'wounded me'.

2 a It emphasises the speaker's solitary, emotional vulnerability.
  b 'groan'.
  c It links the emotional effect of the speaker's loneliness with its cause.

3 a It suggests a 'milder' form of bullet – an aggressive voice which wounds.
  b The relationship seems to be deteriorating – although the speaker is clearly waiting for the call.

5 a/b The speaker squeezes the 'trigger of my tongue' but misses, 'wide of the mark'. The caller succeeds, managing to 'blast me/through the heart'.

6 The only way to kill a werewolf and, figuratively, an almost magical solution to a problem. These kisses seem to heal the rift.

7 Suggests both the taking of a gunshot and a kiss.

Activity 2

The relationship is given strong overtones of violence and aggression in the imagery of phones as guns; yet the poem ends with some kind of reconciliation: the 'silver bullets of your kiss' suggesting that these kisses can solve any argument, and that perhaps this tempestuous relationship relies on physical rather than emotional elements.

Comparison activities

Key points for this activity are provided in **Worksheet 4.16**.

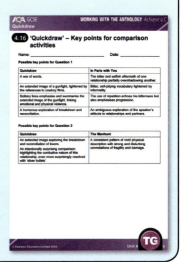

Chapter 4 Relationships

Ghazal by Mimi Khalvati

Assessment Objectives
- **AO1:** respond to texts critically and imaginatively; select and evaluate relevant textual detail to illustrate and support interpretations
- **AO2:** explain how language, structure and form contribute to writers' presentation of ideas, themes and settings

Learning Objectives
- To develop students' responses to the poem
- To relate the Assessment Objectives to the poem

Required resources
- Poem text, available on CD-ROM and video/audio online at http://anthology.aqa.org.uk
- Student Book, page 106
- Worksheets 1.3, 4.17, 4.18, 4.19

1 Starter

Display/distribute **Worksheet 4.17**. Explain that each blank rhymes with the first line ('through me'). How many of the blanks can students guess? Allow only 5 minutes, emphasising that this is a guessing game! Ask volunteers to share their suggestions.

2 Activity 1

a Using the Digital Anthology, listen to/watch/read the poem to the class.

b Students complete questions 1–6 independently. Take feedback to share, ensure and develop understanding. Display the poem using the Digital Anthology, annotating the text with students' responses using Wordbox.

c Take students' initial response to the poem, commenting on the presentation of the relationship in the poem.

d Ask students to write a sentence or two, summing up the content or meaning of the poem. They can begin: *'Ghazal' is about…* .

ACTIVITY 1
Initial responses

1. **a** What things does the **speaker** compare herself and her love to in the first **stanza**? Make a list.
   b What types of things are these?
2. **a** What type of things does she compare herself and her love to in the second stanza?
   b What is the effect of the **enjambment** here – the way that there is a line break between 'hang' and 'on', that makes a pause?
3. Look at stanzas three and four and the use of 'tattoo me'. How do you think the speaker would like the lover to behave here?
4. Look at stanzas five and six. The speaker uses some tree **imagery** here.
   a Why would she like to be 'bark'?
   b What does she want her lover to do?
5. **a** 'Marry' in the seventh stanza can mean 'match'. How would she like the two of them to be matched?
   b What different things would she like the lover to do?
6. How do the speaker's ideas get bigger in the last three stanzas? What does she compare herself and her lover to?

3 Activity 2

a Display the poem using the Digital Anthology.

b Students discuss the question in pairs, writing their response in full sentences to ensure clarity of thought and their ability to express it. Take feedback to share and ensure understanding. Aim to validate all responses supported with evidence from the poem and/or explanation, recording appropriate annotations.

Words/phrases to explore (AO1)

How would you describe the attitude of the speaker to the other person in the poem? Clearly there is love in the poem, but which of the lovers is in control, do you think? Write a paragraph about the relationship, using details from the poem. You could start with 'subdue me'.

4 GradeStudio

a Read the GradeStudio sample answer to the class. Ask: How has the writer of this answer shown 'appropriate comment on ideas/themes'?

b Where else in the poem is there an opportunity for students to explore the poem's ideas/themes? For example, the speaker's request to be subdued and dominated, or the shifting of power in the imagery of hawk and moth.

c Ask students to select a short quotation that will allow them to explore their response to the poem. They then write a paragraph about it, using point-evidence-explanation.

GradeStudio
Sample answer

To achieve a C on this AO1 descriptor, you need to show **appropriate comment on ideas/themes**. The following extract from a sample answer would hit the grade C requirement.

Activity 1, question 6
The love being expressed by the speaker seems to get larger as the poem progresses, from the small beginnings of 'grass' to a comparison with the sun and finally 'heaven and earth to me', which is just about everything.

5 Comparison activities, page 128

Note: In order to do these activities, students would need to have completed their work on 'Praise Song for my Mother.

a In pairs or independently, students complete **Worksheet 4.18**, linking their response to the poems with the relevant Assessment Objective. Take feedback on any areas which students found difficult to grasp or to comment on.

Ghazal

1 **Comparing ideas and themes**
Compare the feelings of the speakers shown in 'Ghazal' and 'Praise Song for My Mother'.

2 **Comparing writers' devices**
Compare the ways in which the writers present the feelings shown in 'Ghazal' and 'Praise Song for My Mother' by the ways they write about the other person.

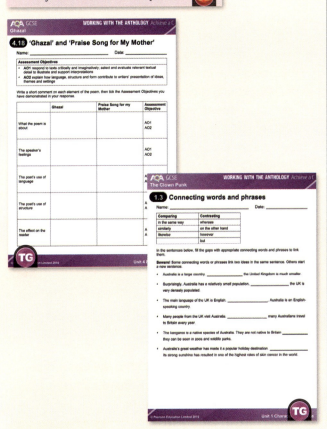

b Students use their notes from **Worksheet 4.18** to write three or four key points comparing the two speakers' feelings and how those feelings are presented in the poems. They should write **in complete sentences using connectives**. Display **Worksheet 1.3** to support them.

c Take feedback, compiling notes on the board. As a class, students find evidence from each poem to support each point.

d Students select three points with supporting evidence from those on the board.

e Students add a sentence or two to each point/piece of evidence, explaining and commenting on how the poets have presented their points of view.

6 Plenary

Take feedback on 'Ghazal', annotating the poem displayed on the whiteboard using Wordbox. Focus on relevant key features, e.g:
- content
- language
- tone.
- interpretation
- structure

If students have studied and compared 'Praise Song for my Mother, take feedback on relevant key similarities and differences in content, interpretation, language, structure or tone.

Suggested answers

Activity 1

1 a I am 'the grass… the rose'; you are 'the breeze… the bird'.
  b Images from nature.

2 a Song/poetry.
  b It reflects the idea of a word hanging on the speaker's lips; also the pace of the lines increases, hurrying towards the rhyme ('cue me').

3 The speaker seems to be asking to be dominated and controlled: to have her poisonous language and behaviour quelled.

4 a If she is bark, then his arms can encircle her as if he were hugging this tree.
  b The speaker then moves on, suggesting that her lover is the 'dew' and could, therefore, drop in the shade of this tree and 'bedew' her. The imagery seems strongly sexual.

5 a The speaker seems to want them to be matched by taking on different shapes, creating matching pairs.
  b She wants her lover to pursue her, yet in the two different examples each is the other's victim: she the shadow and he the hawk that hunts it; she the flame and he the moth, fatally attracted to it.

6 The imagery moves from the specifically earthly to a more universal view: the sun in stanza 8, the intellectual in stanza 9, and the entirety of heaven and earth in stanza 10.

Activity 2

'subdue me' suggests that the speaker wants to be dominated and controlled by her lover. This idea is established with the use of gentler, natural imagery at the start of the poem where she asks her lover to be like 'the breeze' and 'blow through' her: an image of invasion and suffusion. Yet, neither her nor her lover are entirely in control: the images of 'hawk to my shadow, moth to my flame', although suggesting hunting and destruction, reverse the roles of hunter and victim.

Comparison activities

Key points for this activity are provided in **Worksheet 4.19**.

Chapter 4 Relationships

Brothers by Andrew Forster

Assessment Objectives
- **AO1:** respond to texts critically and imaginatively; select and evaluate relevant textual detail to illustrate and support interpretations
- **AO2:** explain how language, structure and form contribute to writers' presentation of ideas, themes and settings

Learning Objectives
- To develop students' responses to the poem
- To relate the Assessment Objectives to the poem

Required resources
- Poem text, available on CD-ROM and video/audio online at http://anthology.aqa.org.uk
- Student Book, page 107
- Worksheets 1.3, 4.20, 4.21

1 Starter
Write the words 'brothers' and 'sisters' on the board. What associations do students have with these words? How does this change if students are presented with the words 'older sisters', 'younger sisters', 'older brothers' and 'little brothers'. Look for responses in which students explore their personal experience of siblings.

2 Activity 1
a Using the Digital Anthology, listen to/watch/read the poem to the class.
b Students complete questions 1–5 independently. Take feedback to share, ensure and develop understanding. Display the poem using the Digital Anthology, annotating the text with students' responses using Wordbox.
c Take students' initial response to the poem, commenting on the presentation of the relationship in the poem.
d Ask students to write a sentence or two, summing up the content or meaning of the poem. They can begin: *'Brothers' is about…* .

Initial responses — ACTIVITY 1
1. a How does the writer show what the **speaker's** attitude to his brother is in the first line?
   b How has the writer chosen the word order to emphasise this?
2. In the first **stanza**, what don't the two older boys like about the young brother?
3. How is the attitude to the young brother shown again in the second stanza?
4. What does the word 'windmilled' suggest about the young boy?
5. The idea of a race runs right through the third stanza.
   a How does line 11 suggest that the two older boys are still children, really?
   b How does line 13 make you think of a race, and perhaps of the 'Olympic Gold'?
   c The speaker 'ran on'. What was he running towards, and what was he running away from at the same time?
   d What 'distance' has the speaker 'set in motion' between himself and his brother, do you think?

3 Activity 2
a Display the poem using the Digital Anthology. Highlight the first and last lines.
b Students discuss the question in pairs, writing their response in full sentences to ensure clarity of thought and their ability to express it. Take feedback, annotating the poem displayed on the whiteboard using Wordbox. Aim to validate all interpretations supported with evidence from elsewhere in the poem and/or explanation.

Words/phrases to explore (AO1 and AO2) — ACTIVITY 2
1. 'Unable to close the distance I'd set in motion'. How has the speaker's attitude changed from the first line of the poem?
2. 'In motion' suggests something moving. What do you think this might imply about the relationship between the speaker and his brother after the time when this incident took place?

4 GradeStudio
a Read the GradeStudio extract to the class. How has the writer of the sample answer shown 'details linked to interpretation'?
b Where else in the poem is there an opportunity to explore the writer's use of language or structure linked to interpretation? For example, the gold medal imagery in the final stanza, or the contrast of the poem's first and last lines.
c Ask students to select a short quotation which will allow them to explore their response to the poem; then write a paragraph about it using point-evidence-explanation.

GradeStudio Sample answer B
To achieve a B on this AO1 descriptor, you need to show **details linked to interpretation**. The following extract from a sample answer would hit the grade B requirement.

Activity 2
'Grown-ups' are supposed to 'stroll the town', but the pace at the end tells of an older person's desperation about his relationship with his brother. He 'chased' and 'ran', but only towards failure. The 'hand' his brother reaches out does not reach him, and he is 'unable to close the distance' he has cr[...]

5 Comparison activities, page 128

Note: In order to do these activities, students would need to have completed their work on 'Sister Maude'.

a In pairs or independently, students complete **Worksheet 4.20**, linking their response to the poems with the relevant Assessment Objective. Take feedback on any areas which students found difficult to grasp or to comment on.

Brothers

1. **Comparing ideas and themes**
   Compare the feelings shown in 'Brothers' and 'Sister Maude'.
2. **Comparing writers' devices**
   Compare the ways in which the writers present feelings in 'Brothers' and 'Sister Maude'.

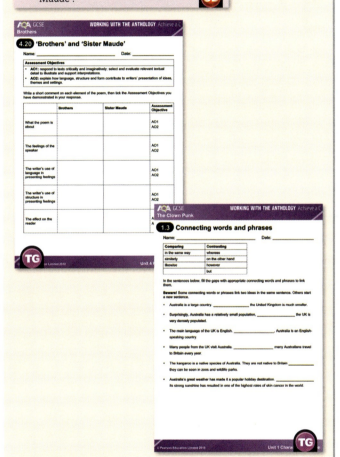

b Students use their notes from **Worksheet 4.20** to write three or four key points comparing feelings shown in the two poems and how they are presented. They should write **in complete sentences using connectives**. Display **Worksheet 1.3** to support them.

c Take feedback, compiling notes on the board. As a class, students find evidence from each poem to support each point.

d Students select three points with supporting evidence from those on the board.

e Students add a sentence or two to each point/piece of evidence, explaining and commenting on how the writers have presented their points of view.

6 Plenary

Take feedback on 'Brothers', annotating the poem displayed on the whiteboard using Wordbox. Focus on relevant key features, e.g:
- content
- language
- tone
- interpretation
- structure

If students have studied and compared 'Sister Maude', take feedback on relevant key similarities and differences in content, interpretation, language, structure or tone.

Suggested answers

Activity 1

1. 'saddled' strongly suggests that his brother's presence is at a parent's request. He is a burden. Placing the word at the start of the poem gives it clear emphasis.

2. His clothes ('ridiculous tank top'), his football team (Rotherham, not Sheffield Wednesday) and his age ('six').

3. The speaker 'sighed', suggesting he is irritated. Their ages are given, and their intention to do 'what grown ups do' suggests they dismiss the little brother as a mere child.

4. It suggests his childish exuberance, in contrast to the older boys who 'stroll'.

5. **a** 'We chased Olympic gold' suggests the ambitions and imagination of children.
   b The hand 'holding out' suggests a relay race, the passing of the baton; the coin suggests and reminds us of the medal.
   c He is running for the bus – and away from his brother.
   d A physical distance – but also an emotional distance.

Activity 2

The opening line suggests he did not want to be close to his brother at this time: he is 'saddled' with him. The closing line, however, suggests that he looks back and regrets the distance which he 'set in motion' at this age. Since then, he has tried to close the emotional gap but is 'unable'.

Comparison activities

Key points for this activity are provided in **Worksheet 4.21**.

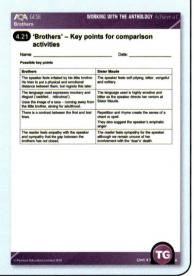

Chapter 4 Relationships

Praise Song for My Mother
by Grace Nichols

Assessment Objectives
- **AO1:** respond to texts critically and imaginatively; select and evaluate relevant textual detail to illustrate and support interpretations
- **AO2:** explain how language, structure and form contribute to writers' presentation of ideas, themes and settings

Learning Objectives
- To develop students' responses to the poem
- To relate the Assessment Objectives to the poem

Required resources
- Poem text, available on CD-ROM and video/audio online at http://anthology.aqa.org.uk
- Student Book, page 108
- Worksheets 1.3, 4.22, 4.23

1 Starter

a Display and read the poem using the Digital Anthology.
b Ask students to select the friend or relation who has had the greatest influence on their life, then write a number of lines which explain and explore that influence. Take feedback, noting and commenting on:
- the kinds of influence that friends and relations can have
- how students have expressed it.

2 Activity 1

a If you have not already done so, listen to/watch/read the poem to the class.
b Students complete questions 1–5 independently. Take feedback to share, ensure and develop understanding. Display the poem using the Digital Anthology, annotating the text with students' responses using Wordbox.
c Take students' initial response to the poem, commenting on the presentation of the relationship in the poem.
d Ask students to write a sentence or two, summing up the content or meaning of the poem. They can begin: *'Praise Song for My Mother' is about…*.

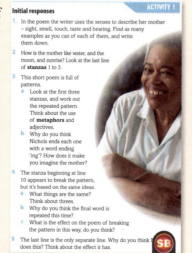

3 Activity 2

a Display the poem using the Digital Anthology.
b Students discuss the question in pairs, recording their response in complete sentences to ensure understanding and the ability to express it. Take feedback, annotating the poem displayed on the whiteboard using Wordbox. Aim to validate all responses.

Words/phrases to explore (AO1 and AO2) — ACTIVITY 2
What is Nichols' attitude to her mother in the poem? Be as exact as you can – there are quite a few things you could say.

4 GradeStudio

a Read the GradeStudio sample answer to the class. Ask: How has the writer of this answer shown an 'identification of effect(s) of writer's choices of language and/or form and/or structure'?
b How could students rewrite or add to this response to show 'explanation of effect(s) of writer's uses of language and/or structure and/or form and effects on readers' and so achieve a C grade? For example: *The effect of all three of these together suggests the all-encompassing nature of her mother's influence.*
c Where else in the poem is there an opportunity for students to explore the poet's uses of language and structure? For example, the use of the senses, or the structure of the first three stanzas.
d Ask students to select a short quotation that will allow them to explore their response to the poem. They then write a paragraph about it, using point-evidence-explanation.

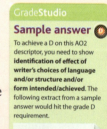

136 © Pearson Education Limited 2010

5 Comparison activities, page 128

Note: In order to do these activities, students would need to have completed their work on 'Sonnet 43'.

a In pairs or independently, students complete **Worksheet 4.22**, linking their response to the poems with the relevant Assessment Objective. Take feedback on any areas which students found difficult to grasp or to comment on.

> **Praise song for My Mother**
> 1 **Comparing ideas and themes**
> Compare the feelings of the **speakers** in 'Praise Song for My Mother' and 'Sonnet 43'.
> 2 **Comparing writers' devices**
> Compare the ways in which the writers use repetitions to show how the characters feel in 'Praise Song for My Mother' and 'Sonnet 43'.

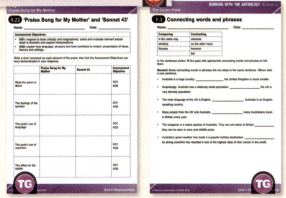

b Students use their notes from **Worksheet 4.22** to write three or four key points comparing the feelings of the speakers in the poems and the use of repetitions. They should write **in complete sentences using connectives**. Display **Worksheet 1.3** to support them.

c Take feedback, compiling notes on the board. As a class, students find evidence from each poem to support each point.

d Students select three points with supporting evidence from those on the board.

e Students add a sentence or two to each point/piece of evidence, explaining and commenting on how the writers have presented their points of view.

6 Plenary

Take feedback on 'Praise Song for My Mother', annotating the poem displayed on the whiteboard using Wordbox. Focus on relevant key features, e.g:
- content
- language
- tone.
- interpretation
- structure

If students have studied and compared 'Sonnet 43', take feedback on relevant key similarities and differences in content, interpretation, language, structure or tone.

Suggested answers

Activity 1

1. Sight: moon's eye (stanza 2)
   Smell/Taste: crab's leg/the fried plantain smell (stanza 4)
   Touch: grained (stanza 2); warm (stanza 3)
   Hearing: you said (stanza 5).

2. Water: 'deep' suggests emotional and perhaps spiritual maturity; 'bold' suggests emotional courage; 'fathoming' suggests an inquisitive, exploratory nature.
   Moon: 'pull' suggests the influence her mother exerted; 'grained' suggests an abrasive quality, perhaps; 'mantling' suggests covering or clothing, implying protection and, perhaps, decoration.
   Sunrise: 'rise' suggests growth and empowerment; 'warm' suggests love and nurture; 'streaming' suggests active constancy.

3. **a** The pattern followed is:
   You were/[Metaphor] to me/[adjective/noun] and [adjective] and [adjective]
   b The use of the present participle, 'ing', suggests the active and enduring nature of her mother's influence.

4. **a** Like the previous three stanzas, it begins 'you were', but is condensed, giving three metaphors in one stanza.
   b It reflects the meaning of the word itself, and the constancy of her mother's active influence.
   c It suggests an acceleration or crescendo of praise.

5. The separation of the final line gives emphasis, reflects a change in speaker (quoting the mother's words), and reflects the separation of the speaker from her mother, suggesting that her mother's absolute and positive influence was not smothering or restrictive, but a preparation for 'wide futures'.

Activity 2

The use of metaphor suggests the range of influences and impressions the speaker's mother had on her: the image of water suggests strength and depth; the image of the moon suggests beauty and nurture; the image of sunrise suggests love. The imagery of the fourth stanza suggests beauty and life and nourishment. Combined, they suggest mutual love, respect, care and admiration.

Comparison activities

Key points for this activity are provided in **Worksheet 4.23**.

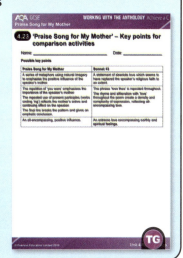

Chapter 4 Relationships

Harmonium
by Simon Armitage

Assessment Objectives
- **AO1:** respond to texts critically and imaginatively; select and evaluate relevant textual detail to illustrate and support interpretations
- **AO2:** explain how language, structure and form contribute to writers' presentation of ideas, themes and settings

Learning Objectives
- To develop students' responses to the poem
- To relate the Assessment Objectives to the poem

Required resources
- Poem text, available on CD-ROM and video/audio online at http://anthology.aqa.org.uk
- Student Book, page 109
- Worksheets 1.3, 4.24, 4.25, 4.26

1 Starter

Display/distribute **Worksheet 4.24**. Explain to students that this is the first stanza of the poem they will be studying in the rest of the lesson. Ask: Which of the options best fit the gaps in the verse? Give students 3 minutes in pairs to make their decisions and write their reasons in full sentences. Take feedback, focusing on language choice: what effect do students' choices create?

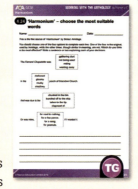

2 Activity 1

a Using the Digital Anthology, listen to/watch/read the poem to the class.

b Students complete questions 1–7 independently. Take feedback to share, ensure and develop understanding. Display the poem using the Digital Anthology, annotating the text with students' responses using Wordbox.

c Take students' initial response to the poem, commenting on the presentation of the relationship in the poem.

d Ask students to write a sentence or two, summing up the content or meaning of the poem. They can begin: *'Harmonium' is about….*

3 Activity 2

1 Display the quotation in close-up using the Digital Anthology. Students discuss the question in pairs, writing their response in full sentences to ensure clarity of thought and their ability to express it. Take feedback, annotating the displayed quotation using Wordbox.

2 Zoom out to display the entire poem. Students discuss the question in pairs, again writing their response in full sentences. Take feedback to share responses. Aim to validate all interpretations supported with evidence and/or explanation, recording appropriate annotations.

4 GradeStudio

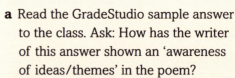

a Read the GradeStudio sample answer to the class. Ask: How has the writer of this answer shown an 'awareness of ideas/themes' in the poem?

b How could students add to or re-write this response to make an 'appropriate comment on ideas/themes' and achieve a C? For example: *Armitage makes connections in the poem between his father and the harmonium because both of them are near the end of their lives.*

c Where else in the poem is there an opportunity for students to comment on its ideas/themes? For example, the speaker's feelings at the end of the poem, or the use of personification.

d Ask students to select a short quotation that will allow them to explore their response to the poem. They then write a paragraph about it, using point-evidence-explanation.

5 Comparison activities, page 128

Note: In order to do these activities, students would need to have completed their work on 'Praise Song for My Mother'.

a In pairs or independently, students complete **Worksheet 4.25**, linking their response to the poems with the relevant Assessment Objective. Take feedback on any areas which students found difficult to grasp or to comment on.

> **Harmonium**
> 1 **Comparing ideas and themes**
>   Compare the feelings about parents in 'Praise Song for My Mother' and 'Harmonium'.
> 2 **Comparing writers' devices**
>   Compare the ways in which the writers show the feelings about parents in 'Praise Song for My Mother' and 'Harmonium' by the way they write about them. **SB**

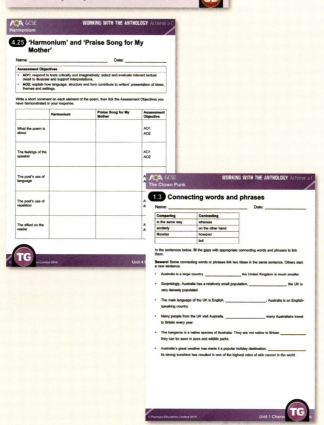

b Students use their notes from **Worksheet 4.25** to write three or four key points comparing the two writers' feelings about parents and how this is presented in the poems. They should write **in complete sentences using connectives**. Display **Worksheet 1.3** to support them.

c Take feedback, compiling notes on the board. As a class, students find evidence from each poem to support each point.

d Students select three points with supporting evidence from those on the board.

e Students add a sentence or two to each point/piece of evidence, explaining and commenting on how the writers have presented their points of view.

6 Plenary

Take feedback on 'Harmonium', annotating the poem displayed on the whiteboard using Wordbox. Focus on relevant key features, e.g:
- content
- language
- tone.
- interpretation
- structure

If students have studied and compared 'Praise Song for My Mother', take feedback on relevant key similarities and differences in content, interpretation, language, structure or tone.

Suggested answers

Activity 1

1 The harmonium was old, dusty, 'yellowed' and 'worn'. The speaker's father helps him carry it out of the church.

2 'aged the harmonium's softwood case/and yellowed the fingernails of its keys', 'lost its tongue', 'holes were worn', 'cart it away'.

3 Reference to 'fingernails' and 'tongue'.

4 **a** Musical puns.
  b The third stanza suggests it is the harmonium's age and history which attract the speaker; perhaps also the history of father-and-son relationships.

5 Like the yellow 'fingernails' of the harmonium, the father's fingers and thumbs are nicotine stained.

6 His father's coffin at his funeral.

7 **a** In addition to the connection of 'boxes' made by the father, the poem suggests the poet's desire to preserve the past: of the harmonium, of his father, of their relationship.
  b It suggests a closeness and, perhaps, reverence for his father: he may not be the figure he once was, but is clearly still a central figure in the speaker's life.
  c The most powerful effect is, perhaps, in the final lines, where the speaker's emotional horror at his father's words sparks our own.

Activity 2

1 The father's reflection on his death is a difficult thought to process and respond to. It winds the speaker.

2 Despite his desire to preserve them, silence is the inevitable conclusion to the lives of the harmonium – and the poet's father.

Comparison activities

Key points for this activity are provided in **Worksheet 4.26**.

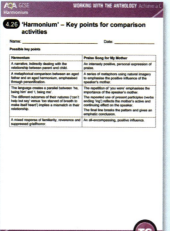

Chapter 4 Relationships

Sonnet 116 by William Shakespeare

Assessment Objectives
- **AO1:** respond to texts critically and imaginatively; select and evaluate relevant textual detail to illustrate and support interpretations
- **AO2:** explain how language, structure and form contribute to writers' presentation of ideas, themes and settings

Learning Objectives
- To develop students' responses to the poem
- To relate the Assessment Objectives to the poem

Required resources
- Poem text, available on CD-ROM and video/audio online at http://anthology.aqa.org.uk
- Student Book, page 110
- Worksheets 1.3, 4.27, 4.28

1 Starter
What is true love? Ask students to write as many definitions as they can in 3 minutes. Take feedback to share responses. To promote discussion, aim for a class consensus, recording it on the whiteboard.

2 Activity 1
a Using the Digital Anthology, listen to/watch/read the poem to the class.

b Students complete questions 1–7 independently. Take feedback to share, ensure and develop understanding. Display the poem using the Digital Anthology, annotating the text with students' responses using Wordbox.

c Take students' initial response to the poem, commenting on the presentation of the relationship in the poem. How does Shakespeare's exposition on the 'marriage of true minds' compare with those definitions discussed in the starter activity?

d Ask students to write a sentence or two, summing up the content or meaning of the poem. They can begin: *'Sonnet 116' is about… .*

Initial responses — ACTIVITY 1
1. The poem suggests true love does not change with time. Which words in the first two lines suggest this?
2. 'Love is not love' repeats the word 'love'. Where else in the next two lines does Shakespeare do this?
3. 'Ever-fixéd' suggests something that cannot be moved by anything. How is this idea shown in the next three lines? Look at the **imagery** Shakespeare uses.
4. How is love not the 'fool' of Time? Think about what Shakespeare is saying about the nature of love.
5. a How does Shakespeare suggest in line 9 that young people are altered by time?
   b What does his 'sickle' do to them?
6. In lines 11 and 12, how is love made to seem everlasting?
7. Look at the last two lines. The **speaker** is very confident that true love does not change with time. How does Shakespeare make this seem final and definite? Think about how the lines are placed on the page and where **rhyme** is used.

3 Activity 2
a Display the poem using the Digital Anthology.

b Students discuss the question in pairs, writing their response in full sentences to ensure clarity of thought and their ability to express it. Take feedback, annotating the poem displayed on the whiteboard using Wordbox. Aim to validate all interpretations supported with evidence and/or explanation.

Words/phrases to explore (AO1 and AO2) — ACTIVITY 2
In the whole poem, how is love seen as an 'ever-fixéd mark'? Think about each part of this phrase.

4 GradeStudio
a Read the GradeStudio sample answer to the class. Ask: How has the writer of this answer shown a 'considered/qualified response to the text'?

b Students add a further sentence to the sample answer, commenting on its effect. For example: *The suggestion is, perhaps, that while love's specific worth is not known, it is its constancy and permanence which are of the greatest value.*

c Where else in the poem is there an opportunity for students to respond to the poet's uses of language and structure? For example, the use of repetition in lines 2, 3 and 4, or the decisive finality of the final couplet.

d Ask students to select a short quotation that will allow them to explore their response to the poem. They then write a paragraph about it, using point-evidence-explanation.

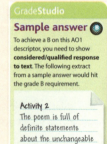

5 Comparison activities, page 129

Note: In order to do these activities, students would need to have completed their work on 'Hour'.

a In pairs or independently, students complete **Worksheet 4.27**, linking their response to the poems with the relevant Assessment Objective. Take feedback on any areas which students found difficult to grasp or to comment on.

Sonnet 116

1. **Comparing ideas and themes**
   Compare the ideas about love shown in 'Sonnet 116' and 'Hour'.
2. **Comparing writers' devices**
   Compare the ways in which the writers present love in 'Sonnet 116' and 'Hour' by the ways they write about it.

b Students use their notes from **Worksheet 4.27** to write three or four key points comparing the views about love and the ways in which the writers present love in the poems. They should write **in complete sentences using connectives**. Display **Worksheet 1.3** to support them.

c Take feedback, compiling notes on the board. As a class, students find evidence from each poem to support each point.

d Students select three points with supporting evidence from those on the board.

e Students add a sentence or two to each point/piece of evidence, explaining and commenting on how the writers have presented their points of view.

6 Plenary

Take feedback on 'Sonnet 116', annotating the poem displayed on the whiteboard using Wordbox. Focus on relevant key features, e.g:
- content
- language
- tone.
- interpretation
- structure

If students have studied and compared 'Hour', take feedback on relevant key similarities and differences in content, interpretation, language, structure or tone.

Suggested answers

Activity 1

1. 'Let me not' (strengthened by the repetition of 'not' in the second line) and 'Admit' suggest that contradiction is impossible.

2. 'alters… alteration', 'remover… remove'.

3. Love cannot be shaken by tempests; it's position is so certain it is like a star by which ships can navigate. Although it can be measured, its value is immeasurable.

4. Time cannot (or should not, if it is true love) be able to diminish love.

5. **a/b** 'rosy lips and cheeks' will not last forever: time's sickle will cut them down and their beauty will fade over time.

6. True love will last longer than hours or weeks: it will last until domesday, the end of the world.

7. The rhyming couplet, indented, presents a final stage in the argument: not an exposition of true love, but the writer's certainty of his belief.

Activity 2

The key points the writer makes are of permanence, contained in the words:
- 'ever' implied in true love's permanence until 'the edge of doom'
- 'fixed', referring to true love's inability to alter, bend or be removed: like the north star (the only star that does not change its position in the sky and which was therefore essential for navigation).

Comparison activities

Key points for this activity are provided in **Worksheet 4.28**.

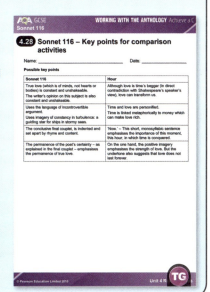

Chapter 4 Relationships

Sonnet 43 by Elizabeth Barrett Browning

Learning Objectives
- To develop students' responses to the poem
- To relate the Assessment Objectives to the poem

Assessment Objectives
- **AO1:** respond to texts critically and imaginatively; select and evaluate relevant textual detail to illustrate and support interpretations
- **AO2:** explain how language, structure and form contribute to writers' presentation of ideas, themes and settings

Required resources
- Poem text, available on CD-ROM and video/audio online at http://anthology.aqa.org.uk
- Student Book, page 111
- Worksheets 1.3, 4.29, 4.30, 4.31

1 Starter

a Without any pre-teaching, give students 5 minutes to write a letter to the (anonymous) person of their choice, declaring their love for them. Explain that the intention is to persuade their loved one to reciprocate, and so the letter should be bold and persuasive!

b Students swap their letters with a partner. What techniques have been used to persuade the recipient of their true love? Ask volunteers to read examples and name effective techniques.

2 Activity 1

a Using the Digital Anthology, listen to/watch/read the poem to the class. What techniques has Barrett Browning used to convince her loved one of her love?

b Students complete questions 1–6 independently. Take feedback to share, ensure and develop understanding. Display the poem using the Digital Anthology, annotating the text with students' responses using Wordbox.

c Take students' initial response to the poem, commenting on the presentation of the relationship in the poem.

d Ask students to write a sentence or two, summing up the content or meaning of the poem. They can begin: 'Sonnet 43' is about... .

> **Initial responses** — ACTIVITY 1
> 1. Count the number of ways in which the **speaker** loves 'thee'.
> 2. 'the ends of Being and ideal Grace' describes a spiritual search. How does the whole sentence in lines 2–4 suggest something very large? Look at the way line 2 is written as well as what the words mean.
> 3. How do lines 5 and 6 suggest small things rather than large, but things for every time of day?
> 4. What has happened to the love that the speaker used to have for her 'lost saints'? Notice that she 'seemed' to lose it.
> 5. Look at the punctuation in lines 12 and 13. Dashes, commas and the exclamation mark have an effect on how you say and hear the line. What does it tell you about the speaker's feelings at this point? Remember that this is near to the end of her thoughts, too.
> 6. How is the final way she mentions she loves 'thee' the biggest?

3 Activity 2

a Display the poem using the Digital Anthology.

b Students work on the task in pairs. Take feedback, annotating the poem displayed on the whiteboard using Wordbox.

c In the same pairings, students now record their response in full sentences to ensure clarity of thought and their ability to express it. The task focuses on the apparent conflict between earthly and godly love, which seems unresolved. Aim to validate (and emphasise the importance of recognising) a range of interpretations supported with evidence and/or explanation, adding relevant annotations to the displayed poem.

> **Words/phrases to explore (AO1 and AO2)** — ACTIVITY 2
> She will love him 'after death', 'if God choose'. This is a religious idea.
> 1. Where else in the poem does the poet use religious ideas? Look for words and phrases associated with religion.
> 2. What does this add to the poem, do you think? What sort of person is the speaker? Write a paragraph about the poem beginning 'speaker of the poem likes ...'.

4 GradeStudio

a Read the GradeStudio sample answer to the class. Ask: How has the writer of this answer shown 'effective use of details to support interpretation'?

b Where else in the poem is there an opportunity for students to explore interpretation? For example, the contrast of the physical and spiritual in lines 2–4, or the conflict of 'life' and 'death' in the final two lines.

c Ask students to select a short quotation that will allow them to explore their response to the poem. They then write a paragraph about it, using point-evidence-explanation.

> **GradeStudio Sample answer**
> To achieve a C on this AO1 descriptor, you need to show **effective use of details to support interpretation**. The following extract from a sample answer would hit the grade C requirement.
>
> The nature of the love the writer expresses changes at line 9. Up to that point the love seems quite spiritual – 'quiet' 'freely' 'purely' all suggest this – but now 'passion' appears

5 Comparison activities, page 129

Note: In order to do these activities, students would need to have completed their work on 'Hour' and 'In Paris with You'.

1 a In pairs or independently, students complete **Worksheet 4.29**, linking their response to the poems with the relevant Assessment Objective. Take feedback on any areas which students found difficult to grasp or to comment on.

Sonnet 43

1 Comparing ideas and themes
Compare the feelings about a loved one shown in 'Sonnet 43' and 'Hour'.

2 Comparing writers' devices
Compare the ways in which love is shown in 'Sonnet 43' and 'In Paris with You'.

b Students use their notes from **Worksheet 4.29** to write three or four key points comparing how the two writers show feelings for a loved one in the poems. They should write **in complete sentences using connectives**. Display **Worksheet 1.3** to support them.

c Take feedback, compiling notes on the board. As a class, students find evidence from each poem to support each point.

d Students select three points with supporting evidence from those on the board.

e Students add a sentence or two to each point/piece of evidence, explaining and commenting on how the writers have presented their points of view.

2 Repeat the above sequence using **Worksheet 4.30**, looking at the ways love is shown in the two poems.

6 Plenary

Take feedback on 'Sonnet 43', annotating the poem displayed on the whiteboard using Wordbox. Focus on relevant key features, e.g.:
- content
- language
- tone.
- interpretation
- structure

If students have studied and compared 'Hour' and/or 'In Paris with You', take feedback on relevant key similarities and differences in content, interpretation, language, structure or tone.

Suggested answers

Activity 1

1 Eight ways (including the final promise to 'love thee' after death).

2 The speaker's choice of language moves from physical dimensions ('depth… breadth… height') to the spiritual ('soul… Being… Grace'), expressing them in exaggerated physical terms ('reach… out of sight… the ends').

The repetitive structure ('and… and') of line 2 emphasises the dimensions of the speaker's love.

3 'everyday's/Most quiet need' suggests the mundanities of everyday life in which her love satisfies even her smallest ('most quiet') needs consistently, day and night: 'by sun and candlelight'.

4 The speaker appears to be suggesting that her religious love for the saints has been replaced with an earthly love. 'Seemed' suggests a loss of faith, although this is countered by the poem's final lines.

5 The effect is of a sudden outburst, an unstoppable expression of the importance of this love in her life. Coming between a reflection on the past ('I seemed to lose') and the future ('I shall'), it brings the power of her present emotions back to the fore of the poem.

6 The final line expresses the eternity of her love.

Activity 2

1 Lines 3 and 4.

2 These lines seem to introduce a conflict between spiritual love and physical love: when 'ideal grace' is 'out of sight', the speaker's love reaches to the very edges of her soul. This implied absence of 'Grace' is echoed in the closing reference to 'lost saints'. Although the final lines emphasise the speaker's religious conviction, there seems to be a reluctance to place her earthly love on an equal footing with her spiritual love.

Comparison activities

Key points for this activity are provided in **Worksheet 4.31**.

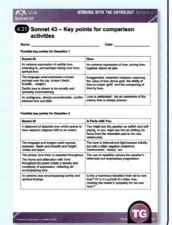

Chapter 4 Relationships

To His Coy Mistress
by Andrew Marvell

Assessment Objectives
- **AO1:** respond to texts critically and imaginatively; select and evaluate relevant textual detail to illustrate and support interpretations
- **AO2:** explain how language, structure and form contribute to writers' presentation of ideas, themes and settings

Learning Objectives
- To develop students' responses to the poem
- To relate the Assessment Objectives to the poem

Required resources
- Poem text, available on CD-ROM and video/audio online at http://anthology.aqa.org.uk
- Student Book, page 112
- Worksheets 1.3, 4.32, 4.33, 4.34, 4.35

1 Starter

Display **Worksheet 4.32**. Explain that the words in the table are comparisons taken from the poem that they are looking at in this lesson. Students match the two elements of each comparison, writing a sentence or two explaining their decision. Take feedback to share ideas and discuss the effect of Marvell's choices.

2 Activity 1

a Using the Digital Anthology, listen to/watch/read the poem to the class.
b Students complete questions 1–6 independently. Take feedback to share, ensure and develop understanding. Display the poem using the Digital Anthology, annotating the text with students' responses using Wordbox.
c Take students' initial response to the poem, commenting on the presentation of the relationship in the poem.
d Ask students to write a sentence or two, summing up the content or meaning of the poem. They can begin: '*To His Coy Mistress' is about…*.

Initial responses — ACTIVITY 1
1. The three **stanzas** are like three stages of an argument, where the speaker is trying to get the woman to sleep with him. What are the stages? Look at the first line of each stanza, and particularly the first two words.
2. In the first stanza the **speaker** suggests what he would do if he had all the world and endless time. Find all the references you can to places and stretches of time. You could start with 'our long love's day'.
3. The speaker allots amounts of time to his mistress's body parts – for example, 'an hundred years' to the eyes.
   a Find other examples in the poem of this?
   b Why do you think he leaves the heart till 'the last age'?
4. The attitude to time changes in the second stanza. Why do you think Marvell describes time as having a 'winged chariot'?
5. a Why does he describe eternity as a 'desert'? Remember what deserts are like, and what he is trying to persuade his mistress to do.
   b What other words and phrases in the stanza suggest emptiness and death?
6. 'Now' begins the third stanza. Look at the first seven lines, and all the suggestions you can of 'now', and speed, and youth, and...

3 Activity 2

a Display the last few lines of the poem in close-up using the Digital Anthology.
b Students discuss the questions in pairs, writing their response in full sentences to ensure clarity of thought and their ability to express it. Take feedback, annotating the quotation using Wordbox. Aim to validate all interpretations supported with evidence from elsewhere in the poem and/or explanation, 'zooming out' to display the whole poem and recording annotations on it.

Words/phrases to explore (AO1 and AO2) — ACTIVITY 2
The last two lines complete the argument ("Thus, …").
1. What is the speaker saying about time here ('we cannot make …')?
2. What does the speaker think the lovers should do to 'make him run'?

You could write a paragraph showing how the whole poem leads to these two lines.

4 GradeStudio

a Read the GradeStudio sample answer to the class. Ask: How has the writer of this answer shown 'explanation of effect(s) of writer's uses of language and/or form and/or structure and effects on readers'?
b Where else in the poem is there an opportunity for students to analyse closely the poet's uses of language and structure? For example, the poem's three-part argument, or the imagery of the second stanza or the final couplet.
c Ask students to select a short quotation that will allow them to explore their response to the poem. They then write a paragraph about it, using point-evidence-explanation.

GradeStudio Sample answer
To achieve a C on this AO2 descriptor, you need to show **explanation of effect of the writer's uses of language and/or structure and/or form and effects on readers**. The following extract from a sample answer would hit the grade C requirement.

Activity 1, question 6
The speaker describes the lovers (as he would like them to be) as being 'like am'rous birds of prey' in the third part. You might expect 'am'rous' birds to be gentle, like doves, but this idea suggests that he wants them to be strong and aggressive when they make love, which goes with 'tear our pleasures'. This is very physical love.

144 © Pearson Education Limited 2010

5 Comparison activities, page 129

Note: In order to do these activities, students would need to have completed their work on 'In Paris With You' and 'Ghazal'.

1 a In pairs or independently, students complete **Worksheet 4.33**, linking their response to the poems with the relevant Assessment Objective. Take feedback on any areas which students found difficult to grasp or to comment on.

To His Coy Mistress

1. **Comparing ideas and themes**
   Compare the attitudes to another person in 'To His Coy Mistress' and 'In Paris with You'.
2. **Comparing writers' devices**
   Compare the ways in which the writers use comparisons drawn from nature to describe things in 'To His Coy Mistress' and 'Ghazal'.

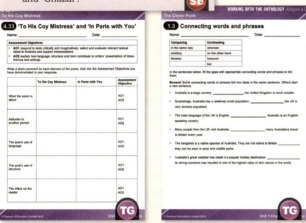

b Students use their notes from **Worksheet 4.33** to write three or four key points comparing the speakers' attitudes to another person in the poems. They should write **in complete sentences using connectives**. Display **Worksheet 1.3** to support them.

c Take feedback, compiling notes on the board. As a class, students find evidence from each poem to support each point.

d Students select three points with supporting evidence from those on the board.

e Students add a sentence or two to each point/piece of evidence, explaining and commenting on how the writers have presented their points of view.

2 Repeat the above sequence using **Worksheet 4.34**, looking at the two poets' use of comparisons drawn from nature.

6 Plenary

Take feedback on 'To His Coy Mistress', annotating the poem displayed on the whiteboard using Wordbox. Focus on relevant key features, e.g:
- content
- language
- tone.
- interpretation
- structure

If students have studied and compared 'In Paris with You' and/or 'Ghazal', take feedback on relevant key similarities and differences in content, interpretation, language, structure or tone.

Suggested answers

Activity 1

1 The first stanza explores how their love might grow if they had all the time in the world.

The second stanza explains that this is not so: time flies; death and decay await.

The third stanza expresses the speaker's conclusion: he wants to 'sport us while we may'.

2 'long love's day', 'Indian Ganges', 'the tide/Of Humber', 'ten years before the Flood', 'Till the conversion of the Jews', 'Vaster than empires and more slow', 'An hundred years', 'Two hundred', 'thirty thousand', 'An age… the last age'.

3 a 'Two hundred to adore each breast… thirty thousand to the rest'.

b The speaker seems to be moving from physical to emotional admiration.

4 The speaker is emphasising the pace at which time moves: a chariot suggests speed.

5 a 'Deserts' implies endless barrenness – in contrast to the fertility which he wishes to take advantage of – before it is too late! The negative image – in conjunction with references to the decay and death of his love's beauty – is intended to persuade.

b 'marble vault', 'echoing', 'worms', 'dust', 'ashes', 'grave'.

6 'youthful', 'morning dew', 'instant fires', 'while we may', 'like am'rous birds of prey… at once our time devour'.

Activity 2

1 Time cannot be stopped.

2 Suggests that they will beat time, frighten it away – or perhaps make it fly, so great will be their pleasure.

Comparison activities

Key points for this activity are provided in **Worksheet 4.35**.

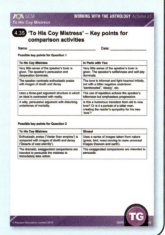

Chapter 4 Relationships

The Farmer's Bride
by Charlotte Mew

Assessment Objectives
- **AO1:** respond to texts critically and imaginatively; select and evaluate relevant textual detail to illustrate and support interpretations
- **AO2:** explain how language, structure and form contribute to writers' presentation of ideas, themes and settings

Learning Objectives
- To develop students' responses to the poem
- To relate the Assessment Objectives to the poem

Required resources
- Poem text, available on CD-ROM and video/audio online at http://anthology.aqa.org.uk
- Student Book, page 113
- Worksheets 1.3, 4.36, 4.37

1 Starter

a Display the **first** stanza of the poem only using the Digital Anthology.

b Ask students to write an extract from the husband's diary, describing his wife and his thoughts on their wedding day; then a similar extract from his wife's diary.

c Take feedback: what impressions have students gained of the couple's appearance and attitudes to each other?

2 Activity 1

a Using the Digital Anthology, listen to/watch/read the poem to the class.

b Students complete questions 1–7 independently. Take feedback to share, ensure and develop understanding. Display the poem using the Digital Anthology, annotating the text with students' responses using Wordbox.

c Take students' initial response to the poem, commenting on the presentation of the relationship in the poem.

d Ask students to write a sentence or two, summing up the content or meaning of the poem. They can begin: *'The Farmer's Bride' is about…*.

ACTIVITY 1
Initial responses
1. Work out the story of the poem – what happened in the past, the time of year now, and where the farmer and his bride are in the house?
2. What clues can you find in the first three lines to what goes wrong in the relationship? Think about the age of the woman.
3. The girl is described as running 'like a hare'.
   a. Find all the other comparisons you can between the girl and parts of nature, rather than 'all things human'.
   b. What evidence can you find that she is happier with animals than humans?
4. The last word of the second **stanza** is 'fast.', which means 'safely locked up' here. How is this word emphasised? Think about where it is placed and the punctuation.
5. The short fourth stanza describes the girl from the point of view of the man. What does it show about how he feels about her?
6. The fifth stanza describes the time of year. How could some of these details relate to the story of the girl and the farmer?
7. a. What do the repetitions in the last stanza show about what the **speaker** is thinking and feeling?
   b. What is the effect on the reader of ending the story like you think?

3 Activity 2

a Display the poem using the Digital Anthology.

b In pairs, students discuss their response to the wife's situation, writing in full sentences to ensure clarity of thought and their ability to express it. Ask volunteers to share their thoughts with the class.

c If time allows, ask students to write a short, imagined monologue in the voice of the wife. Ask volunteers to read their work. Do the class agree with their interpretation of her thoughts?

d In pairs, students discuss the significance of the husband as narrator, again writing their response in full sentences. Aim to validate all interpretations supported with evidence and/or explanation, recording annotations on the displayed poem using Wordbox.

ACTIVITY 2
Words/phrases to explore (AO1 and AO2)
'Alone, poor maid.' How do you feel about the girl's situation in the poem? What difference does it make that the story is narrated by the husband? You could write a paragraph beginning with that p…

4 GradeStudio

a Read the GradeStudio sample answer to the class. Ask: How has the writer of this answer shown 'awareness of a writer making choice(s) of language and/or form and/or structure'?

b How could students re-write or add to the example to show 'identification of effect(s) of writer's choices of language and/or structure and/or form' to achieve a D? For example: *It makes the girl seem timid and frightened…*. Then, in addition, they should re-write or add to their answer to show 'explanation of effect(s) of writer's uses of language and/or structure and/or form' and achieve a C. For example: *…of the human world and much more at home with the natural world.*

GradeStudio
Sample answer
To achieve an E on this AO1 descriptor, you need to show **awareness of writer making choice(s) of language and/or structure and/or form**. The following extract from a sample answer would hit the grade E requirement.

Activity 1, question 3a
The writer uses a simile to describe the girl, 'like a mouse'.

To improve on this, you would have to **identify the effect** and **explain** it (C).

c Where else in the poem is there an opportunity for students to explore the poet's uses of language or structure? For example, the description of the girl's behaviour in the early stanzas, or the repetitions of the final stanza.

d Ask students to select a short quotation that will allow them to explore their response to the poem. They then write a paragraph about it, using point-evidence-explanation.

5 Comparison activities, page 129

Note: In order to do these activities, students would need to have completed their work on 'To His Coy Mistress'.

a In pairs or independently, students complete **Worksheet 4.36**, linking their response to the poems with the relevant Assessment Objective. Take feedback on any areas which students found difficult to grasp or to comment on.

The Farmer's Bride
1 **Comparing ideas and themes**
Compare the attitudes towards another person in 'The Farmer's Bride' and 'To His Coy Mistress'.
2 **Comparing writers' devices**
Compare the ways in which the writers end the poems in 'The Farmer's Bride' and 'To His Coy Mistress'.

b Students use their notes from **Worksheet 4.36** to write three or four key points comparing speakers' attitudes towards another person and the endings of the poems. They should write **in complete sentences using connectives**. Display **Worksheet 1.3** to support them.

c Take feedback, compiling notes on the board. As a class, students find evidence from each poem to support each point.

d Students select three points with supporting evidence from those on the board.

e Students add a sentence or two to each point/piece of evidence, explaining and commenting on how the writers have presented their points of view.

Suggested answers

Activity 1

1 Three years (Summers) ago, the farmer married but his bride shut herself away from other people as if frightened, although she is happy in the company of the farm's animals. As Autumn changes to Winter and Christmas approaches, she now sleeps alone up in the attic.

2 The speaker suggests his bride was too young – and perhaps that his focus on work has not allowed him to give much time to the relationship.

3 a 'she turned afraid', 'Like the shut of a winter's day', 'Out 'mong the sheep, her be', 'her wide brown stare', 'flying like a hare', 'like a mouse', 'Shy as a leveret', 'Straight and slight as a young larch tree/ Sweet as the first wild violets', 'her wild self'.

b She is 'Happy enough to chat and play/With birds and rabbits' and 'beasts in stall/Look round like children at her call.'

4 It is the final word in the stanza and so is followed by a break – and is preceded by the pause of a comma.

5 She seems distant, an unfathomable force of nature who has no feelings for her husband. He seems mystified and disappointed by her.

6 The stanza describes the winter; the initial images are of cold darkness, perhaps suggesting the relationship between husband and wife; the image of the 'one leaf' suggests the husband's loneliness. The 'magpie's feathers' suggest damage and loss. The red of Christmas berries suggests perhaps the contrast of hoped-for joy and actual sadness – and perhaps blood.

7 a The repetitions suggest both incomprehension and desperation: 'the soft young down' and 'her hair' are both physical attributes suggesting sexual longing, while the repetition implies a crescendoing of his disappointment and desperation.

b The reader's focus is returned to the speaker: away from the mysterious bride to his emotional and physical state. Depending on the reader, it may bring a shift in sympathy as he focuses on his purely physical attraction to her.

Activity 2

Likely responses are of sympathy or mystification. The husband's narration allows the bride to remain a mystery – and allows the reader to have some sympathy with both characters.

Comparison activities

Key points for this activity are provided in **Worksheet 4.37**.

6 Plenary

Take feedback on 'The Farmer's Bride', annotating the poem displayed on the whiteboard using Wordbox. Focus on relevant key features, e.g:
- content
- interpretation
- language
- structure
- tone.

If students have studied and compared 'To His Coy Mistress', take feedback on relevant key similarities and differences in content, interpretation, language, structure or tone.

Chapter 4 Relationships

Sister Maude by Christina Rossetti

Assessment Objectives
- **AO1:** respond to texts critically and imaginatively; select and evaluate relevant textual detail to illustrate and support interpretations
- **AO2:** explain how language, structure and form contribute to writers' presentation of ideas, themes and settings

Learning Objectives
- To develop students' responses to the poem
- To relate the Assessment Objectives to the poem

Required resources
- Poem text, available on CD-ROM and video/audio online at http://anthology.aqa.org.uk
- Student Book, page 114
- Worksheets 1.3, 4.38, 4.39, 4.40

1 Starter

Write the words 'brothers' and 'sisters' on the whiteboard. Ask: What are they like? What is the kindest thing your brother/sister has done for you? What is the worst thing your brother/sister has done to you? Aim to collect a range of evidence of sibling love and hate.

2 Activity 1

a Using the Digital Anthology, listen to/watch/read the poem to the class.
b Display **Worksheet 4.38**, an extract from the Witches' spell from *Macbeth*. Explain to students that this will support them in their response to Question 6. Ask: What are the key features of a successful spell? Look for responses that recognise the use of repetition and rhyme.
c Students complete questions 1–6 independently. Take feedback to share, ensure and develop understanding. Display the poem using the Digital Anthology, annotating the text with students' responses using Wordbox.
d Take students' initial response to the poem, commenting on the presentation of the relationships in the poem.
e Ask students to write a sentence or two, summing up the content or meaning of the poem. They can begin: *'Sister Maude' is about…*.

3 Activity 2

a Display the poem using the Digital Anthology.
b Students discuss the questions in pairs, writing their response in full sentences to ensure clarity of thought and their ability to express it. Take feedback, annotating the poem displayed on the whiteboard using Wordbox. Aim to validate all interpretations supported with evidence and/or explanation.

Words/phrases to explore (AO1)
What do you think of the speaker of the poem? Write a paragraph about her, using details from the poem to support your response.

4 GradeStudio

a Read the GradeStudio sample answer to the class. Ask: How has the writer of this answer made 'appropriate comment on ideas/themes'?
b Where else in the poem is there an opportunity for students to explore response to the text? For example, the very physical description of the speaker's 'dear', or her attitude to her sister.
c Ask students to select a short quotation that will allow them to explore their response to the poem. They then write a paragraph about it, using point-evidence-explanation.

5 Comparison activities, page 129

Note: In order to do these activities, students would need to have completed their work on 'In Paris with You'.

a In pairs or independently, students complete **Worksheet 4.39**, linking their response to the poems with the relevant Assessment Objective. Take feedback on any areas which students found difficult to grasp or to comment on.

Sister Maude

1. **Comparing ideas and themes**
   Compare the state of mind of the speakers in 'Sister Maude' and 'In Paris with You'.
2. **Comparing writers' devices**
   Compare the ways in which the writers use repetitions in 'Sister Maude' and 'In Paris with You'.

b Students use their notes from **Worksheet 4.39** to write three or four key points comparing the speakers' states of mind and the writers' use of repetition in the poems. They should write **in complete sentences using connectives**. Display **Worksheet 1.3** to support them.

c Take feedback, compiling notes on the board. As a class, students find evidence from each poem to support each point.

d Students select three points with supporting evidence from those on the board.

e Students add a sentence or two to each point/piece of evidence, explaining and commenting on how the writers have presented their points of view.

6 Plenary

Take feedback on 'Sister Maude', annotating the poem displayed on the whiteboard using Wordbox. Focus on relevant key features, e.g:
- content
- language
- tone.
- interpretation
- structure

If students have studied and compared 'In Paris with You', take feedback on relevant key similarities and differences in content, interpretation, language, structure or tone.

Suggested answers

Activity 1

1. The poem suggests that Maude has betrayed her sister by revealing details of her affair to their mother and father – and perhaps 'stole' her lover.

2. **a/b** 'lurked… spy… peer' suggests she despises Maude for her actions.
   c 'He'd never have looked at you', 'sister Maude shall get no sleep', 'Bide you with death and sin.' All suggest contempt for Maude.

3. The repetition of 'cold' emphasises her regret and sadness at his death.

4. The reader's sympathy for the speaker grows as we realise that she has lost her only love and, effectively, her sister – as well as her parents.

5. **a** An eternity in hell.
   b The poem strongly suggests that sister Maude has committed sin (with the speaker's 'dear') and caused his death.

6. **a** The speaker heaps curses and threats on her sister for wronging her – typical of a spell, e.g. 'Sister Maude shall get no sleep… bide you with death and sin.'
   b Repetition is, similarly, a key feature of spells, creating a hypnotic effect – and perhaps intended to add to the efficacy of the spell.
   c The rhyme pattern is consistent throughout (abcb) until the final stanza, where a further couplet follows the same pattern (abcbdb). It seems to suggest a final nail in Maude's coffin.

Activity 2

Responses are likely to focus on sympathy for the speaker's loss and betrayal and, perhaps, shock at her extreme anger and bitterness.

Comparison activities

Key points for this activity are provided in **Worksheet 4.40**.

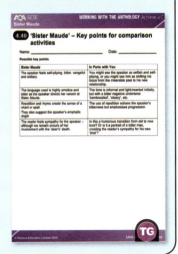

Chapter 4 Relationships

Nettles by Vernon Scannell

Assessment Objectives
- **AO1:** respond to texts critically and imaginatively; select and evaluate relevant textual detail to illustrate and support interpretations
- **AO2:** explain how language, structure and form contribute to writers' presentation of ideas, themes and settings

Learning Objectives
- To develop students' responses to the poem
- To relate the Assessment Objectives to the poem

Required resources
- Poem text, available on CD-ROM and video/audio online at http://anthology.aqa.org.uk
- Student Book, page 115
- Worksheets 1.3, 4.41, 4.42, 4.43

1 Starter

a Ask volunteers to recount stories of accidents from their childhood – there will not be many who cannot contribute! Ask the volunteers the following questions:
- Do they remember these incidents clearly? If so, why?
- How did their parents react at the time?
- Did their parents do anything as a result of the incident – i.e. take preventative measures?
- Do their parents continue to (over-)protect them?

b Ask students what these stories suggest about the relationship between parents and children.

2 Activity 1

a Using the Digital Anthology, listen to/watch/read the poem to the class.

b Students complete questions 1–9 independently. Take feedback to share, ensure and develop understanding. Display the poem using the Digital Anthology, annotating the text with students' responses using Wordbox.

c Take students' initial response to the poem, commenting on the presentation of the relationship in the poem.

d Ask students to write a sentence or two, summing up the content or meaning of the poem. They can begin: 'Nettles' is about… .

Initial responses — ACTIVITY 1
1 What happens to the boy in the poem? What does the father do?
2 The opening line is a simple statement. Find the other sentence which is like this one. Why does Scannell place them where he does?
3 Why does 'bed' seem to be a surprising name for where the nettles grow? Think about the possible contradiction here.
4 'Regiment' is the beginning of an extended **metaphor** comparing the nettles to an army.
  a Find all the other military terms in the poem.
  b Why is the use of military terms an appropriate idea to use for the nettles?
5 A metaphor like this is a way of getting over to the reader the **speaker's** emotions. Which word in line 3 does this more directly?
6 Why do you think the boy's grin is described as 'watery'?
7 'Not a nettle in that fierce parade/Stood upright.' Why is the parade 'fierce'?
8 [What] are the 'recruits' that have been called up?
9 [How] does the father feel in this poem? Suggest more than one feeling.

3 Activity 2

a Display the quotation in close-up using the Digital Anthology.

b Students discuss the questions in pairs, writing their response in full sentences to ensure clarity of thought and their ability to express it. Take feedback, annotating the displayed quotation using Wordbox. Aim to validate all interpretations supported with evidence from elsewhere in the poem and/or explanation, 'zooming out' to display the whole poem and recording annotations on it.

Words/phrases to explore (AO1 and AO2) — ACTIVITY 2
'My son would often feel sharp wounds again' is very general, compared to the specific first line.
1 How does 'wounds' continue the military metaphor?
2 What 'sharp wounds' might the son feel in the future, apart from nettle stings?
3 What does this reveal about the father's feelings and attitude, do you think?

4 GradeStudio

a Read the GradeStudio sample answer to the class. Ask: How has the writer of this answer shown 'identification of effects of writer's choices of language and/or form and/or structure intended/achieved'?

GradeStudio Sample answer
To achieve a D on this AO2 descriptor, you need to show **identification of effects of the writer's choices of language and/or structure and/or form intended/achieved**. The following extract from a sample answer would hit the grade D requirement.

Activity 1, question 4b
Comparing the nettles to 'green spears' makes them seem like something that will hurt the boy.

To move to C, the effects have to be **explained**.

b How could students add to or rewrite this response to show 'explanation of effect(s) of writer's uses of language and/or structure and/or form and effects on readers' and so achieve a C? For example: *It not only describes their physical appearance but also makes them sound like weapons.*

c Where else in the poem is there an opportunity for students to explore interpretation supported by analysis of the poet's uses of language and structure? For example, the father's relationship with his son, or the extended metaphor/personification of the nettles.

d Ask students to select a short quotation that will allow them to explore their response to the poem. They then write a paragraph about it, using point-evidence-explanation.

5 Comparison activities, page 129

Note: In order to do these activities, students would need to have completed their work on 'Born Yesterday' and 'Quickdraw'.

1. **a** In pairs or independently, students complete **Worksheet 4.41**, linking their response to the poems with the relevant Assessment Objective. Take feedback on any areas which students found difficult to grasp or to comment on.

Nettles
1. **Comparing ideas and themes**
   Compare the attitudes towards a child in 'Nettles' and 'Born Yesterday'.
2. **Comparing writers' devices**
   Compare the ways in which the writers use metaphors in 'Nettles' and 'Quickdraw'.

b Students use their notes from **Worksheet 4.41** to write three or four key points comparing attitudes towards a child in the two poems. They should write **in complete sentences using connectives**. Display **Worksheet 1.3** to support them.

c Take feedback, compiling notes on the board. As a class, students find evidence from each poem to support each point.

d Students select three points with supporting evidence from those on the board.

e Students add a sentence or two to each point/piece of evidence, explaining and commenting on how the writers have presented their points of view.

2. Repeat the above sequence using **Worksheet 4.42**, looking at the two poets' use of metaphor.

6 Plenary

Take feedback on 'Nettles', annotating the poem displayed on the whiteboard using Wordbox. Focus on relevant key features, e.g:

- content
- language
- tone.
- interpretation
- structure

If students have studied and compared 'Born Yesterday' and/or 'Quickdraw', take feedback on relevant key similarities and differences in content, interpretation, language, structure or tone.

Suggested answers

Activity 1

1. The boy falls into the nettle bed. The father cuts the nettles down.

2. The first and last lines follow a similar pattern: both begin 'My son'; both are largely simple, monosyllabic sentences. The opening line establishes the stimulus for the poem; the final line concludes, looking to the future and alluding to the nature of this father/son relationship.

3. 'It was no place for rest.'

4. **a** 'that fierce parade', 'the fallen dead', 'recruits'.
   b The extended military metaphor suggests the ongoing battle against the nettles, the enemy that wounded his son – and, by further extension, all the hurt from which this parent will try to protect his child.

5. 'spite' suggests that the pain was intentionally and maliciously inflicted by the nettles and, in doing so, suggests the speaker's anger at this attack.

6. It suggests the tears still streaming down his face.

7. Again, personification is used to suggest the intentional malice of the nettles.

8. The new 'recruits' are the nettles beginning to grow again. It seems that the father is powerless against nature, suggesting that pain and suffering are an implicit part of life.

9. The father seems angry with the malicious nettles, sympathetic in his soothing of his son's pain, vengeful in his cutting the nettles down, and sad that this is not the last pain his son will experience.

Activity 2

1. It continues the military metaphor: the regiment of nettles have wounded his son, as a soldier might be wounded by an enemy.

2. It suggests not only physical wounds but, perhaps, emotional ones.

3. It suggests that the father is not only thinking of his son's future pain, but the impossibility of a parent protecting their child from life.

Comparison activities

Key points for this activity are provided in **Worksheet 4.43**.

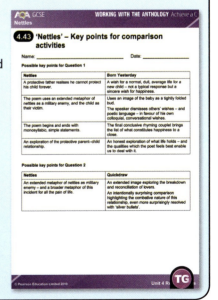

AQA GCSE Working with the Anthology: Achieve a C

Chapter 4 Relationships

Born Yesterday by Philip Larkin

Assessment Objectives
- **AO1:** respond to texts critically and imaginatively; select and evaluate relevant textual detail to illustrate and support interpretations
- **AO2:** explain how language, structure and form contribute to writers' presentation of ideas, themes and settings

Learning Objectives
- To develop students' responses to the poem
- To relate the Assessment Objectives to the poem

Required resources
- Poem text, available on CD-ROM and video/audio online at http://anthology.aqa.org.uk
- Student Book, page 116
- Worksheets 1.3, 4.44, 4.45

1 Starter

a Remind students of the fairy tale, 'Sleeping Beauty'. A number of fairies (the number depends on the version) are invited to a princess's baptism. Each grants the baby a gift. One fairy who was not invited turns up and places a curse upon the child.

b Ask students:
- If you were the child's parents, what gifts would you hope the fairies would bestow on your child? List **twelve**.
- What one gift would you hope the evil fairy would not bestow?

c Take feedback, aiming to conclude: What do we hope for our children?

2 Activity 1

a Using the Digital Anthology, listen to/watch/read the poem to the class.

b Students complete questions 1–6 independently. Take feedback to share, ensure and develop understanding. Display the poem using the Digital Anthology, annotating the text with students' responses using Wordbox.

c Take students' initial response to the poem, commenting on the presentation of the relationship in the poem.

d Ask students to write a sentence or two, summing up the content or meaning of the poem. They can begin: *'Born Yesterday' is about…*.

Initial responses — ACTIVITY 1
1. In what ways is the baby like a 'tightly folded bud'? Think about what a bud is, and how it changes over time.
2. What is 'the usual stuff' that people wish for a baby, according to the **speaker**?
3. Find the first wish that the speaker makes for the child.
   a. How does it sound like a wish? Notice where it comes in the poem, by counting the lines.
   b. Why has the writer made the choice to put it there, do you think?
4. Why might unusual talents be a negative thing, according to the speaker?
5. Wishing for a child to be 'ordinary' and 'dull' may seem unusual, but look at the list of things in lines 21–23 which the speaker wishes for the child. What sort of qualities are these, do you think? Think how the words here are different to the words like 'innocence', 'love', 'ugly', 'good-looking'.
6. a. Which word in the list is not downbeat like the rest of the poem, but actually sounds exciting?
   b. How is the feeling it suggests carried into the final line?
   c. What is the effect on the reader of finishing the poem after the feeling of the earlier part of the poem?

3 Activity 2

a Display the poem using the Digital Anthology.

b Students discuss the question in pairs, writing their response in full sentences to ensure clarity of thought and their ability to express it. Take feedback, annotating the poem displayed on the whiteboard using Wordbox. Aim to validate all interpretations supported with evidence and/or explanation.

Words/phrases to explore (AO1 and AO2) — ACTIVITY 2
What do the wishes for the child make you think about the speaker of the poem? Write a paragraph about what sort of person this is, using details from the poem.

4 GradeStudio

a Read the GradeStudio sample answer to the class. Ask: How has the writer of this answer shown an 'explained response to ideas/themes'?

b How could students add to or rewrite this response to show a 'sustained response to elements of text' and so achieve a C? For example: *…but this is what the speaker thinks will bring the child 'happiness' so, although he seems cynical, he is not completely unsentimental.*

c Where else in the poem is there an opportunity for students to explore the poem's ideas/themes? For example, the image of a 'Tightly-folded bud' or the list of 'Not the usual stuff'.

d Ask students to select a short quotation that will allow them to explore their response to the poem. They then write a paragraph about it, using point-evidence-explanation.

GradeStudio Sample answer
To achieve a D on this AO2 descriptor, you need to show **explained response to elements(s) of text**. The following extract from a sample answer would hit the grade D requirement.

Activity 2
The speaker does not seem very sentimental. He doesn't seem to want the child to be 'beautiful' or to have love, but to be 'average', not 'ugly'. This seems to deny everything most people wish for newly born children.

To move to C, the response below would have to be extended that it became sustained.

5 Comparison activities, page 129

Note: In order to do these activities, students would need to have completed their work on 'Praise Song for My Mother'.

a In pairs or independently, students complete **Worksheet 4.44**, linking their response to the poems with the relevant Assessment Objective. Take feedback on any areas which students found difficult to grasp or to comment on.

Born Yesterday

1. **Comparing ideas and themes**
   Compare the attitudes towards another person in 'Born Yesterday' and 'Praise Song for My Mother'.
2. **Comparing writers' devices**
   Compare the ways in which the writers present what they have to say in 'Born Yesterday' and 'Praise Song for My Mother'.

b Students use their notes from **Worksheet 4.44** to write three or four key points comparing the speakers' attitudes to another person and how the poets present their views in the poems **in complete sentences using connectives**. Display **Worksheet 1.3** to support them.

c Take feedback, compiling notes on the board. As a class, students find evidence from each poem to support each point.

d Students select three points with supporting evidence from those on the board.

e Students add a sentence or two to each point/piece of evidence, explaining and commenting on how the writers have presented their points of view.

6 Plenary

Take feedback on 'Born Yesterday', annotating the poem displayed on the whiteboard using Wordbox. Focus on relevant key features, e.g:
- content
- language
- tone.
- interpretation
- structure

If students have studied and compared 'Praise Song for My Mother', take feedback on relevant key similarities and differences in content, interpretation, language, structure or tone.

Suggested answers

Activity 1

1. A visual image: the baby is curled up and clenched; also a metaphor for a life about to unfold and grow; also imbues the child with the qualities of a flower – beauty, etc.
2. Beauty, innocence, and love.
3. **a** 'May you be ordinary': the first two words make it sound like a wish. It appears on line 12.
   b It comes near the beginning of the second stanza as the writer moves from the traditional wishes for a baby to his own, unconventional thoughts.
4. They might 'pull you off your balance'.
5. 'skilled,/Vigilant, flexible,/Unemphasised, enthralled' are qualities of personal choice rather than physical (e.g. 'ugly') or those given by others ('love'). It suggests that happiness comes from the decisions we make rather than our genetic inheritance or relationships.
6. **a** 'enthralled'.
   b It suggests a vitality continued in 'Catching of happiness'.
   c The tone of the poem is transformed at the end from a mood of mundanity to one of more conventional kindness.

Activity 2

Responses are likely to focus on the speaker's unusual wishes and his cynicism – or perhaps realism! Students may feel that the last four lines of the poem regain our empathy as the speaker more traditionally wishes her happiness.

Comparison activities

Key points for this activity are provided in **Worksheet 4.45**.

Chapter 4 Relationships

Looking at the poems individually: what have you learned?

Assessment Objectives
- **AO1:** respond to texts critically and imaginatively; select and evaluate relevant textual detail to illustrate and support interpretations
- **AO2:** explain how language, structure and form contribute to writers' presentation of ideas, themes and settings

Learning Objective
- To recap and explore students' responses to the poems

Required resources
- Student Book, page 117
- Worksheet 4.46, ideally enlarged to A3 size

1 Starter

Looking at the poems individually: what have you learned?

a Explain to students that this lesson will consolidate, recap and explore their knowledge and understanding of, and response to, the 15 poems they have explored.

b Give students 3 minutes to complete the following task in silence:
Without looking at their Anthology or any notes, how many of the poems can they remember from those they have explored over the last 15 lessons? They can either note down the titles (and poets, if possible) or give a brief description of the poem's content: *The one about… .*

c List the 15 poems aloud so students can check their answers. Ask students to add titles to the poems where the content but not the title had been remembered.

d Take feedback. How many poems could students remember? Based on the class's response as a whole, were some more memorable than others? Why?

The poems		
The Manhunt *Simon Armitage*	Brothers *Andrew Forster*	To His Coy Mistress *Andrew Marvell*
Hour *Carol Ann Duffy*	Praise Song for My Mother *Grace Nichols*	The Farmer's Bride *Charlotte Mew*
In Paris with You *James Fenton*	Harmonium *Simon Armitage*	Sister Maude *Christina Rossetti*
Quickdraw *Carol Ann Duffy*	Sonnet 116 *William Shakespeare*	Nettles *Vernon Scannell*
Ghazal *Mimi Khalvati*	Sonnet 43 *Elizabeth Barrett Browning*	Born Yesterday *Philip Larkin*

2 Activity 1

a Explain that Question 1 of the activity will consolidate their thinking from the starter activity.

b Read Question 1 aloud. Then ask students to choose the **five** poems which they responded to most strongly – it is likely that these will be the first five they listed in the Starter. Ask them to add a sentence explaining why they found this poem memorable: it may be an activity, a word, a line, an idea, a character, or a title which has sparked their engagement. Ask volunteers to share with the class.

c Read Question 2. Ask students: Are your answers to this question likely to feature the same poems as Question 1? Why?

d Give students 5 minutes to list the **five** poems they found it easiest to offer an interpretation about, using their notes from the last 15 lessons. Take feedback. Ask: Is it easier to talk and write about poems that are simpler to understand? Or is there more to be said (and more marks to be gained!) by exploring a variety of different interpretations of more complex poems?

Assessment Objective 1 (AO1) — ACTIVITY 1

1 Which of these poems did you **respond** to most strongly? You may have liked it, or disliked it, or found it the most interesting, or horrible. It might mean that you had a number of things to say about it.
Working with a partner, or by yourself, display your responses as a spider diagram, and then compare it with someone else's, to see if you have responded to the poems in similar ways.

2 Which poems did you find it easiest to offer an **interpretation** about? In other words, you had an opinion about a poem's meaning that you could argue from the text and **select detail** to support your opinion. For instance, you might have found it easy to argue and support the idea that the speaker in 'Praise Song for My Mother' admires her mother.
Suggesting more than one interpretation of a poem, or parts of a poem, gives you opportunities to score more marks. For instance, there are several ways you could interpret the nature of the speaker in 'The Farmer's Bride'.

3 Activity 2

Give students 20 minutes to complete both questions 1 and 2 of the activity. Students can record their responses on **Worksheet 4.46**. Point out that if they cannot think of anything significant in a particular area within, say, 30 seconds, then it does not suggest a ready understanding; they should move on to a new feature or poem. Take feedback to ensure and develop understanding.

Assessment Objective 2 (AO2) — ACTIVITY 2

1. Which features of **language**, **structure** or **form** did you understand best? The most promising ones to write about in the exam will be the ones where you have most to say. For instance, you might have found several things to say about:
   - the effect of the heart not being represented through a metaphor in 'The Manhunt' (**language**).
   - the gradual change in attitude in 'In Paris with You' (**structure**)
   - the effects of the spaces between stanzas in 'Quickdraw' (**form**).

2. What **ideas** did you identify in the poems? Again, the best answers will probably identify several ideas in a poem, or several aspects of one idea. For instance, you might have identified or explored more than one idea about life in 'To His Coy Mistress'.

4 Plenary

Ask students:
- Based on your exploration of content, interpretation, language, structure, form and ideas, which are the most memorable, exam-friendly poems in the 'Relationships' cluster? Do they have any significant links or points of comparison?
- Which poems are particularly difficult to write about?
- Which poems do you feel you need to give more (of your own) time to?

5 Further work

a. Students identify the **five** poems which have the fewest entries on **Worksheet 4.46**.

b. Students complete each column for each poem, using **Worksheet 4.46** and their notes.

4.46 What have you learned?

Name: _____ Date: _____

Title	Language	Structure	Form	Ideas
The Manhunt – Simon Armitage				
Hour – Carol Ann Duffy				
In Paris with You – James Fenton				
Quickdraw – Carol Ann Duffy				
Ghazal – Mimi Khalvati				
Brothers – Andrew Forster				
Praise Song for My Mother – Grace Nichols				
Harmonium – Simon Armitage				
Sonnet 116 – William Shakespeare				
Sonnet 43 – Elizabeth Barrett Browning				
To His Coy Mistress – Andrew Marvell				
The Farmer's Bride – Charlotte Mew				
Sister Maude – Christina Rossetti				
Nettles – Vernon Scannell				
Born Yesterday – Philip Larkin				

Chapter 4 Relationships

Comparing the 'Relationships' poems (1)

Assessment Objective
- **AO3:** make comparisons and explain links between texts, evaluating writers' different ways of expressing meaning and achieving effects

Learning Objectives
- To develop students' abilities to compare the poems
- To relate the Assessment Objectives to the poems
- To develop students' writing skills for the exam

Required resources
- Poem texts, available on CD-ROM and video/audio online at http://anthology.aqa.org.uk
- Student Book, page 118
- Worksheet 4.47

1 Starter

a Read the explanation of the Assessment Objective on page 118 of the Student Book, clarifying understanding of the Assessment Objective's demands.

b Explain to students that in this lesson they are going to compare 'In Paris with You' and 'Quickdraw'.

c Display both poems on the whiteboard, side by side, using the Digital Anthology. Re-read the poems.

d Ask students to describe the content of each poem, providing evidence where appropriate. Draw the events in the poem on the board as they are described, annotating with quotations. Depending on your art skills, you may want to ask a volunteer student to take this role!

Assessment Objective:

The Assessment Objective you will be focusing on in this part of the chapter is:

 make comparisons and explain links between texts, evaluating writers' different ways of expressing meaning and achieving effects.

2 Activity 1

a Using **Worksheet 4.47**, students record all the similarities and differences they can think of in the two poems in the first column on the worksheet. The second column is for their responses to Activity 2.

b Take feedback, ideally compiling students' responses on a copy of the worksheet projected onto the whiteboard.

ACTIVITY 1

Think about the ideas and themes in the two poems. List as many similarities and differences as you can. For example, both poems are about difficulties in love, so you could think about the following points:
1 Are the attitudes to the other people in the poems similar, or different? How?
2 Do the feelings of the characters in the poems change, or stay the same?
3 Which of these poems has stronger feelings for another person

156 © Pearson Education Limited 2010

3 Activity 2

Explain that this is an opportunity for students to develop their points of comparison. Use the example in the Student Book and perhaps one other from the class's responses on the whiteboard. Remind students of the need for evidence to support each point. Take feedback, again compiling notes on the whiteboard.

ACTIVITY 2

Using your list of similarities and differences from Activity 1, decide how different each of the poems are for each point you made. For example, both **speakers** have had difficulties with another person, but in 'In Paris with You' the difficulties seem to be over. The speaker in 'Quickdraw' seems to still be in the middle of her problems.

Use quotations or refer to the poem to support what you think.

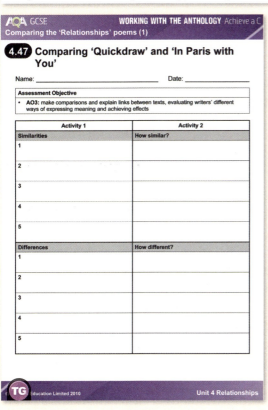

4 Plenary

a Read the GradeStudio sample answer on page 118 to the class. Ask: How has the writer of this answer made 'some comment(s) on similarities/differences, with detail'?

b Explain that they will be exploring this response further in the next lesson. Give students 2–3 minutes to consider in pairs how they could develop this response to show 'structured comments on similarities/differences, with detail' and so achieve a D. For example: *However, the speaker in 'In Paris with You' is reflecting bitterly on a past relationship, while the speaker in 'Quickdraw' is fighting with her lover by phone.*

c Give a further 2 minutes to consider: How could the answer be developed further to show 'sustained focus on similarities/differences, with detail' and so achieve a C? For example: *'Quickdraw' ends happily but violently with 'the silver bullets of your kiss'. 'In Paris with You' ends happily too, but only for the speaker because he is 'in Paris with you'. It seems less happy for his lover who has had to listen to his bitter complaints and 'embarrassing' passion.*

d Take feedback, compiling a class response on the whiteboard to share and develop thinking. If possible, save or note this response for reference next lesson.

GradeStudio

Sample answer E

To achieve a grade E on this AO3 descriptor, you need to make **some comment(s) on similarities/differences, with detail**. The following extract from a sample answer to Activity 4 would hit the grade E requirement.

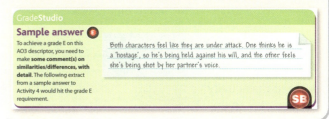

Both characters feel like they are under attack. One thinks he is a 'hostage', so he's being held against his will, and the other feels she's being shot by her partner's voice.

Suggested answers

Activities 1/2

Similarities:
- Both poems focus on love and relationships.
- Both speakers' moods change as the poem progresses.
- Both relationships seem precarious.
- Both use informal and aggressive language.
- Both use repetition for effect.
- Both are written in the first person, suggesting personal experience.

Differences:
- One ends with violent reconciliation, the other with a new relationship.
- One moves from violence to a kind of peace, the other from bitterness to selfish passion.
- One uses an extended metaphor of guns and violence, the other uses Paris as a metaphor for romance.

Chapter 4 Relationships

Comparing the 'Relationships' poems (2)

Assessment Objective
- **AO3:** make comparisons and explain links between texts, evaluating writers' different ways of expressing meaning and achieving effects

Learning Objectives
- To develop students' abilities to compare the poems
- To relate the Assessment Objectives to the poems
- To develop students' writing skills for the exam

Required resources
- Poem texts, available on CD-ROM and video/audio online at http://anthology.aqa.org.uk
- Student Book, pages 119–22, 142–143
- Worksheets 4.48

1 Starter

a Recap the comparison process from the previous lesson.
b Read the explanation of the Assessment Objective on page 118 of the Student Book, clarifying understanding of the Assessment Objective's demands.
c Explain to students that in this lesson, they are going to continue to compare 'Quickdraw' and 'In Paris With You', then use this process to develop their comparison skills further.
d Display both poems on the whiteboard, side by side, using the Digital Anthology. Re-read the poems.

2 Activity 3

a Read the activity aloud, clarifying students' understanding if necessary.
b Students complete the bullet pointed questions independently. Take feedback to share, ensure and develop understanding.

3 Activity 4

a Read the activity instructions, discussing each bullet point as a class.
b Give students 10 minutes to note down their thoughts in bullet points. Take feedback to share, ensure and develop understanding.
c Ask students to write a paragraph comparing the two poems, aiming to achieve a C by showing a 'sustained focus on similarities/differences, with detail'.
d Students swap paragraphs with a partner. Using the mark scheme on page 142–143, what grade do students feel their partners have achieved?

4 Activity 5

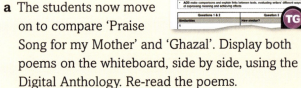

a The students now move on to compare 'Praise Song for my Mother' and 'Ghazal'. Display both poems on the whiteboard, side by side, using the Digital Anthology. Re-read the poems.
b What initial points of comparison, similarities and differences, can students suggest?
c Using **Worksheet 4.48**, students work independently, recording their response to questions 1–3, one at a time. Encourage students to record as wide a range of responses as possible.
d Take feedback after each question, discussing and developing a whole class response, then giving students a minute or two to add to their written response.

5 GradeStudio

a Remind students of the plenary activity from the previous lesson. If available, display the class's written responses.
b Read the GradeStudio sample answer on page 120 to the class. Ask: How has the writer of this answer made 'structured comments on similarities/differences, with detail'?
c How do students feel that the sample answer compares with their own efforts. Would their D answer achieve a similar grade to this one. Is their C answer better? How?

d Now look at the GradeStudio sample answer on page 121 of the Student Book. Ask students to identify how the C has shown 'sustained focus on similarities/differences, with detail'.

e Ask students to identify which elements of the paragraph show 'sustained focus on similarities/differences, with detail', i.e. are key in achieving a C. Which are 'structured comments on similarities/differences, with detail', i.e. without the C elements and so achieving a D? Do they still agree that their C response would achieve the same grade?

f Ask students to look at the B exemplar on page 122. How has this writer further developed the comparison by making a 'developed comparison, with detail'?

6 Activity 6

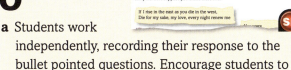

a Students work independently, recording their response to the bullet pointed questions. Encourage students to record as wide a range of responses as possible.

b Take feedback after each question, discussing and developing a whole class response, then giving students a minute to add to their written response.

c Remind students of the GradeStudio activity, and the key features of a C and a B. Give students 10 minutes to write a point-evidence-explanation paragraph comparing the two details from the poem.

7 Plenary

a Students swap their written response to Activity 6 with a partner and, using the grade descriptors on pages 142–143 of the Student Book, decide what grade their partner's response should be awarded.

b Working together, students identify one way in which they could improve or add to their writing to aim for the next grade up.

c Take feedback, summarising those key areas which students have identified as targets to achieve in order to raise their grade.

Suggested answers

Activity 3
- The comparisons on line 4 of 'In Paris with You' are simple metaphors exploring the speaker's feelings. 'Quickdraw' uses an extended metaphor within the poem to explore the nature of the speaker's relationship.
- (See above bullet point.)
- 'In Paris with You' repeats its title, suggesting that this metaphorically romantic city represents his happiness in his new relationship and, at the end, his physical desire. The repetition at the end of 'Quickdraw' suggests a reconciliation: 'the silver bullets of your kiss', connecting kisses and bullets, love and aggression.

Activity 4
- In 'In Paris with You', the speaker is focusing on himself and his self-pity. The word 'maroonded' suggests a child-like mispronunciation, and though the word 'quickdraw' in 'Quickdraw' sounds like an affectionate nickname, the words 'alone… wounded… pellet' create a more serious image of vulnerability and aggression.
- 'Alone' is placed at the start of a line and isolated with a subsequent full stop. Again, we focus on vulnerability rather than the self-pity of 'In Paris'.
- The speaker in 'In Paris' is a 'hostage' to his previous relationship from which he seems unable to progress. In 'Quickdraw' the speaker is under attack from her current relationship creating a more immediate image of danger. While in 'Quickdraw' we may question the nature of this violent relationship, the speaker's selfish words in 'In Paris' may evoke sympathy for his new lover.

Activity 5
1. 'Ghazal' focuses on a sexual relationship which the speaker hopes for; 'Praise Song' on the relationship between the speaker and her mother in childhood.
2. The speaker in 'Ghazal' looks to her lover to enter and dominate every aspect of her life; 'Praise Song' shows a similarly all-encompassing influence.
3. • 'Ghazal' looks to the future; 'Praise Song' the past.
   - Both use the comparison of the sun. 'Praise Song' suggests the speaker's mother was as important as the sunrise, 'rise and warm and streaming', suggesting warmth and love. The sun in 'Ghazal' suggests a mutual relationship but one of opposition: 'If I rise in the east as you die in the west…'
   - The final line of 'Praise Song' breaks the structural pattern and the content of the poem by moving from a dependent past to an independent future. The final couplet of 'Ghazal' continues and expands the idea of mutual dependency and love.

Activity 6
- The idea in 'Praise Song' is simpler: it suggests the love which the mother offered the speaker in childhood. The image in 'Ghazal' is a more complex image of mutual dependency with overtones of sacrifice, rebirth and distance.
- 'Praise Song' looks to the past; 'Ghazal' to the future.
- 'Praise Song' suggests nurturing love and affection. 'Ghazal' suggests a kind of unity in that both the speaker and her lover are compared to the sun. But it seems that the speaker's renewal depends on her lover's metaphorical death – his self-sacrifice.

Chapter 4 Relationships

Writing in the exam

Assessment Objectives
- **AO1:** respond to texts critically and imaginatively; select and evaluate relevant textual detail to illustrate and support interpretations
- **AO2:** explain how language, structure and form contribute to writers' presentation of ideas, themes and settings
- **AO3:** make comparisons and explain links between texts, evaluating writers' different ways of expressing meaning and achieving effects

Learning Objective
- To develop students' ability to structure a successful exam response

Required resources
- Poem text, available on CD-ROM and video/audio online at http://anthology.aqa.org.uk
- Student Book, pages 123–127, 142–143
- Worksheets 1.51, 4.49

1 Starter

a Write the word 'planning' on the board. Ask: What are the advantages and disadvantages of using the first 5 minutes of exam time to plan a written response? Give students 2 minutes to record their thoughts.

b Take feedback. Aim to refute the argument that planning takes up valuable writing time, and that your plan is not marked. Point out that your response **is** marked – and a well-planned response gets the best mark.

2 Writing your response – planning and structuring

Read the sequence of read-think-write-edit to the class, pausing to discuss whether the students agree or disagree that each of these stages is vital. Discuss with students whether anything can be cut out of this process to speed it up and still achieve the best possible grade. Conclude with students that all stages in the process are vital to getting the best possible grade.

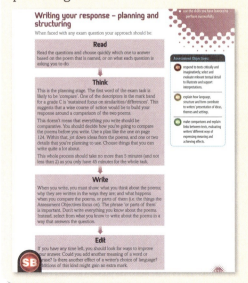

3 Putting it into practice

a Read the material from the Student Book to the class, pausing to clarify understanding where needed.

b Do students think that this is a successful plan? How might they improve it? Point out that the task has to be completed in a limited time, so anything that is added may well mean that something else must be cut. Remind the class that this guide was written by the Chief Examiner – so it's good advice!

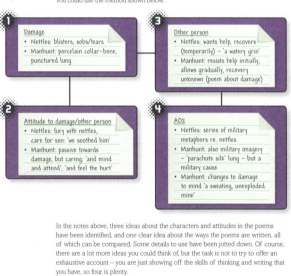

160 © Pearson Education Limited 2010

4 GradeStudio

a Close the Student Book and distribute or display **Worksheet 4.49**.

b Using the grade descriptors on pages 142–143 of the Student Book (also available on **Worksheet 1.51**), ask students to work in pairs to decide which grade they would award Student A and Student B, matching specific features from the mark scheme to specific evidence from each response to justify their decision.

c Take feedback, continually aiming to re-affirm the Assessment Objectives: the importance of responding to, and comparing, the details, ideas, themes, language, structure and form of the poems.

d Return to the Student Book and read through the Examiner comments. Do the class's marks and justifications tally with the Chief Examiner's?

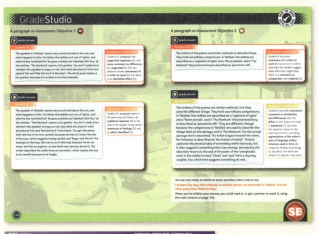

5 Sample exam question

Depending on the confidence of your class, this can be tackled as homework, as entirely independent work, or planned as a whole class prior to independent GCSE writing.

a Ask students to spend 2 minutes noting down the sequence of thinking they would follow before writing. For example:
1 Read the question **carefully**.
2 Identify which parts of the question relate to which Assessment Objective.
3 Consider which poem to compare 'Nettles' with. Think of two or three possibilities. Which will allow you to demonstrate your skill and understanding most fully? Choose one.
4 Note down points comparing the themes and ideas in the poems.
5 Note down points comparing details in the poems.
6 Note down points comparing the writer's choice of language, form and/or structure in the poems and its effect on the reader.

b Give students 10 minutes to follow this sequence, completing their essay plan. Point out that, although this should take 5 minutes in the exam, this is practice to help get students up to exam pace!

> You are now ready to tackle an exam question. Here's one to try:
> Compare the ways that attitudes to another person are presented in 'Nettles' and one other poem from 'Relationships'.
> When you've written your answer, you could mark it, or get a partner to mark it, using the mark scheme on page 142.

6 Plenary

Students swap plans. Does their partner's plan cover all the necessary Assessment Objectives and explore the poem in enough developed detail? What grade do they think the essay based on this plan will achieve? Why? Take feedback, focusing on the grade awarded and the peer marker's justification for that grade. Does the class agree that the grade is justified?

7 Further work

Students can write up their essay in their own time. The following lesson can then be spent peer-marking the essays using the grade descriptors on pages 142–143 of the Student Book – also available on **Worksheet 1.51** – then listening as a class to the peer-marker's choices of:
- the most successful point targeting AO1
- the most successful point targeting AO2
- the most successful point targeting AO3.

AQA GCSE Working with the Anthology: Achieve a C

Chapter 5 The unseen poem (Lesson plan 1)

What to look for when reading and annotating an unseen poem

Assessment Objectives
- **AO1:** respond to texts critically and imaginatively; select and evaluate relevant textual detail to illustrate and support interpretations
- **AO2:** explain how language, structure and form contribute to writers' presentation of ideas, themes and settings

Learning Objectives
- To read an unseen poem
- To annotate an unseen poem

Required resources
- Student Book, pages 130–134 and 136–137
- Worksheet 5.1, 5.2

1 Starter

a Write on the whiteboard:
- What the poem is about.
- How the poet has written the poem.
- The effect on the reader – you.

b Read the Introduction from the Student Book (page 130) to the class. Point out that, although responding to the Unseen Poem in Section B can seem a daunting prospect, there can be no better preparation for it than looking at their interpretation of – and the poet's use of language, structure, tone, etc. in – the 15 poems in their chosen cluster which, 20 or more lessons ago, were all 'unseen'!

c Ask students to close the Student Book. Referring to the bullet points on the whiteboard, ask students to write a short guide, aimed at GCSE students such as themselves, based on their experience of the 15 poems they have already studied, advising what to look for when reading a poem. They should use the three bullet points to prompt their thinking and organise their writing.

d Take feedback to assess understanding. Look for responses that recognise features such as language, structure, imagery, rhythm. Emphasise/reinforce the importance of **commenting on their effect** and the pointlessness of 'technique-spotting' ('The poem has no similes or metaphors…').

Introduction

Section B in the exam asks you to respond to an unseen poem – one that you have not prepared beforehand.

In this chapter of the book you will be:
- learning how to read the unseen poem in the exam
- learning how to annotate it before you write
- learning how to write successfully
- practising exam-style questions.

The skills you need to show are the same ones you worked on in thinking and writing about the poems you studied for Section A of the exam. The two Assessment Objectives tested are the same as those in Section A, so you should be familiar with these from the poems you have studied. You don't have to compare in Section B, so AO3 isn't present here. You have 30 minutes in the exam to answer the question on the unseen poem, and you have to think within this time before you start to write.

2 Reading the poem – what to look for

Read through this section on pages 130–131 of the Student Book. Highlight the information on Assessment Objectives to reiterate the importance of commenting on how and why the writer has written the poem in the way s/he has.

- How does the guide that students wrote in the starter activity compare with this guide?
- What have they missed or forgotten?
- Give students 5 minutes to add to their guide.

My learning

In this section you will learn how to:
- read an unseen poem
- annotate an unseen poem
- write successfully in the exam on the unseen poem.

3 Reading and annotating an unseen poem

a Give students 5 minutes to read the poem 'In Mrs Tilscher's Class' on page 132 of the Student Book, and write a sentence or two beginning *'In Mrs Tilscher's Class' is about…* Take feedback to ensure, share and develop understanding.

b Give students a further 10 minutes to note down or annotate on copies of **Worksheet 5.1** their initial response to the poem, the way it is written and its effect on the reader.

c Take feedback, annotating a displayed copy of the poem with students' responses.

d Return to the Student Book, reading through the sample answers on pages 136–137 of the Student Book. How many of these points did students notice or miss? How many do they agree with – or did they respond differently? Emphasise that a response supported with evidence is rarely 'wrong'.

e Now look at the annotated version of the poem on page 134 of the Student Book. How many of these points correlate with, add to, or develop the points that students have already identified?

ACTIVITY 1

Using the questions on pages 130 and 131 as a guide, list as many relevant points as you can find in the poem 'In Mrs Tilscher's Class'.

You could:
- start with what you think the poem is about
- then think about the way it's written.

Or you could do it the other way round, starting by noticing things like **rhyme** or **metaphors**.

Remember that you do need to do both these things to get as many marks as you can – saying what it's about without writing about methods is only half an answer, and writing about methods without showing what effects they have is only half an answer.

4 Plenary

a Display or distribute **Worksheet 5.2**. Do students agree with the given statement?

b Give students 2 minutes to prepare an argument either for or against. Point out that this should take the form of statements either supporting and explaining the given statement – or replacing it with their own view.

c Take feedback, noting students' arguments in the blank space on the displayed worksheet.

d Give students 2 minutes to note down those points that are relevant to their work on the Unseen Poem.

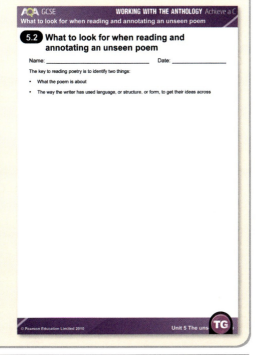

Chapter 5 The unseen poem (Lesson plan 2)

Writing a response in the exam (1)

Assessment Objectives
- **AO1:** respond to texts critically and imaginatively; select and evaluate relevant textual detail to illustrate and support interpretations
- **AO2:** explain how language, structure and form contribute to writers' presentation of ideas, themes and settings

Learning Objectives
- To write successfully about an unseen poem
- To develop awareness of grade descriptors and the key features of higher grades

Required resources
- Student Book, pages 135–138, 143–144
- Worksheets 5.3, 5.4

1 Starter

a Display or distribute **Worksheet 5.3**. Explain that these are the grade descriptors in the mark scheme of Section B, the Unseen Poem.

b Ask students to rank the descriptors from the highest to the lowest grade. Take feedback, confirming the correct answer. What do students feel these phrases mean? How would an answer in which a student is awarded 16 marks specifically differ from one that is awarded 15 marks?

Answer:
1=16–18 marks   4=13–15 marks   3=10–12 marks   2=7–9 marks

2 Writing in the exam

a Read the key points on page 135 of the Student Book to the class.

b How much might students expect to write in 20–25 minutes? Suggest that:
- students should expect to write around a side of A4
- the quality of their writing is more important than the quantity
- it would be difficult to demonstrate the breadth and depth of skills needed for higher grades in much less than a side of A4.

c Students to turn to the grade descriptors on pages 143–144. Display/distribute **Worksheet 5.4**. Give students 5 minutes to read and put these two responses in rank order, and justify their decision. What grade would they award each candidate? Why? Take feedback, focusing on identifying and linking the grade descriptors to specific examples in the three students' responses.

d Look at the Examiner's Comments on pages 136 and 137 of the Student Book. Do students' comments and marks tally with the examiner's?

3 Activity 2

a Explain that you will begin this task in this lesson and continue it in the next. Working independently, students spend 3 minutes reading the poem 'Cynddylan on a Tractor' on page 138 of the Student Book, and completing the sentence 'Cynddylan on a Tractor' is about… . Take feedback to share, ensure and develop understanding.

b Remind students of the notes they made in their initial response to 'In Mrs Tilscher's Class'. Give them 10 minutes to prepare similar notes exploring their response to this poem.

4 Plenary

a Students swap their notes from Activity 2 with a partner, then identify which of their partner's notes are likely to help them achieve 16–18 marks, which 13–15 marks, which 10–12 marks, and which 7–9 marks.

b Ask volunteers to read examples that they feel are likely to achieve 13–18 marks, and to justify their choice. Does the class agree?

164   © Pearson Education Limited 2010

Chapter 5 The unseen poem (Lesson plan 3)

Writing a response in the exam (2)

Assessment Objectives
- **AO1:** respond to texts critically and imaginatively; select and evaluate relevant textual detail to illustrate and support interpretations
- **AO2:** explain how language, structure and form contribute to writers' presentation of ideas, themes and settings

Learning Objectives
- To write successfully about an unseen poem
- To develop awareness of grade descriptors and the key features of higher grades

Required resources
- Student Book, pages 138–139

1 Starter
Recap the previous lesson: give students 3 minutes to re-read 'Cynddylan on a Tractor' on page 138 of the Student Book, and remind themselves of the key points and comments that emerged. Take feedback to ensure all students' awareness of these points.

2 Activity 2, continued
a Depending on the confidence of the class, give students up to 45 minutes to turn their notes into a written response. Explain that they should only allow 30 minutes for this task in the exam, but they are practising before getting up to full exam speed!

b Having completed the task, take students' immediate responses:
  - Were they surprised at how much or how little they could write?
  - Were they surprised at how quickly the time passed?
  - How can they combat any problems which arose? For example:
    - 2–3 minutes' planning will help you select the three or four key points you want to make.
    - Don't plan an answer that you will not have time to write.

c Look again at the Examiner's Comments on students' responses to 'In Mrs Tilscher's Class'. Making similar annotations, ask students to work in pairs, deciding:
  - which mark to award their partner's response
  - a target: one thing that would make a significant contribution to increasing this mark.

3 Plenary
a Give students 3 minutes to address their target. For example, can they add a sentence or two which explains, rather than simply identifying, the effect of the writer's uses of language, form or structure?

b Students swap their improved responses. Does their partner agree that their mark can now be increased?

c Ask volunteers to tell the class about the marking of their response – particularly the target and their attempt to address it. How can they ensure that they achieve this next time they attempt an unseen poem?

4 Further work
Repeat the above for the task in Activity 3, giving students a moment or two at the start of the lesson to remind themselves of the target established above and their strategy for meeting it.

Chapter 6 Controlled Assessment

Unit 3 Literary reading

Introduction

This section of the Teacher Guide provides you with guidance on the Literary Reading Controlled Assessment that forms part of the GCSE English Literature specification. Similar Literary Readings also occur within the GCSE English and GCSE English Language specifications. Extensive guidance for these is available in the corresponding Heinemann Teacher Guides, although this section does on occasion make reference to the Literary Reading requirements in GCSE English Language where this is relevant.

The *Working with the Anthology: Achieve a C* Student Book (accompanied by this Teacher Guide) is predominantly support for centres who choose to study poetry through the examined, external assessment route. This section therefore offers guidance to centres who will be tackling Shakespeare and the English Literary Heritage through Controlled Assessment (i.e. taking route A/Unit 3), although much of the guidance will also be useful for those centres who choose to tackle poetry through Controlled Assessment.

This section aims to:
- familiarise you with the AQA specification requirements
- outline some of the potential advantages and disadvantages of Controlled Assessment
- help you understand the choices available to you
- explain the mark schemes
- offer you some specific guidance and exemplification of the task types available to you.

Literary Reading requirements

In all three specifications, the Controlled Assessment of reading offers a choice of approach. Teachers can choose the texts for study and can also choose a task from the options below. AQA will release a Task Bank in April each year; the task types or headings will be permanent fixtures under which the tasks will change each year.

The task types for centres studying Unit 3 as Controlled Assessment will be as shown in the table below.

Requirements for GCSE English Literature

- In English Literature, teachers will choose for the Controlled Assessment either:
  - route A: Unit 3 The significance of Shakespeare and the English Literary Heritage (ELH); or
  - route B: Unit 5 Exploring poetry

  This Controlled Assessment advice is predominantly for centres choosing route A.
- If the choice is Shakespeare and the ELH, the Controlled Assessment will be based on a link between any play by Shakespeare and any text, from any genre, from the ELH. (This means that it is possible to study two Shakespeare plays.)
- If the choice is Poetry, the Controlled Assessment will be based on links between contemporary poetry and ELH poetry. You could use poems from the AQA Anthology or poems of your own choice.
- Teachers will choose the texts for study in these categories. The ELH text must not be a text studied in any other unit of the course.
- In both Shakespeare/ELH and Poetry, students can draw on multi-modal versions of the texts, showing understanding and appreciation of the way printed texts may be realised and performed by professionals or themselves.
- There is no requirement to compare the linked Shakespeare/ELH texts but Poetry does require comparison of ELH and contemporary texts.
- The Controlled Assessment will be worth 25% of the total marks for English Literature regardless of whether Unit 3 or Unit 5 is chosen.
- The assessed work on Shakespeare/ELH or on Poetry should be no more than 2000 words and the assessment time should be no more than four hours (this can be split over different assessment sessions).
- The task may be selected from the 'Themes and ideas' bank or the 'Characterisation and voice' bank.

Task type	Themes and ideas	Characterisation and voice
Description	Tasks in this area are based on the study of aspects of textual subject matter and content	Tasks in this area are based on authorial technique within a genre

Literary reading

Requirements for GCSE English Language

While this Teacher Guide focuses on GCSE English Literature, it is also useful to be aware of the choices available to you and your students in the Literary Reading Controlled Assessment for GCSE English Language.

- In GCSE English Language, the Unit 3 Controlled Assessment is based on one extended text. This can be a text from any genre. Importantly, this text can also be a text studied for GCSE English Literature.
- It will be worth 15% of the total GCSE English Language marks.
- Teachers will choose the texts for study in these categories.
- The assessed work should be no more than 1200 words and the assessment period should be no more than four hours (this can be split over different assessment sessions).
- The task may be selected from the 'Themes and ideas' bank or the 'Characterisation and voice' bank.

Approaches to texts

The sample assessment tasks in the AQA Task Bank provide a repertoire from which teachers can choose their preferred mode of teaching and assessing, individually or as common departmental policy. Some teachers will prefer traditional, academic essay-type tasks; others will prefer more performance-based and creative tasks involving preparatory group work. What follows are examples of the kinds of Controlled Assessment tasks one might expect to see, grouped into 'traditional' essay-type tasks and 'interactive and creative' type tasks. While the Task Bank first released by AQA does not explicitly include examples of 'interactive and creative' tasks, they will become a feature of future Task Banks as the specification goes live.

Traditional Controlled Assessment tasks

These are generally of a familiar essay type similar to examination questions. Some teachers will prefer these because they prepare students for similar kinds of questions in the Literature exam. The following are examples of what 'traditional' Controlled Assessment tasks might look like in GCSE English Literature if studying Unit 3.

> **Example 1**
> Write about Shakespeare's presentation of Caliban in *The Tempest* and Shelley's presentation of Frankenstein.

> **Example 2**
> Explore the importance of conflict in two Shakespearean comedies.

> **Example 3**
> *The Tempest* and *Lord of the Flies* both employ the setting of an island to explore conflicting characters and ideas. What similarities and differences can you see in the two texts?

Interactive and creative Controlled Assessment tasks

Some teachers will prefer these types of tasks because they want Controlled Assessment responses to be significantly different from exam responses. These tasks generally encourage a more physical, visual, oral and/or group preparation for the assessed task. The emphasis is on the printed text as a public, shared experience rather than a private one, hence encouraging a focus on interpretation, realisation and performance. There is some deliberate overlap in methods and tasks between English Language and English Literature here, and the ability to use the same texts across all three of the specifications.

> **Example 4**
> Explore the ways that a ten-frame snapshot collage could bring out the attitudes, feelings and character of either Shylock in *The Merchant of Venice*, George in *Of Mice and Men* or in any text you have studied. You must write an explanation of your choices and show your understanding of how the writer has used language to draw out the attitudes, feelings and character.

Task guidance: GCSE English Literature

In all specifications, teachers are able to exercise a degree of choice as to the types of tasks they set for students for the Literary Reading Controlled Assessment. The main decision will be the texts you choose to study. While it is compulsory in Unit 3 to study one play by Shakespeare, the other linked text can be from any genre in the English Literary Heritage. This degree of choice is evident when one looks at the sample tasks in the AQA Task Bank.

Choice of texts	Examples from AQA Task Bank
Two Shakespeare plays	Explore the importance of conflict in two Shakespeare comedies.
	Write about the ways in which Shakespeare presents tragic heroes in two of his plays (e.g. *Othello* and *Hamlet*).
Shakespeare play and selection of ELH poetry	Compare the ways in which ideas about war are explored in *Henry V* and a selection of poetry from WW1.
	Explore the presentation of heroism in a Shakespeare play (e.g. portrayals of heroic behaviour in one of Shakespeare's histories) and in poems about WW1.
Shakespeare play and ELH play	How do Shakespeare and Wilde exploit for comic effect the absurdities of people in love in *Twelfth Night* and *The Importance of Being Earnest*?
Shakespeare play and ELH prose	Explore the consequences of ambition in *Macbeth* and *Great Expectations*.
	Write about the ways in which the difficulties of love are explored in the short stories of Thomas Hardy and *Much Ado About Nothing*.

When deciding on the choice of texts, you will no doubt want to consider that the text studied for the reading Controlled Assessment in GCSE English Language may be one of the same texts studied for GCSE English Literature (in either the exam or Controlled Assessment). It is therefore advisable to consider the tasks in the GCSE English Language reading Task Bank as well as those in GCSE English Literature before embarking on tasks and texts.

Another choice available to you is whether to tackle a task from the 'Themes and ideas' column or from the 'Characterisation and voice' column.

'Themes and ideas' in GCSE English Literature

Now let us look at some possible GCSE English Literature tasks under the 'Themes and ideas' heading, how you might approach them and some of the challenges involved.

> **Themes and ideas**
>
> Explore the ways in which family relationships are presented in the texts you have studied.
>
> **Example 1**
>
> How are family relationships presented in *Romeo and Juliet* and *Pride and Prejudice*?
>
> In your response you should explore similarities and differences in the ways the relationships are developed by the writer.
>
> **Example 2**
>
> Explore the similarities and differences in the ways Shakespeare dramatises father/daughter relationships in *King Lear* and *Romeo and Juliet*.

Teachers choosing the kinds of assignment shown in examples 1 and 2 above will tend to prefer entirely print-based approaches, though there is scope for widening the task to embrace some of the ways in which the different genres facilitate or inhibit presentation. Although these two tasks are based on 'Themes and ideas', they do require a grasp of the literary and dramatic techniques used by the writers. For example, 'presented', 'ways' and 'dramatises' should be understood as aspects of the writers' craft in language styles, textual structure and appeal to a public audience/private readers.

> **Example 3**
>
> How does Shakespeare develop the relationship between the cousins Beatrice and Hero in *Much Ado About Nothing* and how does this link to Christina Rossetti's portrayal of female relationships in 'Goblin Market' or some of her shorter poems?

Teachers choosing the kind of assignment shown in example 3 will tend to prefer a stage/screen performance approach to the Shakespeare script, with close observation of the visual, oral, spatial and gestural features of acting and directing. There is scope for interesting classroom interpretation, improvisation and performance prompted by 'your own readings', as well as critical observation and evaluation of dramatic skill in professional performances on stage or screen.

'Character and voice' in GCSE English Literature

Let us now look at some sample GCSE English tasks under the 'Characterisation and voice' heading, how you might approach them and some of the challenges involved.

> **Characterisation and voice**
>
> Explore the way in which the central character is presented and developed in the texts you have studied.
>
> **Example 1**
>
> Write about Shakespeare's presentation of Caliban in *The Tempest* and Shelley's presentation of Frankenstein.

The kind of assignment shown in example 1 on the previous page mainly requires a critical response to the printed text. However, there is scope for including specific devices of the playscript and prose narrative genres, including Shakespeare's use of sound patterns, imagery and attitude, and Shelley's use of narrative, dialogue and varying character point of view.

> **Example 2**
>
> Explore similarities and differences in the presentation of Shylock in *The Merchant of Venice* and Fagin in *Oliver Twist*. Explore the ways that screen representations of these characters reflect the original written representation.
>
> **Example 3**
>
> Explore the ways Shakespeare and Browning reveal deeply unsympathetic characteristics of speakers using Lady Macbeth and the narrator of 'The Laboratory'.
>
> You may want to refer to how actors and readers portray these attitudes in performances of both texts, including your own readings.

The kinds of tasks shown in examples 2 and 3 above favour a focus on public performance, with links between print and stage/screen representation based on acting, directing and production effects. There is scope for interesting classroom interpretation, improvisation and performance prompted by 'your own readings', as well as critical observation and evaluation of dramatic skill in professional performances on stage or screen.

Multi-modal texts

Although the focus of this unit is predominantly on the study of written texts, this should not prevent you from exploring such texts in performance, regardless of the type of task. This can serve to enrich candidates' responses: by seeing the text in performance they may better grasp the impact and effect of the writer's techniques and better understand how characters, themes and ideas might be presented and developed.

Indeed, the AQA Task Bank explicitly states that candidates may study multi-modal versions of the texts, such as stage productions, film and audio versions. The caveat to this is that study of such multi-modal texts should be linked back to the written text and the writer's techniques. When it comes to analysing the mark scheme we will see that the bulk of marks for this unit are allocated to interpretation, comment, analysis and evaluation of the written text: the writer's linguistic and structural techniques, their ideas and attitudes and so on.

Linked texts

As mentioned, the Literary Reading assessment for English Literature focuses on 'linked texts'. In its simplest sense this asks students to make connections and links between chosen texts – for example in the way they present ideas, relationships or characters.

The meaning and significance of this term varies, however, according to whether you have chosen to study Unit 3 or Unit 5 for Controlled Assessment. If studying Unit 3, the study of 'linked texts' does not mean that students must make close comparison of the similarities and differences between texts. This particular skill is assessed predominantly through the Unit 2 Poetry examination.

Candidates would need to write about, say, the theme of conflict in both texts, but not in such a way that compares the techniques, attitudes and ideas of the writer. It would be perfectly acceptable, for example, for a candidate to write about the theme of conflict in *Henry V* in one paragraph and then write about the theme of conflict in poetry from WW1 without drawing any attention to the similarities and differences.

That is not to say that students will be penalised for drawing detailed comparisons, however, it is not a requirement of this Controlled Assessment in the way that it is for the Unit 2 Poetry examination.

If studying Unit 5 for Controlled Assessment, the study of 'linked texts' has a slightly different significance. This route means students will not have studied the Unit 2 Poetry exam, therefore more onus is placed on the Controlled Assessment to test students' ability to compare texts in detail.

The mark scheme

The mark scheme for GCSE English Literature sees you awarding marks in five bands. The total mark for this unit is 40 marks. For the purposes of this Teacher Guide, with its grade focus of E through to B, the focus is on bands 1, 2 and 3.

For Unit 3, each band has four bullet points that rank the degree to which students can:
- understand, appreciate and interpret writers' ideas and attitudes using supported detail
- understand and analyse features of language and structure
- understand and explore links and points of comparison between texts
- grasp and comment on the significance of the contexts of texts.

Chapter 6 Controlled Assessment

The Assessment objectives against which students will be assessed for reading in GCSE English Literature are:

AO1 Respond to texts critically and imaginatively; select and evaluate textual detail to illustrate and support interpretations.

AO2 Explain how language, structure and form contribute to writers' presentation of ideas, themes and settings.

AO3 Make comparisons and explain links between texts, evaluating writers' different ways of expressing meaning and achieving effects.

AO4 Relate texts to their social, cultural and historical contexts; explain how texts have been influential and significant to self and other readers in different contexts at different times.

There is, therefore, a direct correlation between the four bullet points in each band and the four assessment objectives, providing you with four key areas upon which to focus the teaching and learning.

Students working at or around notional grades G/F will be hitting the following descriptors:

Band 1 1–8 marks

- limited awareness of writers' ideas using a limited range of textual detail
- limited awareness of obvious features of language and structure
- limited awareness of links between texts
- limited awareness of contexts but very limited comment on their significance.

Students working at or around notional grades E/D will be hitting the following descriptors:

Band 2 9–16 marks

- some familiarity with writers' ideas supported by a range of textual detail
- some familiarity with obvious features of language and structure supported by some relevant textual detail
- some relevant comments about links between texts
- some relevant comments about the significance of the contexts.

Students working at or around notional grades C/B will be hitting the following descriptors:

Band 3 17–24 marks

- clear understanding of writers' ideas and use of relevant appropriate supporting textual detail
- clear understanding of features of language and structure supported by relevant and appropriate quotation
- clear understanding of links and some points of comparison between texts
- a clear grasp of the significance of some aspects of the contexts.

At its simplest level then, we can identify the bands as follows:

Band	Description
Band 1 – 'Limited'	Students working at this level are likely to deliver partial or restricted responses that suggest only a very basic understanding of the text(s) and its ideas and features. Students may pick out the most obvious ideas, features and links, but supporting detail may be very sparse, while the response as a whole is likely to include irrelevant material.
Band 2 – 'Some'	Students working at this level will not display the clarity or consistency that is characteristic of a Band 3 response. For example, a Band 2 response may pick up on some key ideas but miss others, and likewise reference to supporting detail or comment on significance of contexts may be erratic.
Band 3 – 'Clear, consistent'	Students working at this level will have a secure grasp of writers' ideas and how they use language to convey those ideas. They will be able to make links between texts and understand the significance of some aspects of contexts.

From this we can see that the essential distinction between the bands above lies in the scope and consistency of the response. At the bottom band, responses are likely to be limited to the most basic ideas, using textual details infrequently or not at all, and with portions of the response irrelevant to the task at hand. As we progress up the bands, the responses become more relevant and sustained, grounded in a greater degree of textual detail and displaying more familiarity with the ideas, features and links between texts.

The exemplars that follow go some way to demonstrating the differences between responses at these bands.

GCSE English Literature exemplar 1

Task: Explore the ways in which family relationships are presented in the text(s) you have studied.

My assignment is about family relationships in *Romeo and Juliet*. The family relationships I have been studying are the Capulet family, which is a father and mother and daughter relationship. Juliet is the daughter and she is fourteen years old. Her mother and father are rich people in Verona and they have a maid who has looked after Juliet since she was a baby. She is called the Nurse, and she is quite close to Juliet and Juliet is quite close to her. Juliet is not close to her mother and father in the play. This is because they want her to get married to a man called Paris. She has never met Paris and he is a lot older than her, but her father thinks he would be a good choice because he is rich. This is where the trouble starts because Juliet is in love with Romeo but Romeo belongs to the Montague family and there is a big fued between these two families. Her mother and father would never let her marry Romeo because of the fude. "My only love born of my only hate" is Juliet saying she is in a bad state because of the fude and loving Romeo, so she decides to marry him in secret. This causes big problems. Her father doesn't know about Romeo and thinks she is going against him by not wanting to marry Paris and her mother is the same. Her father calls her terrible names like "unworthy" and "baggage" and loses his temper. He even says she can go on the streets for all he cares, which is not a good thing for a father to say to his daughter. They treat her like a child who has done something wrong, not like a person who has got a right to make up their own mind. Her mother says "I would the fool were married to her grave" and her father says "You mumbling fool". You can tell from this that this is not a good family relationship. In a good family relationship there is trust and respect and parents look after their children and listen to them but in this family relationship the parents are more bothered about getting a rich husband for her than what she feels. It's like they care about appearances more than her. Money before people. Even the Nurse goes against Juliet. She says "Romeo's a dishclout to him" because she thinks Paris is a good catch, so Juliet has no-one to turn to. This is why she takes the potion, to get out of the fix she is in, and this is what, at the end of the day, causes her and Romeo to die. It is down to her parents who should have listened. That's what sort of family relationship you see in the play.

I am going to write about family relationships in Great Expectations by Charles Dickens. In this book, the family I am going to write about is the Gargerys. They are Joe gargery the blacksmith, Mrs Joe Gargery his wife, and Pip, who is Mrs Joes's brother but she has adopted him because his mother and father have died. Pip is only small when the book starts and you get to see how he feels about things from what he describes. The books is written as if Pip was telling the story, so he says he thought his mother and father were strong and frail because of the way the letters looked on their gravestones.

"From the letters on her tombstone I formed the impression that…" So he is an orphan and small and he needs someone to look after him. This is where the family relationships come in. Mrs Joe is horrible to him and Joe is kind, so it's a mixed family relationship. Mrs Joe is always hitting him with a stick she calls Tickler and when she is annoyed with him, like all the time, she says things like "She had wished me in my grave"

At the Christmas dinner, she says children are naturally vicious and only gives him the bad bits of chicken and pork so that all the other people start on him as well. The worst thing she does is blame him for doing things a child can't help, like waking up in the night, as if he was a criminal "all the illnesses I had been guilty of and all the acts of sleeplessness I had committed"

> The other part of the family relationship is better. Joe is kind to him but he can't always show it because it makes Mrs Joe cross. When everyone is getting at him at the Christmas dinner, Joes tries to make him feel better by giving him more gravy. And he warns her about Mrs Joe being in a bad mood and he protects him when she is trying to hit him with the Tickler by putting him behind him. Pip is only small so he doesn't understand why Mrs Joe is so horrible. It's not like she hates him but she can't like anyone, even her husband,. It says she had pins in her blouse that would stick in you if you get too close to her and this is a way of saying she's prickly.
>
> All in all, Pip's family relationships are not good but at least there is some love and kindness he gets from Joe. This is why he ends up going home with Joe after he has been to London. This shows that a good family relationship is important when you are young and can last a long time into your life when you grow up.

Examiner commentary

This student is operating within band 2. After an opening heavy on description but light on comment, the student does eventually start to draw on a range of textual references to support his ideas. Further marks would be gained through attempts to make links between the texts and to comment on the significance of the contexts. A more rigid structuring of the response to *Romeo and Juliet* – currently captured as one large paragraph – may have helped this student hone his ideas and begin to explore some features of language.

GCSE English Literature exemplar 2

Task: Explore the ways in which family relationships are presented in the text(s) you have studied.

I am going to look at similarities and differences in the ways Shakespeare dramatises father/daughter relationships in *Romeo and Juliet* and in *Hamlet*.

In *Romeo and Juliet*, the relationship between Juliet and her father, Lord Capulet, is not a good one because he doesn't treat her as someone who has a right to make important decisions about her life, like who to marry. She is only fourteen but he thinks he can decide that she is old enough to get married, and he thinks he has the right to decide who she will marry. He decides that Paris is a good choice of husband because he has money and comes from a so-called good family and that's it. He's not interested in what Juliet thinks about getting married and he's not interested in how she feels about Paris. He's more like a lord and master than a father because he thinks she should obey him because he's right. Shakespeare was writing about Italy in the sixteenth century, so perhaps this was a more normal way for fathers to behave with their daughters. Girls got married younger in those days, and arranged marriages would not have been as big a deal as they would be to a fourteen-year-old girl in Britain today.

Lord Capulet first mentions this marriage to Paris, then asks his wife to tell Juliet what he has decided! When Lady Capulet tells her husband Juliet is crying, his only thought is 'Doth she not give us thanks? Doth she not count her blest, unworthy as she is, that we have wrought So worthy a gentleman to be her bride?' That's not a nice way to talk to your daughter, even in Shakespeare's time. Then he gets angry and shows that he doesn't care for her feelings and doesn't even think she has the right to her own opinion.

When Juliet stands up to her father, or tries to, the relationship between them gets worse. He doesn't even listen to her or give her a chance to speak. He starts to threaten her and he says some really awful things like she can go out on the street and starve and die if she doesn't marry Paris, which is a cruel thing to say and shows that he thinks of her as something he can give away to someone or throw away if he can't give her away. She's only fourteen and she can't argue with him.

He says if she doesn't agree to marry Paris 'I will drag thee on a hurdle thither. Out you green-sickness carrion, out you baggage, you tallow-face'. This is really insulting and cruel and not what a father/daughter relationship should be. This is where you start to hate him and to feel sorry for Juliet. Even Juliet's mother sides with her father because he is the boss in the house and she is a woman. That's how it was in those days, with women not having the same rights as men. It's only Juliet's Nurse who sees things from her point of view and tries to help, but after a while she gives up and takes the same side as Lord Capulet. She even says that 'Romeo's a dish-clout to him' meaning Paris, which shows how she's changed from when she thought Romeo was the best thing since sliced bread.

In conclusion, Shakespeare is dramatising the parent/daughter relationship in a way that is a warning to other parents. He is saying that if you carry on like this you will drive your daughter into doing something desperate, or even cause her death, which is what happens in the end.

In his play *Hamlet*, Shakespeare shows another father/daughter relationship which is quite similar, so he may think a lot of relationships in life are like this. Ophelia is the daughter of Polonius, who is the King's Counsellor, so he is an important man in the palace. He has a son, too, called Laertes, who is going away to Paris. Polonius gives him advice about how to behave when he's living on his own, telling him that he should drink, gamble and have women in moderation. But he actually sets a spy on Laertes to report what he's doing, so he's a bit of a control freak. Imagine paying a man to spy on your own son when he's away! He controls Ophelia, too, but not like Lord Capulet, forcing her to marry someone. Ophelia is in love with Hamlet and they have had a relationship for some time. Polonius knows this and tries to find things out about Hamlet. He's sort of using her like a spy. He asks her what Hamlet has been doing and how he's been behaving, so that he can go back and tell his boss, the King.

In Act 1 Scene 3 Polonius overhears a conversation between Laertes and Ophelia and asks her what it was about. She says that it was about Hamlet. He asks what is going on and she says that 'He hath made many tenders of his affection to me'. Polonius tells her that she will make a fool of herself if she takes Hamlet seriously. He is a Prince 'with a larger tether may he walk than may be given you.' He tells her she must not spend any more time with, or talk to, Hamlet from now on and she must give him back all his presents. This is different to Lord Capulet, who would probably think a Prince was a good prospect for his daughter, so Polonius's attitude here is caring for his daughter so she doesn't get hurt.

All this changes when Ophelia comes to Polonius and tells him that she has seen Hamlet behaving strangely, and sighing, with his stockings 'fouled, ungyved and ungartered' and his knees knocking. Polonius thinks this is a bad sign and reports it to the King, and gets told by King Claudius to find out more about what Hamlet is up to. (Claudius thinks Hamlet may know about him killing his father.) The relationship now becomes him using his daughter to find out things to please his King and the Queen. He reads the Queen some of Hamlet's love letters to his daughter, which shows no respect for her. In the famous 'To be or not to be' scene it gets worse and the relationship is nothing like a good father/daughter one. He says to the King he'll 'loose my daughter to him' so that they can hide behind an arras and eavesdrop on the conversation. This is an awful thing to do because Ophelia knows that she is being used and that Hamlet may think she is part of the trick to get him to say something. After the speech, Hamlet gets suspicious and turns on her, telling her to go and spend the rest of her life in a nunnery. She is hurt by this but her father doesn't care about her feelings now she's been useful to the King, 'You need not tell us what Lord Hamlet said. We heard it all.' This is a bad side of the parent/daughter relationship because he puts her second to his job and he doesn't care how she feels now Hamlet has turned on her. Polonius may not be as bad as Lord Capulet but in the end his way of being a parent has the same result. Ophelia, like Juliet, kills herself and this is directly down to her relationship with her father.

Examiner commentary

This student is operating within band 3. There is clear and consistent understanding of the text and of the task. Shakespeare's ideas are clearly explained and comments are supported with relevant textual detail. There are links between the texts and a clear grasp of the significance of some aspects of the context of the texts, particularly *Romeo and Juliet*. There is no focus on language used to convey aspects of character, attitude or ideas.

Heinemann is an imprint of Pearson Education Limited, a company incorporated in England and Wales, having its registered office at Edinburgh Gate, Harlow, Essex CM20 2JE. Registered company number: 872828

www.pearsonschoolsandfecolleges.co.uk

Heinemann is a registered trademark of Pearson Education Limited

Text © Person Education Limited

First published 2010

14 13 12 11 10
10 9 8 7 6 5 4 3 2 1

British Library Cataloguing in Publication Data
A catalogue record for this book is available from the British Library.

ISBN 978 0435 11853 2

Copyright notice
All rights reserved. The material in this publication is copyright. Pupil sheets may be freely photocopied for classroom use in the purchasing institution. However, this material is copyright and under no circumstances may copies be offered for sale. If you wish to use the material in any way other than that specified you must apply in writing to the publishers.

Edited by Jane Anson
Designed and produced by Kamae Design, Oxford
Original illustrations © Pearson Education Ltd 2010
Cover design by Wooden Ark Studios, Leeds
Cover photo © Bill Brooks/Masterfile
Printed and bound in the UK by Ashford Colour Press

Acknowledgements
The author and publisher would like to thank the following individuals and organisations for permission to reproduce copyright material:

'Clown Punk' from *Tyrannosaurus Rex versus The Corduroy Kid* published by Faber and Faber; 'Checking Out Me History' © 1996 by John Agard reproduced by kind permission of John Agard c/o Caroline Sheldon Literary Agency Limited; 'Horse Whisperer' from *Fear of Thunder* by Andrew Forster, published by Flambard Press © Andrew Forster, 2007. Used by permission of Flambard Press; 'Medusa' from *The Worlds Wife* by Carol Ann Duffy, published by Picador. Used by permission of Picador, a division of Macmillan Books; 'Singh Song' from *Look We Have Coming to Dover* by Daljit Nagra, published by Faber and Faber; 'Brendon Gallacher' (25 lines) from *Two's Company* by Jackie Kay (Blackie, 1992) Copyright © Jackie Kay, 1992. Used by permission of Penguin Group (UK); 'Give' from *Dead Sea Poems* by Simon Armitage, published by Faber and Faber; 'Les Grands Seigneurs' from *Hare Soup* by Dorothy Molloy published by Faber and Faber; 'The River God' from *New Selected Poems* published by New Direction Books. Used by permission of The Estate of James MacGibbon; 'The Hunchback in the Park' by Dylan Thomas from *The Poems* published by J.M. Dent. © Dylan Thomas. Granted by permission of David Higham Associates; 'The Ruined Main' artwork reproduced with permission of Punch Ltd, www.punch.co.uk; 'Case history: Alison (head injury)' by U A Fanthorpe, from *Collected Poems 1978-2003*, published by Perterloo Poets. © U A Fanthorpe. Used by permission of the Estate of U A Fanthorpe; 'On A Portrait of a Deaf Man' from *Best Loved Poems of John Betjeman* published by John Murray. Used by permission of John Murray and Aitken Alexander Associates; 'The Blackbird of Glanmore' from *District and Circle* by Seamus Heaney, published by Faber and Faber; 'A Vision' from *Tyrannosaurus Rex versus The Corduroy Kid* published by Faber and Faber; 'The Moment' by Margaret Atwood from *Eating Fire*, published by Virago, a division of Little Brown. Reproduced with permission of Curtis Brown Ltd. London on behalf of Margaret Atwood. © Margaret Atwood 1998; 'Cold Knap Lake' taken from *Collected Poems* by Gillian Clarke. © Gillian Clarke. Published by Carcanet Press Limited. Used by permission of Carcanet Press; 'Price We Pay for the Sun' from *The Fat Black Woman's Poems* published by Virago. © Grace Nichols, reproduced with permission of Curtis Brown Group Ltd.; 'Neighbours' taken from *Collected Poems* by Gillian Clarke. © Gillian Clarke. Published by Carcanet Press Limited. Used by permission of Carcanet Press; 'Crossing the Loch' from *Jizzen* by Kathleen Jamie. © 1999 Kathleen Jamie. Published by Picador. Used by permission of Picador, a division of Macmillan books; 'Hard Water' by Jean Sprackland © 2003. Published by Jonathan Cape. Used by permission of Random House UK; 'Below the Green Corrie' from *The Poems of Norman MacCaig* by Norman MacCaig is reproduced by permission of Polygon, an imprint of Birlinn Ltd. (www.birlinn.co.uk); 'Wind' from *Collected Poems* by Ted Hughes, published by Faber and Faber; 'Flag' from: *Half-Caste and other Poems* by John Agard © 2007. Published by Hodder Arnold; 'Out of the Blue' by Simon Armitage is reproduced from *Out of the Blue* (Enitharmon Press © 2008) Used by permission; 'Mametz Wood' from *Skirrid Hill* by Owen Sheers. First published by Seren Books. © 2005 Owen Sheers. Reproduced by permission of the author c/o Rogers, Coleridge & White Ltd., 20 Powis Mews, London, W11 1JN; 'The Yellow Palm' taken from Selected Poems by Robert Minhinnick. © Robert Minhinnick. Published by Carcanet Press Limited. Used by permission of Carcanet Press; 'The Right Word' taken from: *Terrorist at my Table* by Imtiaz Dharker. Published by Bloodaxe Books, © 2006. Used by permission; 'The Right Word' artwork reproduced with permission of Imtiaz Dha 'At the Border' taken from: *Life for Us* by Choman Hardi. Published by Bloodaxe Books © 2004. Used by permission; 'Belfast Confetti' by Ciaran Carson. Used by kind permission of the author and The Gallery Press, Loughcrew, Oldcastle, County Meath, Ireland from *Collected Poems* © 2008; 'Poppies' by Jane Weir. Used by kind permission of Templar Poetry; 'Bayonet Charge' from *Hawke in the Rain* by Ted Hughes, published by Faber and Faber; 'The Falling Leaves' by Margaret Postgate Cole, used by permission of David Higham Associates; 'Come On, Come Back' from *Not Waving but Drowning* by Stevie Smith published by Penguin Books. Used by permission of The Estate of James MacGibbon; 'next to of course god america' Copyright 1926, 1954 © 1991 by the Trustees for the E.E. Cummings Trust. Copyright © 1985 by George James Firmage, from COMPLETE POEMS: 1904-1962 BY E.E. Cummings, edited by George J. Firmage. Used by permission of Liveright Publishing Corporation United States and WW Norton, United Kingdom; 'Hawk Roosting' from *Selected Poems* by Ted Hughes, published by Faber and Faber; 'The Manhunt' from *The Not Dead* by Simon Armitage, Published by Pomona Books. Used by permission; 'Hour' from *Rapture* by Carol Ann Duffy, published by Picador. Used by permission of Picador, a division of Macmillan Books; 'In Paris With You' by James Fenton from *Selected Poems* published by Penguin Books. Reprinted by permission of United Agents on behalf of James Fenton; 'Quickdraw' from *Rapture* by Carol Ann Duffy, published by Picador. Used by permission of Picador, a division of Macmillan Books; 'Ghazal' by Mimi Khalvati. Used by kind permission of the poet; 'Brothers' from *Fear of Thunder* by Andrew Forster, published by Flambard Press © Andrew Forster, 2007. Used by permission of Flambard Press; 'Praise Song for My Mother' from *The Fat Black Woman's Poems* published by Virago. © Grace Nichols, reproduced with permission of Curtis Brown Group Ltd.; 'Harmonium' by Simon Armitage © Simon Armitage. Used by permission of David Godwin Associates; 'Nettles' from *New and Collected Poems* by Vernon Scannell. Used by permission of The Estate of Vernon Scannell; 'Born Yesterday' by Philip Larkin, taken from *The Less Deceived* published by The Marvell Press; 'In Mrs Tilscher's Class' is taken from *The Other Country* by Carol Ann Duffy published by Anvil Press Poetry in 1990. © Carol Ann Duffy. Used by permission; 'Cynddylan on a Tractor' from Collected Poems 1945–1990 by RS Thomas, published by Phoenix, an imprint of the Orion Publishing Group, London. Used by permission; 'Even Tho' from *Lazy Thoughts of a Lazy Woman* by Grace Nichols, published by Virago. Copyright © Grace Nichols 1989, reproduced with permission of Curtis Brown Group Ltd.; 'My Bus Conductor' from The Mersey Sound by Roger McGough.

Every effort has been made to contact copyright holders of material reproduced in this book. Any omissions will be rectified in subsequent printings if notice is given to the publishers.